No Rooms of Their Own

OTHER BOOKS BY HEYDAY

No Rooms of Their Own

Women Writers of Early California

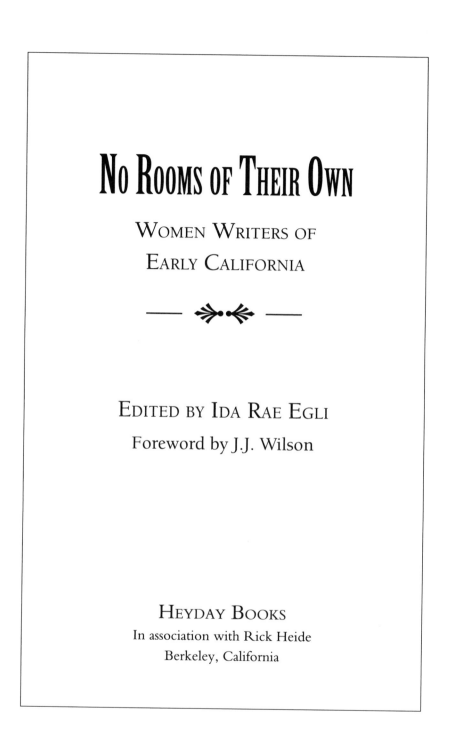

Edited by Ida Rae Egli

Foreword by J.J. Wilson

HEYDAY BOOKS
In association with Rick Heide
Berkeley, California

Published by Heyday Books, P.O. Box 9145, Berkeley, CA 94709

Cover design by Jeannine Gendar
Interior design by Tracey Broderick
Production coordination by Tracey Broderick
Cover photograph of Josephine Clifford McCrackin courtesy of the Bancroft Library.
Typeset in Bembo by Rick Heide, Redwood City, CA

Printed in the United States of America
10 9 8 7 6 5 4 3 2 1

ISBN: 0-930588-54-1
Library of Congress Card Catalog Number: 91-073798

Portions of "A Frontier Lady" by Sarah Royce, copyright © 1977, reprinted with the permission of Yale University Press.

Portions of "Out of the Past: Lucy's Story" by Lucy Young, copyright © 1978, reprinted with the permission of the Held Poage Research Library, Ukiah.

"My Grizzly Bear" and "Sierra Neighbors" by Jessie Benton Frémont, copyright © 1970, reprinted with the permission of Lewis Osborne Press, Ashland.

"Delirium" by Hipolita Orendain de Medina printed with the permission of the California Historical Society, San Francisco.

Portions of Georgiana Kirby's unpublished journal printed with the permission of the California Historical Society, San Francisco.

ACKNOWLEDGMENTS

When researching and editing a book such as this, one quickly realizes that the name credit on the front of the book is at least partly erroneous. One cannot possibly put together such a body of work alone. In the end what I feel, as editor of *No Rooms of Their Own,* is that the whole process from beginning to end was a community effort, almost a birthing, and that by deciding I wanted such a book, I somehow ended up with the billing. But truthfully, the book is born of a society that supports free libraries, academic research, commercial and academic publishing, and eager audiences ready to consume interesting written material. Aides to such projects are dedicated librarians like Lila Lee (and photographer, Robert Lee) at the Held Poage Research Library in Ukiah, Michael Harvey and Robert McKimmie of the California Historical Society Library in San Francisco, Franz Enciso and the others at the Bancroft Library in Berkeley, and our own college and university librarians at Santa Rosa Junior College and Sonoma State University. Also involved and supportive in a hundred ways, from the beginning, are college and university professors like Dr. Tom MacMillan, Dr. J.J. Wilson, Dr. Eugene Soules, Dr. Michael S. Gregory, and Dr. Daniel B. Knapp—and translators, like Dr. Gustavo Calderon of San Francisco State University, who not only give freely of their time but also join in the celebration of the nineteenth century women whose thoughts they reveal. Publishers provide the facilities and quarters for the event, serve as hand-holders, and become respected, valued friends—at Heyday Books, Malcolm Margolin, Tracey Broderick, Rick Heide, and Jeannine Gendar. Family friends also play an important role, as did Andy Mattern, Pauline Herme and Susan Forrest, and the family of staff and faculty at Santa Rosa Junior College.

A special fond thanks is due J.J. Wilson, whose initial curiosity initiated my research into California women writers, and who stayed with me full circle to the publication of the book, writing a foreword for the collection we have talked about so often.

Parenting such a book also becomes day to day reality—the late nights, poor meals, discussing, rehashing, stopping and starting, Alka-Seltzer headache job of family members—husband, father, editor, omelette chef Gus P'manolis; daughter, editor, graphics and computer coordinator Heidi Harting; son, editor, advisor and receptive ear Daniel Harting; mentor and grandfather Dan Egli; grandmother Ruth Egli, and on and on.

To all the people who helped bring this book into the world, I offer my deepest thanks and respect, and to those I have forgotten to thank personally, I ask pardon for my unintentional oversight. In the end, when the book is a public entity with a life of its own, and in this case reintroduces the lives of women who experienced California more than a hundred years ago, many people feel proud, many people call for a celebration. But it is these women—Sarah Royce, Lucy Young, Dame Shirley, Helen Carpenter, Frances Fuller Victor, Josephine Clifford, Jessie Benton Frémont, Hipolita Orendain de Medina, Georgiana Kirby, Ina Coolbrith, Mary Hallock Foote, Charlotte Brown, Ella Sterling Cummins Mighels, Adah Menken, and Ada Clare—that we celebrate!

I. R. E.

TABLE OF CONTENTS

———Questioning Roles———

FOREWORD

Is it because we are coming up to a new century that we find ourselves looking longingly backward, seeking some hints as to what lies ahead? For some reasons anyway, local history and regional literature are both much in demand now, which is part of what makes Ida Rae Egli's book so timely and so satisfying. What is more, it fills in on the distaff side the territory previously described mainly through the masculine eyes of Mark Twain, Bret Harte, and company.

When I travel through the picturesque Mother Lode area, stopping dutifully to read every historical marker, I am usually left with a feeling of coming up light, of getting history out of classic comic books. What is lacking is diversity and depth. Fortunately, we are now moving, albeit slowly, to a post-colonial consciousness which understands the importance of the margins to the mainstream. Serious scholars, museum curators, and other specialists are undertaking the long work of revising western history away from the pernicious folklore it has become. That old-fashioned and never really accurate picture of the miners as boys on a bachelor holiday, happily playing in the dirt and placer mining poor mother earth to make her give up what she would not relinquish willingly, has outlived its usefulness, even as myth.

Interestingly, one of the authors from this new anthology, Ada Clare, complains (and this in the 1860s) that "Few of us value our past sufficiently. Most people look upon it as a game that has been played and ought to be forgotten." Too much history does read like a game, and all too often a game where we are not told of all the players. No wonder we ignore our past, when it has been so distorted.

Joan Jensen and Darlis Miller, in their 1980 revisionist article from the respected journal *Pacific Historical Review,* warn that as recently as 1976 a textbook on the West (Ray Allen Billington's monumental *Westward Expansion*) listed only three women in the index: Helen Hunt Jackson, Queen Liliuokalani, and Sacajewea. They describe some of the effects of this neglect on our view of our history and of ourselves:

> By virtually excluding women from western studies on the
> one hand, and emphasizing their rareness on the other, the
> impression is left that women played insignificant roles in
> settling the American West. As the frontier advances with all
> its romance and color across the pages of [this book], it is a
> robust masculine domain that emerges, and the few women
> who appear, Calamity Jane and Mary Lease, for example, do
> so on a masculine stage.

Stereotypes beget stereotypes and the images of women in the west have
been reduced to four main categories which the *Review* authors designate
as "gentle tamers, sunbonneted helpmates, hell-raisers, and bad women."
I am delighted to report that not one of Professor Egli's writers fits into
these prefabricated slots! Indeed, there will be some surprises here because
as soon as you leave the B movie script fantasy for real women who
write about their real lives, history becomes more satisfactorily complex,
sophisticated, and absorbing.

Readers will absorb these previously unavailable authors thirstily; we
are, as a recent conference on women's biography discovered, all writing
and reading about women's lives, searching for some new friends. And
Professor Egli's breezy biographies provide an introduction to some
charming characters. Readers will come to cherish, as she does, these
women with voices if not rooms of their own.

From Dame Shirley's comparatively well known and compulsively
readable letters and the assured professional story-telling voice of Mary
Hallock Foote to the bare, basic narrative of Charlotte Brown's oral court
testimony, we get the satisfaction of hearing some new and different
voices, truthful, tactful, and to the point, telling us about the West.

Some of these voices sound not all that different from our own. As
has been pointed out by Jo Ann Levy in *They Saw the Elephant,* by Ruth
Saxton in her studies at Mills College, and by others, the western experience could not be anything other than a liberation for these 19th century
women. Here is Ada Clare again with a satiric reversal that still works
against the double standard: "The sacred precinct of home is the real
sphere of man . . . we love to see the sweet male violets hidden under
domestic greens." In the early eco-feminism of Josephine Clifford Mc-
Crackin, we get a refreshingly different view of the not so wild West.
Alas, even Ella Mighels' views on birth control and the purity of the
white race sound curiously current. I found myself wondering what I
would have said to Jessie Benton Frémont about her support for her

husband, were she in my women's group. And I would have loved to have known Adah Menken and Ada Clare and gone to their parties.

The title of this collection is, of course, derived from Virginia Woolf's influential book, *A Room of One's Own,* but I keep hearing another oft-repeated phrase of hers, an injunction that we should all be "thinking back through our mothers." Today, as we stand at the frontier of a new century, let us take courage from the words of one of our mothers, Sarah Royce, written about the day of her setting out:

> I would not consent to delay our departure for fear of the weather. Had I not made up my mind to encounter many storms? If we were going, let us go, and meet what we were to meet, bravely.

J.J. Wilson, Professor of English
Sonoma State University

CALIFORNIA

Weaverville

Fort Seward

Rich Bar &
Indian Bar

Round Valley
Reservation

Potter Valley

Donner Pass

Ukiah   Grass Valley

Sacramento

Sonoma   Sutter's Mill

Yosemite

San Francisco   Oakland

Bear Valley

Santa Cruz

Salinas

Monterey   Gabilan Range

Salinas Valley

Santa Ynez Mountains   San Fernando
Valley

Santa Barbara

San
Buenaventura   Los Angeles

INTRODUCTION

"A Woman must have money and a room of her own
if she is to write fiction . . ." — *Virginia Woolf,*
from A Room of One's Own

FIRST CONTACT

The Gold Rush of 1848. The California gold rush opened floodgates of adventure and opportunity and within one year brought 250,000 argonauts from half a continent or several seas away to participate in the "bonanza" experience. It also drew a rather small but impressive crowd of women who were as anxious as their male counterparts to challenge the brave new world in the West. In the beginning there was but a single woman for every twelve men, but even outnumbered these women were not intimidated. Quite the contrary. Their rarity gave them an enhanced value—and perhaps more power than they had ever dared hope possible.

That they came at all was testament to their strong character and sense of adventure. Those not robust stayed at home. Those who came were open to change. Louisa Clapp, better known as Dame Shirley, called herself "a regular Nomad" in her "passion for wandering." Georgiana Kirby wanted to "share in the general prosperity." Helen Carpenter enthusiastically shouted "Ho to California!" to set her wagon train in motion. Along the trail many women dropped their hoop skirts even before they reached the Sierra Nevada in favor of simple unencumbering dresses, split skirts, or even bloomers that allowed them to ride a horse astride, walk more freely across the desert, or scale the mountain passes. The closer they came to California, the further behind they left their preconceived notions about what women should wear, should do, should be.

California was different. Its men were different. Its women were different. The miners were aggressive, unfettered by law, tradition or family expectations. They joined in a frenzy for gold and free land. Every man wanted a piece of the prosperity. The law that pervaded was Darwinian, survival of the fittest—and it called for quick thinking and improvisation. This law applied equally to women. Because in the early years they were few in number they were sometimes guarded, yet often given a freer rein than their eastern counterparts. They were welcomed into the male world of pioneer California knowing they had to work hard alongside the men to survive and get ahead—and they proved they could.

In the beginning some were even miners. In 1850 two Florida women scraped the beds of California's creeks, accumulating upwards of $10,000 worth of gold. Mrs. H. H. Smith discovered a "lump" weighing more than ninety-five pounds, which was two-thirds pure gold and worth $13,000. Most women, of course, were wives and mothers, but wives and mothers who plowed fields, planted potatoes, kept books, delivered calves, sheep, horses, and other women's babies.

Many immigrating women had come from homogeneous cultures, but in California were brought face to face with a multi-cultural population that offered new perspectives on living. Thousands of Native American women, speaking a hundred separate languages, were enjoying the last years of their traditional existence. Wives and daughters of Spanish descent, some called "Rancheras"—widows and single women like Doña Vicente Sepulveda of Rancho Sepulveda and Catarina Manzaneli de Munras who lived near Monterey—tended their own ranches, supervising the raising of cattle, managing dairies, vineyards, orchards. Other women in their culture were mothers of large families, living within a Catholic tradition that was quite foreign to most of the newcomers. In Los Angeles in the 1850s there was a multi-cultural population that freely intermarried made up of Hispanic, black, and mestizo men and women, the women maintaining a slight majority over the men.

By the 1860s California's population was enlarged by African-American women escaping the slavery of the south or the difficulties of the north; by Chilean women brought by boat to be sold as prostitutes or wives; by Irish women fleeing the potato famine in Ireland or the crowded Irish neighborhoods in New York City or Chicago; by Chinese women sold to ship's captains after the Tai-ping Rebellion and famine in Southeastern China and resold in San Francisco as prostitutes, wives or domestics, sometimes right off the docks. Nearly 40 percent of all the women in early California were foreign born. For many, California offered "newness," an atmosphere ripe for change, where hard work was expected of them and huge rewards might be won.

Quickly the women proved they were enduring. Fewer women than men died of disease or accident. Cholera took significantly more men than women and the statistics for survival of the 1846 Donner party were similar to others of the early frontier period: of the forty people who died at Donner Pass only seven were women, and of the fifteen who were sent out to bring back a rescue group, all five of the women survived but only two of the ten men. Women were also less susceptible to the high suicide rate. However, women died in childbirth, and this single factor kept the death rates of the two sexes fairly even.

Over and over in the writings left by women of this period there appear images of California's exciting newness, its promise, and its challenge. Dame Shirley was awed by groups of Indian women harvesting grass seeds near Indian Bar mining camp and by the coarse, perilous nature of the camps; Sarah Royce and Helen Carpenter describe the hopes they cling to and the toil they encounter while taking advantage of the "free" land in California; Georgiana Kirby discusses in her diary her fears of birthing her baby unaided and alone, and the hardships of planting and harvesting potatoes on her ranch while pregnant. Over and over women overcame these challenges.

MAKING ROOM

A Unique Frontier—and Opportunity for Women. The gold rush set the stage for what became the unique personality of California. It produced $80,000,000 worth of gold in 1850 alone, and this instant prosperity became the base for a new society. Within a year travel to California became easier; both the California and Southwestern trails were clearly marked with the telltale signs of earlier wagon companies, and sea voyagers, instead of rounding Cape Horn, could now cross Panama and catch another steamship to San Francisco. Businessmen, doctors, lawyers, publishers, engineers, farmers, and dressmakers now came in large numbers. By 1860 there were more college graduates in California, per capita, than in any other state. Each year the ratio of women to men narrowed as more women came to California with husbands, brothers, fathers—or not uncommonly, alone.

Slowly, as the surface gold ran out, argonauts began to pursue more common frontier endeavors: farming, ranching, operating small businesses or professional practices. But California never followed the historical pattern set by other frontiers. As Franklin Walker commented in *San Francisco's Literary Frontier,* "Most frontiers insisted on settling down; this one refused to." Ordinarily, farmers, blacksmiths and horse traders gradually moved into new frontiers, bringing order with them, as happened in Virginia and Pennsylvania in the 1700s. But the gold strike in California brought instant wealth to the state and encouraged exciting and paradoxical disorder. Saloons and gambling houses flourished within shouting distance of schools and churches; stage robbers were hanged within minutes, but fraudulent land speculators were ignored; vigilantes were in direct and blatant competition with law enforcement officials; there was a rowdy, working class and an equally large refined, monied class; legislators created a "free state" for slaves but simultaneously pursued active "Indian extermination."

Rather primitive living conditions in frontier California paralleled those in earlier colonial America to some degree, and "made for greater sexual as well as economic mobility—a rough egalitarianism better served the needs of frontier communities to survive and prosper." There were exceptions, of course, among them prostitutes, who generally fared poorly as their earning ability determined their value. If they became ill they received no care, and most died young. But a few came freely to set up brothels and saloons, like Belle Cora, the "Countess," and Irene McCready, who were not only financially successful, but also tolerated in respectable San Francisco society.

Often pioneer women complained they missed the safety, refinement, and fellowship of Eastern cities. But for all the hardships and losses, they exulted in newfound freedoms and what was for many a newfound status. Thwarted in her attempts to become a nurse in the East, Sophia Eastman came to San Francisco and within months had accomplished her dream. Julia Shannon was respected as a midwife and daguerrean artist; Mrs. E. S. Sleeper and Charlotte B. Brown (no relation to the Charlotte L. Brown whose oral testimony is included in this collection) were medical doctors; Madame St. Dennis was a consultant on "matters of love, law and business"; and Mrs. Lee Whipple-Haslam identified three bandits that robbed the stage she was riding as an agent for Wells, Fargo & Co. Many more owned their own boarding houses, worked as barbers, taught school, even drove stage coaches. Catherine Oliver, a seamstress working in San Francisco in 1850, wrote enthusiastically back to a friend in Boston of opportunities for women:

> A smart woman can do very well in this country—true
> there are not many comforts and one must work all the time
> and work hard, but is plenty to do and good pay. If I was in
> Boston now and knew what I now know of California, I
> would come out here if I had to hire the money to bring me
> out. It is the only country that I was ever in where a woman
> received anything like a just compensation for her work.

Many women took advantage of the window of opportunity, although generally it was those of European ancestry who could. By the 1860s women were pushing for suffrage, for entrance into medical schools and law schools, for Indian reform, and for legislation beyond the "separate ownership" guaranteed by the California constitution. They also began to push to be heard as writers—columnists, novelists, poets, and playwrights. Because the time was right they found an eager audience.

Women Writers and their Audience. As early as the mid-1850s residents of the golden state were ready—eager actually—for a literature of their own, one that reflected the unique populations, landscapes and social philosophies of early California. Stories like Dame Shirley's mining camp narrative, first published in 1854, received enthusiastic response. Young writers saw this as a new opportunity. California, they knew, was a cornucopia of untold tales, poems, and dramas. Also, the intellectual spirit of revolution and personal freedom unique to the west coast helped bolster the creatives juices of even the most reticent artists. In and out of California readers wanted to see the real California. With publishing houses popping up in San Francisco, Sacramento and Los Angeles, the demanding California readership soon got what it wanted. Luckily, missing from the scene were dignified members of the literary establishment who would have censured, mocked or suppressed the fresh flow of creativity.

From the beginning, California literature sold because readers were cut off from the literature of their past, because shared experiences on the rough plain had provided an immediacy and commonality between audience and writer, and because everyone wanted a part in defining the new world in California. The creation of a new homeland had involved all Californians in a spontaneous burst of creativity that provided an instant connection between writer and audience. They were an educated, sophisticated audience, discriminating in their tastes but egalitarian in their concepts of class and station, supportive of local writers, open to new trends and forms. The women of California had a special opportunity because they were still outnumbered. Men were hungry for women's voices, as were women from Eureka to Los Angeles who coveted the intimacy between woman writer and woman reader in order to momentarily bridge the physical distances that separated women. And most Californians, regardless of gender, religion or social background, were lonely at least a few hours of every day and therefore eager to establish a connection with others in a precarious pioneer world.

These connections are seen often in this collection. The short stories and essays Helen Carpenter wrote in northern Mendocino County for the *Golden Era* and the *Overland Monthly* testify to her long-distance but firm connection with writers and readers throughout the state who shared her interest in revealing abuses to Native Americans, as well as the beauty of the valley in which she lived. The feminine poems of Ina Coolbrith as well as the strong and explicit works of Adah Menken touched audiences who wrote to editors pleading for more.

QUESTIONING ROLES

A Literary Tradition Is Born in California. From its embryonic state in 1860, California literature soon grew and prospered in the heat of San Francisco entrepreneurialism. During this period "San Francisco was the west coast," as literary historian Franklin Walker put it, the city that controlled state economic markets. Per capita, California was the wealthiest state in the nation, and there were schools, theaters, opera houses and Grange halls popping up as quickly as contracts could be written.

San Francisco also became the base for publishing houses and booksellers. In the early 1850s there were no fewer than fifty printers working in San Francisco alone, and by the early 1860s the *Pioneer*, the *Golden Era*, the *Hesperian*, the *Californian*, and the *Overland Monthly* could compare with the best Eastern journals. The wealth to produce these journals and the leisure to read them made the marriage of readers and printed material possible. In the ten years following the gold rush 132 periodicals took to the presses in San Francisco alone. Some folded, but those that survived proudly boasted a "total per capita circulation and . . . variety greater than in New York, London, or anywhere else." They printed in six languages and served the worldly, cosmopolitan population of and around San Francisco. At about this time in the Bay Area there were seven black newspapers and at least one printed in Chinese. Every town of consequence had its own paper, and so did many of the smallest mining camps. Hubert Bancroft, author of *Bancroft's Works,* was buying and printing books, and along with San Francisco booksellers Anton Roman, Bosqui, and Towne & Bacon enjoyed a brisk turnover of local selections. Printed matter was transported by stage, wagon or mule to readers in even the most remote corners of the state.

These newspapers and periodicals offered the opportunities young writers standing in the wings needed. Mark Twain established himself at the *Territorial Enterprise,* then moved to San Francisco where he wrote *"The Jumping Frog of Calaveras County."* He joined Bret Harte, Joaquin Miller, Charles Warren Stoddard, Prentice Mulford, and others who were "literizing" the rough and ready characters of frontier California. Women joined in, encouraged by an eager audience and a supportive publishing industry. Ina Coolbrith received flattering reviews for "A Mother's Grief" and "When the Grass Shall Cover Me." Literary historian Franklin Walker praised her work: "It was commonly acknowledged that her poetry was the best that was appearing in the *Overland.*" Alongside Adah Menken, whose form showed the influence of Walt Whitman, they represented the two poles of the poetry spectrum from romantic lyric to outspoken free verse. Coolbrith was reflective, Menken sensual and evocative. Frances Fuller Victor wrote not only Greek and Roman classic parodies, but also historic fictions and biographies, novels and a column for the *Evening Herald.* Josephine Clifford's European literary background was transformed into western tales and a woman's novel.

Ada Clare was invited to San Francisco to write a literary column for the *Golden Era,* and joined Helen Carpenter and Georgiana Kirby who were both publishing short stories and exposés in San Francisco papers and periodicals. Through their writings and social interaction, these women collaborated to push for more intellectual freedom, questioning women's roles and encouraging their rather liberal audiences to rise and support them. All through the 1860s and sometimes into the 1870s, these writers experienced encouraging responses, a writer's bonanza, the golden era of California frontier literature.

Inspired by early successes of men and women writers alike—some encouraged also by Bret Harte, editor of the *Overland Monthly* and author of *"M'Liss"* and *"The Luck of Roaring Camp"*—the early writers coined a literary genre they felt captured their style: the Sagebrush School. They were storytellers who mixed reality with a little western mythology and a bonanza hyperbole that their audiences loved. Their characters were often picturesque, and selections contained pathos or humor and some-times an abnormality that was intimately exclusive to California. They had fun, but they were serious about writing and their Sagebrush Realism mirrored common images seen in the state. The poets even found them-selves in two popular collections—*Outcroppings: Selections of California Verse,* 1866, and *Poetry of the Pacific,* 1867.

Published women represented a wide range of California's society, yet still did not cover the actual diversity of women's experiences in early California. In the two decades that followed the discovery of gold, Euro-American women made up less than 60 percent of the female population, but nearly all the published writers were from this group. The reasons are many. Minority women of the time were rarely fluent enough in English to write and publish for the English-speaking world, nor was the act of writing necessarily a part of their cultural value system. Their voices are hard to come by, yet when heard present cultural points of view which complement the voices of women of European descent. Lucy Young, a Lassik Indian girl who saw white soldiers annihilate the men in her tribe, finally passed on her oral narrative in broken English to a white female friend when she was nearly 93. Mary Ellen Pleasant, known as Mammy Pleasant, was a well-known figure in San Francisco's early black community who was immortalized for her philanthropy with black emigrants to California and her financial support of John Brown. Her life experiences in the Bay Area would have made for evocative reading, and indeed she began an oral narration of her life but publication of the narrative was halted for unknown reasons after the first episode. Mexican-American and Asian women seldom tested the strong cultural and religious taboos against writing, or the family patriarchy which forbade it, as in the case of Asian women. Also, in this time of American colonial expansion and jingoism minority women faced a deep-seated racism, an overwhelm-ing contempt for the experiences of those who did not belong to the dominant culture, a racism which surfaces at times even in this collection.

Digging deep into the archives of magazines and newspapers for stories by white women in early California meant digging far deeper for even momentary glimpses into the lives of minority women. But when found, these glimpses were electrifying: Charlotte Brown testifying to the humiliation of being removed from a public transport because of her skin color, Hipolita Orendain de Medina longing for romance and medi-tating on the mysteries of death in the privacy of her spirit journal. We are stunned yet privileged to get a glimpse of these women's experience in California. Hopefully, in years to come, as more of these minority women's writings are drawn from shelves and family chests, they will further illuminate and complete our understanding of the female experience in the west.

The Frontier Era Dies—and its Literature Wanes. California frontier literature did not live long—only about twenty-five years. Just as wordsmiths were beginning to hope that they could support themselves by their writing, the Transcontinental Railway steamed into San Francisco in 1869. Aside from the gold rush, nothing in early California history had such a dramatic impact on residents as the railway that connected them to the East. New immigrants did not leap in great numbers from passenger cars ready to buy land, hats and fencing material as speculators had planned—a deep recession hit California in 1870 and three years later spread eastward. Still, the serpentine body of railcars, relentless in its swaying trek from coast to coast, soon changed the face of California and its literature.

California was no longer an entity unto itself. Once the whole continent was connected by the spreading arteries of railroad tracks, California farmers were competing with those in the Midwest and California manufacturers with those in Pittsburgh and Milwaukee. Also, the slower but still constant stream of new emigrés who now made their way west no longer appreciated the emancipated climate that had been California's in the early days. These later pioneers wanted the order and safety of a more homogeneous society. They wanted to replicate the streets, schools, operas and attitudes they had left in New York City, St. Louis, and Charleston. Church social halls sprung up across the state, along with Masonic Temples and orders of the Daughters of the American Revolution.

Feeling the beginning of the end most of the popular male writers of the frontier period left for greener literary pastures, many practicing travel writing, a genre that was developing to entertain Eastern audiences. Mark Twain headed for Europe to write *Innocents Abroad,* Bret Harte accepted a hefty increase in pay to become editor of the *Atlantic* magazine in New York City, Joaquin Miller and Prentice Mulford both headed for London and Paris. Along with them went Adah Menken and Jessie Benton Frémont, following her husband. Some escapees were personally successful: Twain, Bierce, Harte, others. Their defection, however, sealed the fate of the new literary tradition that was developing in the West. Many of the women writers remained in the state, but after the golden years found few publishing opportunities and faced mainly conservative audiences not particularly interested in women's literature.

California was enduring a rite of passage and the initiation was painful. The price exacted for settlement and assimilation into the continental United States was a loss of individual state identity. For years to come, Californians weren't sure of their cultural personality nor did they call for a literature that reflected their own cultural profile. They were overwhelmed by boxcar after boxcar loaded with texts, novels and periodicals from New York and the eastern seaboard. They were also enduring the eclipse of their own native Sagebrush literature by the new genres eastern publishing and literary figures prescribed for the entire nation: Realism—an offshoot in part of the bloody Civil War and America's loss of national innocence; Regionalism—perhaps the result of a collective desire to know and understand the cities and valleys of the octopus that was the expanding United States; and Naturalism—almost certainly the subconscious manifestation of the desire of an industrialized society to return to a simpler life close to nature.

The golden era of the California frontier was dead, and buried with it were the budding lives of Sagebrush Realism and frontier California literature. Stories and poems of California by its own writers still sold; some writers like the prolific Mary Hallock Foote continued to write professionally to eager audiences years after most of the other early writers had fallen into obscurity. Gertrude Atherton, Frank Norris and Jack London were in later decades successful in their individual careers. But the collective spirit had been lost. The unique literary genre that might have developed in California, suited to its geography, demography and liberal character, had been overwhelmed by the eastern literary monopoly. With it went the promise of a women's literature that might have fully flowered had it been granted more time in its nurturing environment. The novels and collections of short stories and poetry that women writers had produced during the frontier period slowly slipped further back on library shelves and were eventually sold at Friends of the Library sales for pennies.

Of the fifteen women represented here, seven died in poverty, and nearly all were grossly unappreciated as writers in their lifetimes; this void in California women's literature initiated the research that has ended in this anthology. Now united after more than a century of obscurity, these women writers have a respectability and a power they could not attain individually in the 1860s. They wrote without "rooms of their own," often without even desks or tables, yet what they say to us about the birthing process of California is as vital as our own individual histories. In their broad diversity—from Sarah Royce waxing religious to the sexually liberated Adah Menken, from literary scholar Frances Fuller Victor to Lassik Indian Lucy Young retelling her life in broken English, from Dame Shirley's crude mining camp to Jessie Benton Frémont's marble-tabled Mariposa Ranch—we can follow the wise women who march through the annals of California history. Through their narratives we see a gentler, more malleable and somehow more cyclical and ongoing local heritage. We see and feel the presence women brought to California.

Josephine Clifford McCrackin wrote to Ina Coolbrith as an old woman: "The world has not used us well, Ina; California has been ungrateful to us." Perhaps the time has finally come to prove her wrong.

First Contact

Sarah Eleanor Royce (1819–1891)

When she was sixty, Sarah Royce revised and edited the diary she had started as a westering woman thirty years before, in the spring of 1849. Her son, Josiah, was by this time a noted Harvard historian, and it was he who encouraged her to edit and refine the overland journal she had maintained during her months enroute to California. He asked her to finish the diary for his pleasure, and for his use as a historian—not for publication.

Sarah Royce probably thought that when she died she would best be remembered as the mother of Josiah Royce and the grandmother of children who would recall her berry pies and organ hymns. Perhaps because she was writing for her family, her diary is straightforward, personal and philosophic. By the time she rewrote the diary, she had seen her son mature into a nationally recognized academic—but one who had fairly rejected his mother's Christian philosophy. Some, including Ralph Henry Gabriel, who wrote the introduction when the diary was later published as *A Frontier Lady,* thought that Sarah Royce inserted religious overtones into her narrative to win her son back to her faith. But the personal presence we find in Sarah Royce's diary, her command of memory and language, are not merely a reflection of her faith in God. In lively prose, she presents a purity of conviction and altruism that exemplifies the noble character we have stereotypically come to attribute to "pioneer women."

Born in England, at Stratford on Avon in 1819, Sarah Royce was carried on board a ship sailing for America when she was six weeks old. Church bells ringing in the background marked the birth of Queen Victoria. Raised in New York, in various city settings, she was given a solid academic education. She met and married Josiah Royce Sr. in New York, and became the mother of a daughter, Mary. While still nursing the baby, she traveled to Missouri and began preparing for the moment, on April 30, 1849, when she, Josiah and Mary would embark for California.

Their trek was not an easy one—none were. When trouble presented itself in outbreaks of cholera, threats from Indians, low water supply, loss of cattle or other privations, she would draw from a storehouse of Christian faith. Her descriptions of these difficult times draw us back to the nineteenth century and the crude conditions that faced overland travelers daily.

The Royces arrived at the Sierra foothill mining camps in October, and immediately set up a tent alongside a creekbed and began panning for gold. They were unsuccessful, and by the new year they had made their way to Sacramento, bought a plot of land on which to build a store and home, and made ready to set up shop. Sacramento was brimming with new settlers who had followed the rumors of gold—in less than a year it had grown from a four-family settlement to a tent city of more than 10,000.

For two weeks the Royces enjoyed the warm, sunny days that often mark January in California. Then the Great Flood of 1850 began to pour upon them and within days they had to be rescued by boat and flee to San Francisco, rowing away from their cash stake and the land that they had bought. They rented a house in San Francisco, then moved back to the mining settlements, finally settling in Grass Valley where they managed a farm.

In Grass Valley, Sarah gave birth to three more children. A lively woman with a generous heart, Sarah was soon leading others to her church and helping pioneer families in need. She educated not only her own children but others as well, long before schools were established. A lover of music and literature, she had brought her Bible and a copy of Milton's works with her overland, and soon she secured a set of encyclopedias and other books of science and letters. She even had a melodeon shipped to California—the first to come around the Horn—which she played from her tent home. And although she had feared living in the camps, her experience soon told her these fears were unfounded. The miners from whom she had feared rowdy and evil behavior watched out for her and her children, and gathered quietly on the creekbank to listen to her play hymns as the sun sank in the western sky.

For Sarah Royce, the horrendous overland journey to California resulted in a transcendent and conversionary experience. Lonely and on the verge of physical collapse, she felt the presence of God in a burning sage bush, and when she spoke to Him, a strange, illogical peace was the answer to her prayer. She became a mystic, and from that hour mysticism was one of the foundation stones of her life. The other was family.

No Rooms of Their Own

In 1932 Josiah Royce had his mother's diary published as *A Frontier Lady*, selections of which are reprinted here. Perhaps it was the strength of these foundations—religious faith and devotion to family—that allowed Sarah Royce to construct such a vivid, believable, and unforgettable narrative of what it was to travel to California by land.

A FRONTIER LADY
PLAINS

———— ❧•❦ ————

On the last day of April, 1849 we began our journey to California. Our out-fit consisted of a covered wagon, well loaded with provisions, and such preparations for sleeping, cooking etc., as we had been able to furnish, guided only by the light of Fremont's *Travels,* and the suggestions, often conflicting, of the many who, like ourselves, utter strangers to camping life, were setting out for the "Golden Gate." Our wagon was drawn by three yoke of oxen and one yoke of cows, the latter being used in the team only part of the time. Their milk was of course to be a valuable part of our subsistence.

Nearly a year before we had bidden farewell to all our friends in the East, and we had been living for several months in a pleasant village in Iowa, about twenty miles from the Mississippi. So we had nearly the whole state of Iowa to cross, as merely introductory to the journey proper to California. Council Bluffs was the point for which we were to aim first, and that was to be the place of starting upon the grand pilgrimage.

The morning of that 30th of April was not very bright; but neither was it very gloomy. Rain might come within an hour, but then the sun might come out—I would not consent to delay our departure for fear of the weather. Had I not made up my mind to encounter many storms? If we were going, let us go, and meet what we were to meet, bravely. So I seated myself in the wagon, my little two-year old Mary was placed beside me, my husband

and the other man of our little company started the team, and we were on our way. The day turned out by no means unpleasant. Our first noon lunch was eaten by the whole party, seated in the front part of the wagon, while the cattle, detached from the wagon but not unyoked, grazed near by. After a short rest we again moved on. The afternoon wore quietly away, the weather being rather brighter and warmer than in the morning—and now night was coming on. No house was within sight.

Why did I look for one? I knew we were to camp; but surely there would be a few trees or a sheltering hillside against which to place our wagon. No, only the level prairie stretched on each side of the way. Nothing indicated a place for us—a cozy nook, in which for the night we might be guarded, at least by banks and boughs. I had for months anticipated this hour, yet, not till it came, did I realize the blank dreariness of seeing night come on without house or home to shelter us and our baby-girl. And this was to be the same for many weeks, perhaps months. It was a chilling prospect, and there was a terrible shrinking from it in my heart; but I kept it all to myself and we were soon busy making things as comfortable as we could for the night. Our wagon was large, we were provided with straw and plenty of bed clothes; and soon a very tolerable resting place was ready for us. Our little Mary had been happy as a lark all day, and now sank to sleep in her straw and blanket bed, as serenely as though she were in a palace, on a downy pillow. At first the oppressive sense of home-lessness, and an instinct of watchfulness, kept me awake. Perhaps it was not to be wondered at in one whose life had so far, been spent in city or town, surrounded by the accompaniments of civilization and who was now, for the first time in her life "camping out." However, quiet sleep came at last, and in the morning, there was a mildly exultant feeling which comes from having kept silent through a cowardly fit, and finding the fit gone off.

But the oxen and cows were found to be "gone off" too, and my first entry in my "Pilgrim's Diary" was made at very unwelcome leisure, "staying by the stuff" with my little one, while the men were recovering the animals. It was late in the forenoon when they were brought and yoked up, and our second day's journey was begun. It soon became plain that the hard facts of this pilgrimage would require patience, energy, and courage fully equal to what I had anticipated when I had tried to stretch my imagination to the utmost. These facts came first in such mean, vexing forms. Deep mud-holes in which the wagon would stick fast, or, still worse, sloughs—called by the western people "sloos"—covered with turf that appeared perfectly sound, but which would break when the full weight came upon it, and let the wheels in nearly to the hubs; closing round the spokes so tightly that digging, alone, would free them. In these cases, the whole, or nearly the whole, of the contents of the wagon had to be unloaded, often in very miry places sometimes in the rain, while the men had to "put shoulder to the wheels" and lift them out by main force. Several times while we were all busy, in such a scene the cattle wandered off, into a wood or over a hill, and hours would be lost in getting them together. Oftener they were lost in the morning—for they must be turned out to graze during the night, and then the best traveling part of the day would be gone, before we could move on. This happened on our fourth day out.

Looking into my old diary, which I kept in those days, though in a very broken, desultory manner, I find the following entry, for May 3rd, 1849. "The sloughs were very bad, stopping us repeatedly during the day; and just at dusk we found ourselves fast, in a most dreary swamp." We had encountered in the middle of the afternoon a tremendous blow and rain while out on the open prairie—the night looked threatening, and before morning we were visited by a heavy thunder storm. The next day, Friday, was so inclement as to prevent traveling. I cooked as well as I could by a log fire in a strong north-east blow. My little Mary, to my great surprise, was cheerful and happy, playing in the wagon, with various simple things I provided for her, singing and laughing most of the time.

Saturday morning, though the weather still continued cloudy, we attempted to proceed, but the rain had softened the ground so much that we found ourselves *"stuck"* almost every half mile. After a hard day's work we succeeded in reaching the little town of Tipton, only three miles from where we started in the morning. Here we spent our first Sabbath out; the clouds still threatening and the rain falling every few minutes. At this point we met with three other wagons, and three days after, at Cedar River, with several others, all bound for California. There was certainly satisfaction in having company, for we could, by uniting teams help each other over hard places, saving much time. But the weather still continued unfavorable, and I find recorded for Friday, May 11th, which was the day after crossing the Cedar River, that "we had a hard day's drive through a drenching rain, arriving at Iowa City toward night." Here we spent our second Sunday, and on Monday morning crossed the Iowa River which I see I noted as "A pretty stream, reminding me of my own, old Genesee; especially when I saw one, solitary steamboat lying at the landing some distance from the City."

Storms, bad roads and swollen streams, continued to impede our way nearly every day till we reached Council Bluffs. Referring again to my journal, I find on the 20th of May we "were visited by a thunder storm," and, on the 21st, "Were overtaken, during the afternoon by two tremendous storms of thunder, lightning and wind. Encamped, just as the last one burst upon us, on the lee side of a beautiful grove; and, at the close of the storm, as the clouds broke, the most brilliant and perfect rain-bow I ever saw completely arched the lovely scene."

"May 22. Reached Indian Creek which was so swollen by the late rains as to be impassable. Had to remain there until the men built a bridge; which took them till the next day at noon; and after crossing the stream, our way for some distance lay through flat, bottom-land, where in several places the water stood two feet deep."

When we reached Fort Des Moines we fell in with several more little companies from different points, nearly all of whom gave discouraging reports of their own progress, and of the news they were receiving, at this point, in various ways, from others who were on the way to California. From Council Bluffs, and other crossing places on the Missouri River, came word that cholera was raging among the emigrants; with various other depressing stories about difficulties in obtaining proper supplies of wholesome provisions, such as could be carried on so long a journey. To this was added the assertion that such an immense number had already left the Missouri, and were far on their way, that the grass was all eaten up, and no more animals could live on the great plains.

All this we heard, and all this we talked over, but still we went on, and at the end of one month and four days after beginning our travels, we reached Council Bluffs. Here we found a city of wagons, some of which had been there many days waiting their turn to cross the great river. But we were consoled by being assured that the ferry men were working as fast as possible, and that probably in a week or so, all now camped ready for crossing, would be over the Missouri. Notwithstanding the crowd of people, most of them strangers to each other, thrown together in such new and inconvenient circumstances, with much to try patience— and all standing necessarily more or less in the position of rivals for the local conveniences which campers so soon learn to look for and prize—still the utmost quiet and good humor . . . prevailed. The great majority of the crowd were men, generally working men of ordinary intelligence, farmers and mechanics—accustomed to the comforts and amenities of domestic life, and, most of them evidently intending to carry more or less of these agreeable things with them 'across the plains.' Occasionally these men were accompanied by wife and children, and their wagons were easily distinguished by the greater number of conveniences, and household articles they carried, which here, in this time of prolonged camping, were often, many of them, disposed about the outside of the wagon, in a home-like way. And, where bushes, trees or logs formed partial enclosures, a kitchen or sitting room quite easily suggested itself to a feminine heart, yearning for home. The few women who caught glimpses of each other, or, in some cases, were thrown nearer together in this motley gathering were in general very kind to each other, and to each other's children. But, waiting as they were for the very first chance to cross the Missouri, and expecting after that to travel in different companies, there was no motive for any particular mutual interest.

After patiently waiting some days for our turn to cross the river, it came at last, and on Friday the 8th of June we ventured ourselves and our little all, on board a very uncertain looking ferryboat and were slowly conveyed across the turbid and unfriendly-looking Missouri. The cattle were "swum" across the stream; the men driving them in and frightening them off from the shore in various ways, until a few of the leaders reached the flats on the opposite side. As soon as they were seen to come out of the water there, the others easily followed. A few of the many thus crossed were driven by the strong current beyond the flats and lost, but most of them crossed safely. From the place where we landed the ascent up the bluff was steep and dusty. Arriving at the top we were on an almost level plain, with only here and there a tree or two, though there was a body of timber a mile or two to the southwest. Not very far from the river we began to see the few scattering buildings of Trader's Point, the Indian Agency for this part of Nebraska Territory.

So few . . . were the houses that I scarcely remember any thing but a blacksmith's shop and, not far from it, a pretty good sized log house. Yet, on that spot Omaha City soon after grew to fair proportions, and has now for many years flourished. A slight accident had broken something about the wagon, and we stopped at the blacksmith-shop to have it repaired. The other wagons passed on to the place of encampment for the night which was to be in the edge of the before mentioned timber. Just as the blacksmith began work on our wagon, the gentlemanly Indian Agent, whom we had seen at Council Bluffs, came to us and kindly insisted upon my going, with my little girl to his home, which proved to be the good-sized log house I had noticed, and resting there till my husband was ready to proceed. I gratefully accepted, and his hospitality did not cease until we had all three partaken of a bountiful supper prepared by his kind-hearted old negro cook, and had enjoyed a good rest and social chat beside his ample fire place. He then helped us into our wagon, directed us to our camp grounds, two miles distant, expressed his good wishes for our long journey, and bade us good night. That was my farewell to the fag-end of civilization on the Atlantic side of the continent. I saw no house from that time till we passed within view of the few dwellings at Fort Laramie; and did not again eat a meal in a house, until urged to do so once only by a hospitable Mormon woman, beside whose garden fence we had permission to locate our wagon, during our stay in Salt Lake City.

From our first arrival at Council Bluffs we had been annoyed by begging and pilfering Indians, male and female. To attempt to satisfy them was out of the question, for the most trifling thing bestowed on one, would bring a dozen more. So our only defence was to keep them decidedly and quietly at a distance. Few of them could understand our words and we had to act with most emphatic dignity to keep them at all in their proper place. On the western side of the Missouri they became more numerous, swarming about us at every pause in our way from the crossing of the ferry till night closed in, but then they disappeared; and the agent assured us that they were gone, not "to bed," but to their sleep among the bushes and sand hills; and that they would not dare to molest us so near the Agency; so, we might go, without fear, to camp. His words proved true, and we arrived safely at our place of stopping for the first night in an Indian country.

The next day was spent mostly by the men in organizing a regular company, with captain, and subordinate officers whose duties and prerogatives were set forth in rules and by-laws then and there adopted. The few women in the company were busy meantime in cooking, washing, mending up clothes, etc. Notwithstanding the disheartening reports circulated among us for the past two weeks at different points in our way, hopefulness and unflinching resolution upon the whole prevailed. Some few there were, no doubt, who would have turned back, but they were involved either in family or business relations with others more resolute—or more rash—and, seeing the uselessness of resistance, they took up their part of the daily toil, in most cases, without complaining.

A number in the company tried to incorporate in the by-laws, a rule that every Sunday should be a day of rest; but they only succeeded in gaining a general assent to camping on Sundays when the necessities and dangers of the way did not demand uninterrupted traveling. The majority insisted that the lateness of the season—we being nearly the last emigrants to cross the Missouri—and the importance of keeping near to larger companies just ahead, made it imperative that we should set out the very next morning; although it was Sunday. Accordingly on the 10th of June we left our first camp ground west of the Missouri, and launched forth upon a journey in which, we all knew, from that hour there was not the least chance of turning back.

The morning was bright and the scene animating. We were up early, breakfast was dispatched, and then came the bustle of packing our wagons, which was done by one man belonging to each wagon, while the other one, or two yoked the cattle. In the few cases where there were women they were, without exception, seen doing their full share of the work. When all was ready the Captain gave the word of command, "Roll out!" and wagon after wagon fell into line in the order which had been assigned them. For an hour or two we moved on with as lively a pace as oxen could well keep up. The sun shone brightly, and all looked hopeful. We were approaching rolling hills between which, we could see, our road lay.

Suddenly, numerous dark moving objects appeared upon the hills in the distance, on both sides of the road. What could they be? Had some of the large companies ahead camped, and turned out their cattle? Or, could it be, that we were about to have our first sight of a herd of buffalo? As we drew nearer they proved to be Indians, by hundreds; and soon they had ranged themselves along on each side of the way. A group of them came forward, and at the Captain's command our company halted, while he with several others went to meet the Indians and hold a parley. It turned out that they had gathered to demand the payment of a certain sum per head for every emigrant passing through this part of the country, which they claimed as their own. The men of our company after consultation, resolved that the demand was unreasonable, that the country we were traveling over belonged to the United States, and that these red men had no right to stop us. The Indians were then plainly informed that the company meant to proceed at once without paying a dollar. That if unmolested, they would not harm anything; but if the Indians attempted to stop them, they would open fire with all their rifles and revolvers. At the Captain's word of command all the men of the company then armed themselves with every weapon to be found in their wagons. Revolvers, knives, hatchets, glittered in their belts; rifles and guns bristled on their shoulders. The drivers raised aloft their long whips, the rousing words "Go 'long Buck"—"Bright!"—"Dan!" were given all along the line, and we were at once moving between long but not very compact rows of half naked redskins; many of them well armed; others carrying but indifferent weapons; while all wore in their faces the expression of sullen disappointment, mingled with a half-defiant scowl, that suggested the thought of future night attacks, when darkness and thickets should give them greater advantage. For the present, however, they had evidently made up their minds to let us pass, and we soon lost sight of them.

But another enemy, unseen, and without one audible word of demand or threat, was in that very hour advancing upon us, and made our wagon his first point of attack. The oldest of the men who had joined company with my husband, complained of intense pain and sickness, and was soon obliged to lie down in the wagon, which, being large, gave room for quite a comfortable bed behind the seat where Mary and I sat. Soon, terrible spasms convulsed him; the Captain was called, examined the case, and ordered a halt. Medicine was administered which afforded some relief. About this time a horseman or two appeared, with the intelligence that some companies in advance of us were camped at the ford of the Elkhorn River, not more than two miles distant, and that there was a physician among them. We therefore made the sick man as comfortable as we could, and went on. Arrived at the encampment the Doctor pronounced the disease Asiatic Cholera. Everything was done that could be under the circumstances, but nothing availed, and in two or three hours the poor old man expired.

The most prompt and energetic sympathy was shown by our fellow travelers. The fact was at once recognized that close contact with the disease for several hours, had exposed us to contagion, and had also made necessary the disinfecting of our wagon and all it contained. There were in the encampment those who had tents as well as wagons, and soon a comfortable tent, with a cot bed and other conveniences, was placed at our disposal till our things could be disinfected. That Sunday night was one never to be forgotten by me. I positively refused to lie down, because there was room and covering for only one besides Mary—my husband had been on guard the night before, and on most exhausting duty all day; so I insisted upon his resting, while I sat by my little one, leaning my head on her pillow, and tried to sleep.

But a storm began in the evening. The wind moaned fitfully, and rain fell constantly. I could not sleep. I rose and walked softly to the tent door, put the curtains aside and looked out. The body of the dead man lay stretched upon a rudely constructed bier beside our wagon a few rods off, the sheet that was stretched over it flapped in the wind with a sound that suggested the idea of some vindictive creature struggling restlessly in bonds; while its white flutterings, dimly seen, confirmed the ghastly fancy. Not many yards beyond, a party of Indians—who had, for a day or two, been playing the part of friendly hangers-on to one of the large companies—had raised a rude skin tent, and built a fire, round which they were seated on the ground—looking unearthly in its flickering light, and chanting, hour after hour, a wild melancholy chant, varied by occasional high, shrill notes as of distressful appeal. The minor key ran through it all. I knew it was a death dirge.

Morning came at last. In the early dawn the body of the old man was laid in the grave that had been dug in a hill-side nearby. Then came the work of cleansing the wagon, washing bed clothes and thoroughly sunning and airing everything; for the storm was over and the sun shone very warmly. Before we had half done this work, the crossing of the Elkhorn was begun by the other companies. The wagons and people crossed on rafts and the cattle were "swum." By one or two o'clock P.M. we were all across and we finished our drying and airing on the west side. Soon after leaving the Elkhorn we struck the Platte River and now felt ourselves fairly launched out "on the plains."

The next Wednesday morning, June 13th, before dawn we were visited by one of the most terrible storms I ever recollect witnessing. Thunder, lightning and wind seemed combined to tear our frail tenements to pieces; but the same Almighty Power that sent the tempest, tempered it to us defenseless ones; and though the rain drove into our wagons, our food and clothing were not seriously injured. The next morning, just three days from the time old Mr. R—— had been buried, the first news that met our ears was, that two more of our company were ill with the same fatal disease. Before the first watch of that night was set, one of them was laid in his lonely grave. I here quote again from my diary, which I "wrote up" a few days after these events.

"Now indeed a heavy gloom hung round us. The destroyer seemed let loose upon our camp. Who would go next? What if my husband should be taken and leave us alone in the wilderness? What if I should be taken and leave my little Mary motherless? Or, still more distracting thought—what if we both should be laid low, and she be left a destitute orphan, among strangers, in a land of savages? Such thoughts would rush into my mind, and for some hours these gloomy forebodings heavily oppressed me; but I poured out my heart to God in prayer, and He gave me comfort and rest. I felt a full assurance that He would not afflict us beyond our strength to bear. I committed my precious child into His hands entirely, claiming for her His promises, and His guardianship. I said from my heart 'Thy will be done.' Then peace took possession of my soul, and spite of threatening ills, I felt strong for duty and endurance."

The second of the two sick men soon began to show favorable symptoms and in a few days recovered. From that time we had no more cases of cholera among our fellow travelers; though we passed a number of graves of its victims, and heard of deaths in other companies who camped not far from us.

On Saturday evening June 16th we arrived at the crossing of the Loup Fork of the Platte River. Here we found two companies, who had been camped there some days waiting for the waters to go down so that they could find a fording place. The bed of the Loup is, for miles, formed of quick-sand, so that where teams crossed in safety one day there might be deep holes the next. Especially after the waters had been swollen by heavy rains as had lately been the case, it was impossible to be sure of a fording place without the most careful exploration, which of course involved considerable danger. A man had been drowned only a short time before our arrival, by venturing too hastily forward, when nearly across. He had found the water so shallow thus far, that he became too sanguine, and stepped suddenly into a deep channel, where the rushing water and sand soon swallowed him up.

On the third day it was announced that the water had sufficiently subsided for us to attempt the passage; though there was still rather an ugly current near the farther shore. On our side there was shallow water for some rods through which our ordinary teams could pull a lightly-loaded wagon. Then there was an island of sand; and beyond that, the current was so deep and strong that teams would have to be doubled, and long ropes used. Moreover the greatest dispatch was necessary; for the sands shifted so constantly that the bottom changed more or less every hour. As the quickest way of working, our own teams were to take to the island two or three wagons at a time, then, fastening all the cattle to one wagon, with several men to drive, they were to rush that one rapidly across the deeper stream, and return for another. As fast as one standing-place on the island was vacated another wagon was driven over the shallow water to be ready for its turn; and thus one fresh team was used to each wagon at the hardest point. It was a little exciting for us women to take our seats, with our children beside us, and be drawn upon these treacherous sands we had heard so much of for two or three days; and it became startling when we felt the wagon trembling under us, as in a lively earthquake. The vibrations did not cease while we stood on the island, the wheels perpetually settling with short jerks into the sand: had we been obliged to stay there long we should have sunk to the hubs. But the men and faithful cattle worked nobly, and in due time we were west of the treacherous Loup Fork.

A few days after this we had a new and unexpected experience in the way of a stampede of cattle. On camping for the night each company of wagons always formed a corral by placing the wagons one before the other in such a position as to make a large circle. The tongue of each wagon dropped its end to the ground, as the cattle were loosed from it, and the wagon in front was backed up so close as to leave barely room for a person to step in and out. A space, large enough to form a gateway, was left between the back of the first wagon and the front of the last, and into this gateway the cattle were driven at night, after they had well pastured; and the gateway was closed by ox-chains, securely fastened to the wheels of the two terminating wagons. Then a guard of two or three men, was set, who patrolled on the outside of the corral, and were changed after midnight. On the night of the 19th of June our wagon was one of the terminating ones with its back to the gateway. On Wednesday morning June 20th I was awakened between three and four o'clock, by the sound of rain upon the wagon-top. It was quite a moderate shower, and I lay thinking, in a calm mood, when a flash of lightning came, followed in a moment by a strange, rushing sound, which quickly became loud as thunder. The wagon began to shake violently, then to move as if pushed sideways by a great force, then it was lifted and thrown violently over on its side; there was a crash of breaking wheels and chains, the rapid tramp of cattle became distinct for a minute, and then was lost in the distance.

When we and our neighbors on the other side of the gateway, had picked ourselves up, and out, and found that none of us were much hurt, we began to try to account for the catastrophe, and examine its extent. The cattle must have been frightened by the flash of lightning. Those near the entrance of the corral instinctively tried to escape, others near, pressed upon them, the panic grew, till, in their frantic struggles, they overturned the two chained wagons. At that moment the chains must have broken and cleared the passage-way, or they would have trampled us to death. There were some unimportant injuries done to both the wagons and to some of their contents; but the grand calamity was the breaking of three wheels; one of ours, and two of the other. We had, a day or two before, entered upon a stage of the journey marked in our guide-books as being destitute of timber for nearly two hundred miles, with the exception of one, solitary tree—about midway of the distance—marked down as "The Lone Tree." Just as we had found out the worst of our breakage, the Captain of the company came near, and, after gazing a moment in speechless consternation, exclaimed, "Three wheels broke all to smash, and fifty miles from timber!" It was true, and the fact was a hard one, yet, strange elasticity of mind, we laughed heartily at the grotesque speech.

But now, what was to be done? In the first place, the cattle had "stampeded," and were all gone. How, and when could they be got back? Often in such cases they ran themselves to death. But even while we thus questioned, we were told that at the first alarm, some of the men had mounted the few horses owned in the company, and were last seen gaining upon the swiftest fugitives; while others, on foot, had already succeeded in turning back some of the more gentle ones. But those broken wheels—how could they be repaired in this desert? It soon turned out that there was a blacksmith in the company, with some tools, and a few odd pieces of hard wood; there were also two families who had brought with them wide, hard-wood boards, two or three feet long, which they used for tables while camping. These were freely contributed to the necessities of the occasion; and, as some of the spokes of the broken wheels were still whole, as well as parts of the rims, it was soon decided that enough material for repairs was at hand, though we *were* 'fifty miles from timber.' In a few hours the lost cattle were all recovered, and had plenty of time to rest and feed while the wagons were mended, which took all the remainder of that day, and the whole of the next.

On Sunday the 29th of July we determined to remain in camp and rest till the next day. One family of our fellow travelers, Mr. B—— and his wife with their three little boys, did the same. We enjoyed a quiet rest, held a social meeting for prayer, reading and singing, and the next morning resumed our journey, much re-freshed. From this time till we reached Salt Lake we had no earthly company or protection except that mutually afforded and enjoyed by two men, two women and four children, the oldest not more than eight, and the youngest not yet three. Twice we met with Indians, but they did not molest us. We passed the company we had been traveling with, kept in advance of them, notwithstanding Sunday rests, and arrived in Salt Lake valley the day before they did. Saturday the 4th of August we reached the South Pass of the Rocky Mountains.

Our Guide Book gave very elaborate directions by which we might be able to identify the highest point in our road, where we passed from the Atlantic to the Pacific Slope. Otherwise we could not have noticed it, so gradual had been the ascent, and so slightly varied was the surface for a mile or two on all sides. But I had looked forward for weeks to the step that should take me past the point. In the morning of that day I had taken my last look at the waters that flowed eastward, to mingle with the streams and wash the shores where childhood and early youth had been spent; where all I loved, save, O, so small a number, lived; and now I stood on the almost imperceptible elevation that, when passed, would separate me from all these, perhaps forever. Through what toils and dangers we had come to reach that point; and, as I stood looking my farewell, a strong desire seized me to mark the spot in some way, and record at least one word of grateful acknowledgment. Yes, I would make a little heap of stones, and mark on one of them, or on a stick, the word "Ebenezer."

Nobody would notice or understand it; but my Heavenly Father would see the little monument in the mountain wilderness, and accept the humble thanks it recorded. So I turned to gather stones. But no stone could I find, not even pebbles enough to make a heap—and no stick either, not a bush or a shrub or a tree within reach. So I stood still upon the spot till the two wagons and the little company had passed out of hearing; and when I left not a visible sign marked the place.

We were now for several days crossing the extreme northern end of the great Colorado Valley. Many of the springs were so strong with alkali as to be powerfully poisonous, and the grass in their vicinity was the same. One of our oxen died on the second day after entering this section, and we were obliged to yoke up the rest, and travel all night, so as to get to safer feed and water. On Saturday of that week we camped at night by Black Fork where we rested over Sunday. The next day reached Fort Bridger where was a rude log fort and one or two log huts. We got what information we could about the road and passed on.

The next day August 14th we crossed the dividing ridge between the Colorado Valley and the Great Salt Lake Basin. Here, in the Wasatch Mountains, our road was by far the most precipitous and the scenery the wildest, we had yet seen. At the greatest elevation our altitude was seven thousand some hundred feet. Looking up to the high peak which towered above us on our left, we distinctly saw snow driving and eddying about in the strong wind. The clouds settled down nearer to us and we had a lively sprinkling of rain for a short time, but as we descended we were soon again in the hot sunshine; the dust, which had been excessive for two days, growing deeper and deeper, lighter and lighter, till it was like wading through a bed of fine ashes; so that when, at the entrance of Great Salt Lake Valley, we paused to take breath, and faced each other with mutual looks of wonder, we agreed that we did not know each other; and it was not till after a free use of the pure valley waters, aided in some instances by the hot mineral springs, that we recovered our identity.

It was near sunset on the 18th of August when we got our first view of the Great Salt Lake, with its back-ground of mountains; and in its foreground the well laid-out city, of snug dwellings and thrifty gardens. The suddenness with which we came upon the view was startling. From narrow mountain gorges and rough crooked turns, our road abruptly led us through an opening, almost like an immense doorway, unarched at the top. Here we were on a small plateau some hundreds of feet above the valley, with nothing to obstruct one's view for many miles. It is impossible to describe how, in the transparent atmosphere, everything was brought out with a distinctness that almost ignored distance. From here the road wound gradually down the mountain side to the plain and then into the City. As it was near sunset we camped on the second plateau, rested there through Sunday, and then moved into the City of Great Salt Lake.

At this point, company organizations were broken up, almost without exception, and every man proceeded to make such arrangements as seemed best to himself and those belonging to the same wagon. In many cases, even those owning teams and wagons together, sold out and parted goods, each taking his own way. Some few hurried on at once, but nearly all remained, a few days at least, to recruit. There was a general selling of tired out cattle; and buying of fresh.

DESERT

— ✥ —

Our only guide from Salt Lake City consisted of two small sheets of note paper, sewed together, and bearing on the outside in writing the title "Best Guide to the Gold Mines, 816 miles, by Ira J. Willes, GSL City."

This little pamphlet was wholly in writing, there being at that time no printing press at Salt Lake. It was gotten up by a man who had been to California and back the preceding year. The directions, and the descriptions of camping places, together with the distances seemed pretty definite and satisfactory until they reached the lower part of the Mary's or Humboldt River; when poor camping and scarcity of water were mentioned with discouraging frequency. From the sink of the Humboldt, all seemed confusion. We were told by our writer, to look out for a new track which "was to be made last fall" and which *might be better,*" and just here, for several stages, all seemed uncertainty. Indeed the man from whom we got the Guide Book told my husband he must be guided in this part of the way, by information which he must get from a returning Mormon Train, which we would meet before reaching the Humboldt.

The only man who now accompanied my husband was considerably advanced in years, and not in perfect health. He was extremely anxious to reach California, but had no means in the world save one solitary ox, a little clothing and sufficient food to sustain him till he reached El Dorado, if he could go straight through. He offered to put his ox into the team, to help drive and take care of the cattle and assist otherwise, so far as able, for the privilege of traveling in company and having his few things carried. Thus we set forth on the last, and by far the most perilous, stage of our great journey.

We had traveled but a few days, when, after camping one evening, we saw approaching, a couple of young men, scarcely beyond boyhood, having with them a horse and a mule. They stopped not far from us, turned out their animals to feed, made a fire and took their evening meal, as we were doing; and, after awhile, came over to our camp to talk. They also had launched out alone, and would be very glad to keep in company with us. As they appeared civil, and one of them rather gentlemanly, we of course did not object. This seemed like a little more protection; but it had its drawbacks; for we soon found out they had very little to eat; and in a few days they began to plead for some of our flour; promising they would hunt, away from the road, every day and bring in game to keep up the supply of provisions. But game was scarce, and very few were the times along the whole way that they caught any. We had allowed a very small margin of provisions for contingencies, because the necessity for the fastest possible traveling was so great.

Still we kept on, sharing, and hoping for the best. Their efforts at hunting, fruitless as they usually were, kept the young men away from the road most of the time, so that we were nearly as much alone as ever. On the morning of the 11th of September they had been away from us for some hours. We were moving quietly along our way, no living creature, save our plodding team and our own feeble company, within sight, when, suddenly, there appeared from between the hills a party of Indians. As they came nearer we saw they were all armed; and presently several arranged themselves in a sort of semi-circle closing the road, and one of them laid his rifle across the foreheads of our leaders, and stopped the team.

From my seat in the wagon I had from their first appearance observed every movement. I saw we were completely in their power. Their numbers and their arms were enough to destroy us in a few moments. Even if the young men with their guns were at hand there would be no hope in battle. If firing once commenced those savages would not cease till they had laid low, at least every man of the company. There was no hope, save in an influence that should change their purpose, in so far as it was hostile, and supply motives for letting us go. With my whole soul I prayed that God would wield that influence, and supply those motives; and as they closed around us I cast all into His hands without any other hope.

At first every appearance was hostile. They were importunate in demanding various things, acted with the air of victors, some of the younger ones pressed close to the wagon, and looked in, with boisterous exclamations and impertinent gestures. But I was enabled to keep a firm unblenching front, taking care that my little Mary did not stir from my side. She was too young to realize any danger, and thought the whole rather amusing. My husband met them from the first with a calm, business-like air, as if he thought they wanted to hold a consultation with him; and when they became overbearing, he still kept on making speeches to them, though we could not perceive that they understood what he said. Their behavior changed several times quite strangely. They would draw nearer together and consult with puzzled looks, some of them still guarding the team. Then they would scowl and seem to differ among themselves. Thus they kept us for perhaps an hour, when, all at once, my husband raised the big ox-whip, shouted to the cattle, and rushed them forward so suddenly that those nearest Indians instinctively stepped aside, then pompously exclaiming "I'm going to move on" he called the old man to follow, and we were once more in motion. But would they let us keep on? I looked through a small gap in the wagon. They were evidently puzzled by such unusual behavior, and as evidently divided in their counsels. Some were vociferating—with their guns in threatening positions—others plainly differed from them, but it was certain they had not quite decided what to do, when a turn of the road took us out of sight.

We expected they would way-lay us again; for we were passing through several narrow defiles that day—but the hours went by and night came, without another sight of the enemy. My husband kept guard that night, and I slept very little. The others of our little company disappeared among the bushes and seemed to sleep as well as usual.

Two days after this we met a band of Mormons who had been gold-hunting in California for the summer, and were on their return to Salt Lake. This was the company whose leader was to tell us how we might get from the Sink of the Humboldt, otherwise Mary's River, to Carson River; for that was a part of our journey which yet lay shrouded in grim mystery. The directions given us seemed very plain. He traced out the road in the sand with a stick—I think it was his whip handle. It was taken for granted that we knew our way to the "Sink of the Mary's [Humboldt] River" so he took *that* for his starting point in giving us directions, and showed us that, soon after passing there, we would see a plain wagon track leading to the left, which we were to follow, and it would bring us to grassy meadows, lying two or three miles from the main road, and so, still abounding in feed. Here also, he said, we would find several shallow wells, dug but recently—in the last part of the season—by Mormons, who had gone to spend the winter in California, and on their way there had found these meadows, cut feed in them for use on the forty mile desert and, on arriving in California had given to him and his company—then just about to start for Salt Lake—directions to find the spot. The wells, he said had good water in them when he was there a few days before. None of them were deep, but the water was near the surface all about there, and we could, if we found it desirable, scoop out one or two of the holes deeper, let them settle all night, and in the morning have plenty of fresh water.

He was evidently an old and experienced traveler of deserts, plains and mountains. He advised us to camp in the meadows he described, for at least two or three days, let the cattle rest and feed freely, while the men made it their first business to cut as much hay as there was room for in the wagon. This would partly dry while the cattle were recruiting; then load it up, fill every available vessel with water, and set out on the desert about noon of the day, if the weather were cool—otherwise toward evening. When once out on the desert we were to stop at intervals of a few hours, feed some of the hay to the cattle, give them a moderate drink, let them breathe a short time and then go on. In this way, he said, we would be able to reach Carson River in about twenty-four hours from the time of starting on the desert.

After hearing his instructions, and having the road made thus plain to us, we went on with renewed cheerfulness and energy. On Sunday the 16th of September we camped on the head branch of Mary's River, and on Monday morning passed through a cañon which brought us to the River itself, down which we continued to travel for several days. It was now getting late in the season, and we could not help feeling it rather ominous that a thunderstorm overtook us one evening followed by cold nights; and on the evening and night of the 1st of October a terrific wind blew, threatening for hours to strangle us with thick clouds of sand, and to blow our wagon, with all our means of living, over the steep bluff. But a good Providence preserved us and, with the morning calm returned. We had now nearly reached the head of Humboldt Lake, which, at this late period in the dry season, was utterly destitute of water, the river having sunk gradually in the sand, until, hereabout it entirely disappeared. Still, the name "Sink of Mary's or Humboldt River" was applied in our Guide Book, as well as in conversations at Salt Lake City, to the *southern* or *lower end* of Humboldt Lake, a point some ten miles farther on our way, where, we were told, there were several holes dug, close to the road. Having always understood it to be thus applied, it of course never came into our minds to suppose, that our Mormon friend, when he so particularly marked in the sand "The Sink of Mary's," meant the point where at that time the river actually disappeared.

When, therefore, on the night of October 2nd, we camped in the neighborhood of the last mentioned point, we said, "Now, we must be about twelve or thirteen miles from where that road to the meadows leads off to the left; and thence it will be only two or three miles to the meadows, where we are to rest and prepare for the desert. If we rise *very* early tomorrow morning, we shall get there by noon, and have a half day to settle camp, and get ready for work." Accordingly the first one who woke the next morning roused all the rest, and, though we found it was not much past two o'clock, we agreed it was not best to sleep again; so, by our fire of sage-brush we took some hot coffee, and the last bit of rabbit pot-pie—the result of a very rare success the day before—yoked up the oxen, and went resolutely on our way.

It was moonlight, but the gray-white sand with only here and there a sage-brush looked all so much alike that it required care to keep the road. And now, for the first time in my life, I saw a mirage; or several repetitions of that optical illusion. Once it was an extended sheet of water lying calmly bright in the moonlight, with here and there a tree on its shores; and our road seemed to tend directly towards it; then it was a small lake seen through openings in a row of trees, while the shadowy outlines of a forest appeared beyond it; all lying to our left. What a pity it seemed to be passing it by, when our poor animals had been so stinted of late. Again, we were traveling parallel with a placid river on our right; beyond which were trees; and from us to the water's edge the ground sloped so gently it appeared absurd not to turn aside to its brink and refresh ourselves and our oxen.

But, as day dawned, these beautiful sights disappeared, and we began to look anxiously for the depression in the ground, and the holes dug, which we were told would mark the Sink of the Humboldt. But it was nearly noonday before we came to them. There was still some passable water in the holes, but not fit to drink clear, so we contrived to gather enough sticks of sage to boil some, made a little coffee, ate our lunch and, thus refreshed, we hastened to find the forking road. Our director had told us, that within about two or three miles beyond the Sink we might look for the road, to the left, and we did look, and kept looking, and going on, drearily, till the sun got lower and lower, and night was fast approaching. Then the conviction, which had long been gaining ground in my mind, took possession of the whole party. We had passed the forks of the road before daylight, that morning, and were now miles out on the desert without a mouthful of food for the cattle and only two or three quarts of water in a little cask.

What could be done? Halt we must, for the oxen were nearly worn out and night was coming on. The animals must at least rest, if they could not be fed: and, that they might rest, they were chained securely to the wagon, for, hungry and thirsty as they were, they would, if loose, start off frantically in search of water and food, and soon drop down exhausted. Having fastened them in such a way that they could lie down, we took a few mouthfuls of food, and then, we in our wagon and the men not far off upon the sand, fell wearily to sleep; a forlorn little company wrecked upon the desert.

The first question in the morning was, "How can the oxen be kept from starving?" A happy thought occurred. We had, thus far on our journey, managed to keep something in the shape of a bed to sleep on. It was a mattress-tick, and, just before leaving Salt Lake, we had put into it some fresh hay—not very much, for our load must be as light as possible; but the old gentleman traveling with us had also a small straw mattress; the two together might keep the poor things from starving for a few hours. At once a small portion was dealt out to them and for the present they were saved. For ourselves we had food which we believed would about last us till we reached the Gold Mines if we could go right on: if we were much delayed anywhere, it was doubtful. The two or three quarts of water in our little cask would last only a few hours, to give moderate drinks to each of the party. For myself I inwardly determined I should scarcely take any of it as, I had found, throughout the journey, that I could do with less drink than most land travelers. Some of the men, however, easily suffered with thirst, and, as to my little girl, it is well known, a child cannot do long without either water or milk. Everything looked rather dark, and dubious.

Should we try to go on? But there were miles of desert before us, in which, we knew, neither grass or water could be found. We had been told by those who had crossed it with comparatively fresh teams, that, with plenty of hay and water to bait with, we might get over it in about twenty-four hours, though it was acknowledged it might take us longer. Here we were, without water, and with only a few mouthfuls of poor feed, while our animals were already tired out, and very hungry and thirsty. No, it would be madness to go farther out in the desert under such conditions. Should we then turn back and try to reach the meadows with their wells? But, as near as we could calculate, it could not be less than twelve or fifteen miles to them. Would it be possible for our poor cattle to reach there? Their only food would be that pitiful mess still left in our mattresses. It might be divided into two portions, giving them each a few mouthfuls more at noon, and then, if they kept on their feet long enough to reach the holes at the Sink, we might possibly find enough water to give them each a little drink, which, with the remainder of the fodder might keep them up till the meadows were reached. It was a forlorn hope; but it was all we had.

The morning was wearing away while these things were talked over. Precious time was being wasted; but, the truth was, the situation was so new and unexpected, that it seemed for awhile to confuse—almost to stupefy—most of the little party; and, those least affected in this way, felt so deeply the responsibility of the next move, that they dared not decide upon it hastily. The least responsible and efficient of the company had been most of the morning, wandering aimlessly about, sometimes keeping within a small circle, then again branching off nearly out of sight. Perhaps they all had a vague hope they might find another track. But now, as noon approached, they gathered near the wagon, tired, moody, and evidently very near "giving up." But this would never do. So the more hopeful ones proposed that we should all eat something and, as soon as the noon heat abated, prepare for a move. So we took some lunch, and soon the men were lying upon the sand at short distances from each other, fast asleep. My little Mary slept too. But I was not sleepy. With unwearied gaze my eyes swept, again and again, the shimmering horizon. There was no help or hope there. Then I looked at what lay nearest. How short-lived our few remaining resources would be, unless fresh strength came soon from somewhere. How still it was. Only the sound of a few feeble breaths. It would not take many hours of starvation to quiet them forever.

All the human aid we had could do but little now; and if, in trying to do that little, one more mistake were made, it must be fatal. When then this calm strength which girded me round so surely, while I, and all surrounding me were so weak? I had known what it was to *believe* in God, and to pray that He would never leave us. Was it thus then, that when all other helpers failed, He came so near that I no longer simply *believed* in Him, but *knew* His presence there, giving strength for whatever might come? Soon some of the party awoke and, after a little talk, concluded that two of them would walk to a bald ridge that rose out of the flat waste, about a mile and a half distant, and take a view from thence, in the faint hope that we might yet be mistaken, and the forking road and the meadows might still be in advance. My husband said he would go, and the best of the two young men went with him, while the other two wandered listlessly off again. I made no opposition; I felt no inclination to oppose; though I knew the helplessness and loneliness of the position would thus be greatly increased. But that calm strength, that certainty of One near and all sufficient hushed and cheered me. Only a woman who has been alone upon a desert with her helpless child can have any adequate idea of my experience for the next hour or two. But that consciousness of an unseen Presence still sustained me.

When the explorers returned from their walk to the ridge, it was only to report, no discovery: nothing to be seen on all sides but sand and scattered sagebrush interspersed with the carcasses of dead cattle. So there was nothing to be done but to turn back and try to find the meadows. Turn back! What a chill the words sent through one. *Turn back*, on a journey like that; in which every mile had been gained by most earnest labor, growing more and more intense, until, of late, it had seemed that the certainty of *advance* with every step, was all that made the next step possible. And now for miles we were to *go back*. In all that long journey no steps ever seemed so heavy, so hard to take, as those with which I turned my back to the sun that afternoon of October 4th, 1849.

We had not been long on the move when we saw dust rising in the road at a distance, and soon perceived we were about to meet a little caravan of wagons. Then a bright gleam of hope stole in. They had doubtless stopped at the meadows, and were supplied with grass and water. Might it not be possible that they would have enough to spare for us? Then we could go on with them. My heart bounded at the thought. But the hope was short lived. We met, and some of the men gathered round our wagon with eager inquiries, while those who could not leave their teams stood looking, with wonder, at a solitary wagon headed the wrong way.

Our story was soon told. It turned out that they were camping in the meadows at the very time we passed the forking road without seeing it, the morning we so ambitiously started soon after midnight. Ah, we certainly got up too early that day. If we had only seen that road and taken it, we might now have been with this company, provided for the desert, and no longer alone. But, when the question was asked whether they could spare sufficient grass and water to get our team over the desert, they shook their heads, and unanimously agreed that it was out of the question. Their own cattle, they said, were weak from long travel and too often scant supplies. They had only been able to load up barely enough to get to the Carson River. The season was far advanced and the clouds, hanging of late round the mountain tops, looked threatening. It would be like throwing away their own lives without any certainty of saving ours; for once out in the desert without food we would all be helpless together. One of the men had his family with him, a wife and two or three children; and while they talked the woman was seen coming towards us. She had not, when they first halted, understood that any but men were with the lone wagon.

As soon as she heard to the contrary, and what were the circumstances, she hastened, with countenance full of concern, to condole with me; and, I think, had the decision depended alone upon her, she would have insisted upon our turning back with them and sharing their feed and water to the last.

But fortunately for them, probably for us all, other counsels prevailed, and we resumed our depressing backward march. Two or three things, before uncertain, were settled by this meeting. The first was the distance to the meadows, which they agreed could not be less than fourteen or sixteen miles from where we met them, which seemed, in our circumstances, like an appalling interval. But there was relief in being assured that we should find a pretty good supply of water in the holes at the Sink, where we were to camp that night, and that, when we once reached the meadows, there was food and water enough for a number of teams during many days. We had also definite directions as to the shortest road, and were assured it was perfectly plain, and good except that it was rather sandy.

I had now become so impressed with the danger of the cattle giving out, that I refused to ride except for occasional brief rests. So, soon after losing sight of the dust of the envied little caravan, I left the wagon and walked the remainder of the day. For a good while I kept near the wagon but, by and by, being very weary I fell behind. The sun had set, before we reached the Sink, and the light was fading fast when the wagon disappeared from my sight behind a slight elevation; and, as the others had gone on in advance some time before, I was all alone on the barren waste. However, as I recognized the features of the neighborhood, and knew we were quite near the Sink, I felt no particular apprehension, only a feeling that it was a weird and dreary scene and instinctively urged forward my lagging footsteps in hope of regaining sight of the wagon.

Suddenly I caught sight of an object a few rods distant on the left of the road, moving steadily but rather stealthily toward the road, in a line that would intercept it some paces ahead of me. I stopped—the creature stopped too, looking steadily at me. It was a coyote. I had several times during the journey heard them howling at night but, as the season had advanced, they had been seldom heard, and to meet one thus almost face to face with no human being in sight was a little startling. But, calling to mind what I had heard of their reluctance to face a steady look and determined resistance, I lifted my hands with threatening gestures, raised a shout, and sprang forward a step or two. Mr. Coyote stood a moment as if questioning the resistance offered; but when I repeated, more violently, the gestures and the shouts, he turned and retraced his steps into the dim distance, only looking back once or twice to see if the enemy retained the ground. As he disappeared I hastened forward, and in a few minutes came within sight of the wagon, now halted for the night near the camp fire, which the men had just lit.

The next morning we resumed our backward march after feeding out the last mouthful of fodder. The water in the little cask was nearly used up in making coffee for supper and breakfast; but, if only each one would be moderate in taking a share when thirst impelled him, we might yet reach the wells before any one suffered seriously. We had lately had but few chances for cooking; and only a little boiled rice with dried fruit, and a few bits of biscuit remained after we had done breakfast. If we could only reach the meadows by noon. But that we could hardly hope for, the animals were so weak and tired. There was no alternative, however, the only thing to be done was to go steadily on, determined to do and endure to the utmost.

I found no difficulty this morning in keeping up with the team. They went so slowly, and I was so preternaturally stimulated by anxiety to get forward, that, before I was aware of it I would be some rods ahead of the cattle, straining my gaze as if expecting to see a land of promise, long before I had any rational hope of the kind. My imagination acted intensely. I seemed to see Hagar, in the wilderness walking wearily away from her fainting child among the dried up bushes, and seating herself in the hot sand. I seemed to become Hagar myself, and when my little one, from the wagon behind me, called out, "Mamma I want a drink"—I stopped, gave her some, noted that there were but a few swallows left, then mechanically pressed onward again, alone, repeating, over and over, the words, "Let me not see the death of the child."

Just in the heat of noon-day we came to where the sage bushes were nearer together; and a fire, left by campers or Indians, had spread for some distance, leaving beds of ashes, and occasionally charred skeletons of bushes to make the scene more dreary. Smoke was still sluggishly curling up here and there, but no fire was visible; when suddenly just before me to my right a bright flame sprang up at the foot of a small bush, ran rapidly up it, leaped from one little branch to another till all, for a few seconds, were ablaze together, then went out, leaving nothing but a few ashes and a little smouldering trunk. It was a small incident, easily accounted for, but to my then over-wrought fancy it made more vivid the illusion of being a wanderer in a far off, old time desert, and myself witnessing a wonderful phenomenon. For a few moments I stood with bowed head worshiping the God of Horeb, and I was strengthened thereby.

Wearily passed the hottest noon-day hour, with many an anxious look at the horned-heads, which seemed to me to bow lower and lower, while the poor tired hoofs almost refused to move. The two young men had been out of sight for sometime; when, all at once, we heard a shout, and saw, a few hundred yards in advance a couple of hats thrown into the air and four hands waving triumphantly. As soon as we got near enough, we heard them call out, "Grass and water! Grass and water!" and shortly we were at the meadows. The remainder of that day was spent chiefly in rest and refreshment. The next day the men busied themselves in cutting and spreading grass; while I sorted out and re-arranged things in the wagon so as to make all possible room for hay and water; and also cooked all the meat we had left, and as much of our small stock of flour, rice, and dried fruits, as might last us till we could again find wood.

The day after that was Sunday, and we should have had a very quiet rest, had we not been visited by a party of some eight or ten Indians, who came from the Humboldt Mountains on Saturday afternoon, and remained near us till we left. They professed to be friendly; but were rather troublesome, and evidently desirous of getting something out of us if they could. Two or three of them had rifles; and when the young men went to talk to them they began to show off their marksmanship by firing at particular objects. The young men felt this to be rather of the nature of a challenge; and thought it would be safer to accept than to ignore it. So they got the arms from the wagon, set up a mark, and, as one of them—the gentleman of the two—proved to be a remarkable shot, the Indians were struck with surprise, which, as, time after time, W——'s ball hit within an inch of his aim, grew to admiration, and ended in evident awe; for not one of their party could quite equal him. How much our safety, and exemption from pillage were due to that young man's true aim we might not be quite sure; but I have always been very willing to acknowledge a debt of gratitude to him.

On Monday morning we loaded up, but did not hurry, for the cattle had not rested any too long; another day would have been better; but we dared not linger. So, giving them time that morning thoroughly to satisfy themselves with grass and water we once more set forward toward the formidable desert, and, at that late season, with our equipment, the scarcely less formidable Sierras. The feeling that we were once more going forward instead of backward, gave an animation to every step which we could never have felt but by contrast. By night we were again at the Sink where we once more camped; but we durst not, the following morning, launch out upon the desert with the whole day before us; for, though it was now the 9th of October, the sun was still powerful for some hours daily, and the arid sand doubled its heat. Not much after noon, however, we ventured out upon the sea of sand; this time to cross or die.

Not far from the edge of night we stopped to bait, at no great distance from the scene of our last week's bitter disappointment. Once beyond that, I began to feel renewed courage, as though the worst were passed; and, as I had walked much of the afternoon, and knew I must walk again by and by, I was persuaded to get into the wagon and lie down by Mary, who was sleeping soundly. By a strong effort of will, backed by the soothing influence of prayer, I fell asleep, but only for a few minutes. I was roused by the stopping of the wagon, and then my husband's voice said, "So you've given out, have you Tom?" and at the same moment I knew by the rattling chains and yokes that some of the cattle were being loosed from the team. I was out of the wagon in a minute. One of the oxen was prostrate on the ground, and his companion, from whose neck the yoke was just being removed, looked very likely soon to follow him. It had been the weak couple all along. Now we had but two yoke. How soon would they, one by one, follow?

Nothing could induce me to get into the wagon again. I said I would walk by the team, and for awhile I did; but by and by I found myself yards ahead. An inward power urged me forward; and the poor cattle were so slow, it seemed every minute as if they were going to stop. When I got so far off as to miss the sound of footsteps and wheels, I would pause, startled, wait and listen, dreading lest they had stopped, then as they came near, I would again walk beside them awhile, watching, through the darkness, the dim outlines of their heads and horns to see if they drooped lower. But soon I found myself again forward and alone. There was no moon yet, but by starlight we had for some time seen, only too plainly, the dead bodies of cattle lying here and there on both sides of the road. As we advanced they increased in numbers, and presently we saw two or three wagons. At first we thought we had overtaken a company, but coming close, no sign of life appeared. We had candles with us, so, as there was not the least breeze, we lit one or two and examined. Everything indicated a complete break down, and a hasty flight. Some animals were lying nearly in front of a wagon, apparently just as they had dropped down, while loose yokes and chains indicated that part of the teams had been driven on, laden probably with some necessaries of life; for the contents of the wagons were scattered in confusion, the most essential articles alone evidently having been thought worth carrying. "Ah," we said, "some belated little company has been obliged to pack what they could, and hurry to the river. Maybe it was the little company we met the other day." It was not a very encouraging scene but our four oxen still kept their feet; we would drive on a little farther, out of this scene of ruin, bait them, rest ourselves and go on. We did so, but soon found that what we had supposed an exceptional misfortune must have been the common fate of many companies; for at still shortening intervals, scenes of ruin similar to that just described kept recurring till we seemed to be but the last, little, feeble, struggling band at the rear of a routed army.

From near midnight, on through the small hours, it appeared necessary to stop more frequently, for both man and beast were sadly weary, and craved frequent nourishment. Soon after midnight we finished the last bit of meat we had; but there was still enough of the biscuit, rice and dried fruit to give us two or three more little baits. The waning moon now gave us a little melancholy light, showing still the bodies of dead cattle, and the forms of forsaken wagons as our grim way-marks. In one or two instances they had been left in the very middle of the road; and we had to turn out into the untracked sand to pass them. Soon we came upon a scene of wreck that surpassed anything preceding it. As we neared it, we wondered at the size of the wagons, which, in the dim light, looked tall as houses, against the sky. Coming to them, we found three of four of them to be of the make that the early Mississippi Valley emigrants used to call "Prairie Schooners": having deep beds, with projecting backs and high tops. One of them was specially immense, and, useless as we felt it to be to spend time in examining these warning relics of those who had gone before us, curiosity led us to lift the front curtain, which hung down, and by the light of our candle that we had again lit,

{ 37 }

look in. There from the strong, high bows, hung several sides of well cured bacon, much better in quality than that we had finished, at our last resting place. So we had but a short interval in which to say we were destitute of meat, for, though, warned by all we saw not to add a useless pound to our load, we thought it wise to take a little, to eke out our scanty supply of food. And, as to the young men, who had so rarely, since they joined us, had a bit of meat they could call their own, they were very glad to bear the burden of a few pounds of bacon slung over their shoulders.

After this little episode, the only cheering incident for many hours, we turned to look at what lay round these monster wagons. It would be impossible to describe the motley collection of things of various sorts, strewed all about. The greater part of the materials, however, were pasteboard boxes, some complete, but most of them broken, and pieces of wrapping paper still creased, partially in the form of packages. But the most prominent objects were two or three, perhaps more, very beautifully finished trunks of various sizes, some of them standing open, their pretty trays lying on the ground, and all rifled of their contents; save that occasionally a few pamphlets, or, here and there, a book remained in the corners. We concluded that this must have been a company of merchants hauling a load of goods to California, that some of their animals had given out, and, fearing the rest would they had packed such things as they could, and had fled for their lives toward the river. There was only one thing, (besides the few pounds of bacon) that, in all these varied heaps of things, many of which, in civilized scenes, would have been valuable, I thought worth picking up. That was a little book, bound in cloth and illustrated with a number of small engravings. Its title was "Little Ella." I thought it would please Mary, so I put it in my pocket. It was an easily carried souvenir of the desert; and more than one pair of young eyes learned to read its pages in after years.

Morning was now approaching, and we hoped, when full daylight came, to see some signs of the river. But, for two or three weary hours after sunrise nothing of the kind appeared. The last of the water had been given to the cattle before daylight. When the sun was up we gave them the remainder of their hay, took a little breakfast and pressed forward. For a long time not a word was spoken save occasionally to the cattle. I had again, unconsciously, got in advance; my eyes scanning the horizon to catch the first glimpse of any change; though I had no definite idea in my mind what first to expect. But now there was surely something. Was it a cloud? It was very low at first and I feared it might evaporate as the sun warmed it. But it became rather more distinct and a little higher. I paused, and stood till the team came up. Then walking beside it I asked my husband what he thought that low dark line could be. "I think," he said, "it must be the timber on Carson River." Again we were silent and for a while I watched anxiously the heads of the two leading cattle. They were rather unusually fine animals, often showing considerable intelligence, and so faithful had they been, through so many trying scenes, I could not help feeling a sort of attachment to them; and I pitied them, as I observed how low their heads drooped as they pressed their shoulders so resolutely and yet so wearily against the bows. Another glance at the horizon. Surely there was now visible a little unevenness in the top of that dark line, as though it might indeed be trees. "How far off do you think that is now?" I said. "About five or six miles I guess," was the reply. At that moment the white-faced leader raised his head, stretched forward his nose and uttered a low "Moo-o-oo." I was startled fearing it was the sign for him to fall, exhausted. "What is the matter with him?" I said. "I think he smells the water" was the answer. "How can he at such a distance?" As I spoke, the other leader raised his head, stretched out his nose, and uttered the same sound. The hinder cattle seemed to catch the idea, whatever it was; they all somewhat increased their pace, and from that time, showed renewed animation.

But we had yet many weary steps to take, and noon had passed before we stood in the shade of those longed-for trees, beside the Carson River. As soon as the yokes were removed the oxen walked into the stream, and stood a few moments, apparently enjoying its coolness, then drank as they chose, came out, and soon found feed that satisfied them for the present, though at this point it was not abundant. The remainder of that day was spent in much needed rest. The next day we did not travel many miles, for our team showed decided signs of weakness, and the sand became deeper as we advanced, binding the wheels so as to make hauling very hard. We had conquered the desert.

Mountains

— ❧·❦ —

But the great Sierra Nevada Mountains were still all before us, and we had many miles to make, up this [Carson] River, before their ascent was fairly begun. If this sand continued many miles as looked probable, when should we ever even begin the real climbing? The men began to talk among themselves about how much easier they could get on if they left the wagon; and it was not unlikely they would try starting out without us, if we had to travel too slowly. But they could not do this to any real advantage unless they took with them their pack-mule to carry some provisions. All they had was the bacon they found on the desert, and some parched corn meal; but they felt sanguine that they could go so much faster than the cattle with the wagon, they could easily make this last them through. But the bargain had been, when we agreed to supply them with flour, that the pack mule, and the old horse if he could be of any use, should be at our service to aid in any pinch that might occur, to the end of the journey. Having shared the perils of the way thus far, it certainly seemed unwise to divide the strength of so small a party when the mountains were to be scaled.

I wished most heartily there was some more rapid way for Mary and me to ride. But it was out of the question; for only a thoroughly trained mountain animal would do for me to ride carrying her. Besides this, all the clothing and personal conveniences we had in the world were in our wagon, and we had neither a sufficient number of sound animals nor those of the right kind, to pack them across the mountains. So the only way was to try to keep on. But it looked like rather a hopeless case when, for this whole day, we advanced but a few miles.

The next morning, Friday the 12th of October, we set out once more, hoping the sand would become lighter and the road easier to travel. But, instead of this, the wheels sank deeper than yester-day, there was more of ascent to overcome, the sun shone out decidedly hot, and, towards noon, we saw that we were approach-ing some pretty steep hills up which our road evidently led. It did not look as though we could ascend them but we would at least try to reach their foot. As we neared them we saw dust rising from the road at one of the turns we could distinguish high up in the hills a few miles off. Probably it was some party ahead of us. There was no hope of our overtaking anybody, so when we lost sight of the dust we did not expect to see it again. But soon another section of the road was in sight, and again the dust appeared; this time nearer, and plainly moving toward us. Conjecture now be-came very lively. It was probably Indians; but they could not be of the same tribes we had seen. Were they foes? How many were there? Repeatedly we saw the dust at different points, but could make out no distinct figures.

We were now so near the foot of the hills that we could distinctly see a stretch of road leading down a very steep incline to where we were moving so laboriously along. Presently at the head of this steep incline appeared two horsemen, clad in loose, flying garments that flapped, like wings on each side of them, while their broad-brimmed hats blown up from their foreheads, revealed hair and faces that belonged to no Indians. Their rapidity of motion and the steepness of the descent gave a strong impression of coming down from above, and the thought flashed into my mind, "They look heaven-sent." As they came nearer we saw that each of them led by a halter a fine mule, and the perfect ease with which all the animals cantered down that steep, was a marvel in our eyes. My husband and myself were at the heads of the lead cattle, and our little Mary was up in the front of the wagon, looking with wonder at the approaching forms.

As they came near they smiled and the forward one said "Well sir, you are the man we are after!" "How can that be?" said my husband, with surprise. "Yes, sir," continued the stranger, "you and your wife, and that little girl, are what brought us as far as this. You see we belong to the Relief Company sent out by order of the United States Government to help the late emigrants over the mountains. We were ordered only as far as Truckee Pass. When we got there we met a little company that had just got in. They'd been in a snow storm at the summit; 'most got froze to death themselves, lost some of their cattle, and just managed to get to where some of our men had fixed a relief camp. There was a woman and some children with them; and that woman set right to work at us fellows to go on over the mountains after a family she said they'd met on the desert going back for grass and water 'cause they'd missed their way. She said there was only one wagon, and there was a woman and child in it; and she knew they could never get through them cañons and over them ridges without help. We told her we had no orders to go any farther then. She said she didn't care for orders. She didn't believe anybody would blame us for doing what we were sent out to do, if we did have to go farther than ordered. And she kept at me so, I couldn't get rid of her. You see I've got a wife and little girl of my own; so I felt just how it was; and I got this man to come with me and here we are, to give you more to eat, if you want it, let you have these two mules, and tell you how to get right over the mountains the best and quickest way."

While he thus rapidly, in cheery though blunt fashion, explained their sudden presence with us, the thought of their being heaven-sent—that had so lightly flashed into my mind as I at first watched their rapid descent of the hill, with flying garments—grew into a sweetly solemn conviction; and I stood in mute adoration, brea-thing, in my inmost heart, thanksgiving to that Providential Hand which had taken hold of the conflicting movements, the provoking blunders, the contradictory plans, of our lives and those of a dozen other people, who a few days before were utterly unknown to each other, and many miles apart, and had from those rough, broken materials wrought out for us so unlooked for a deliverance.

Having made their hasty explanation, our new friends advised us to keep on some little distance farther, to a point where there was a spring in the hills, and excellent camping, to which they would guide us. There we were to rest the remainder of the day, while they would help to select, put into proper shape and pack, everything in the wagon that could be packed. The rest we must be content to leave. As we moved leisurely on to our camping place, they explained more fully the details of our situation—which they understood so much better than we could—and told us what we were to do. There had been two nights of snow storm at the summit: had there come much more they could not have got through. But the weather had cleared, the snow was fast going off the roads as they came over; and, if no other storm occurred, the pass would be in good order when we reached it. But we must hasten with all possible despatch, for, when the storms once again set in, they were not likely at that season to give any more chance for crossing the mountains. As to keeping on with the wagon, even supposing the cattle to grow no weaker than now—it would take us two weeks at the least to ascend the Carson Valley to the cañon. That cañon could not in several places be traversed by wheels. Wagons had been taken through; but only by taking them apart and packing, at the most difficult points; which of course could only be done by strong companies with plenty of time. Our only hope, therefore, was to pack. They then went farther into details about packing. The oxen, they said, could easily be made to carry, each, two moderate sized bundles, if snugly packed and well fastened on. Then the old horse could carry something though not very much. And the mule the young men had brought along, they said must carry most of the provisions.

"And now as to these two mules we brought," continued the chief speaker, "this white one is a perfectly-trained, mountain saddle-mule. My wife has rode him for miles, over steep and slippery roads, and he'll be perfectly safe for this lady to ride, with her little girl in front of her. And this dark mule is just as good for carrying packs, and the lady is to have him for her things and the little girl's. Now," he continued, turning to me, "as soon as we stop, and have all had some dinner, you just pick out all the things you care most about, and put them by themselves—you can save out enough for two good sized packs: he's strong, and understands it—and we'll do them up snug for you, and show the men how to fasten them on safe; and you remember, now, that these two mules are yours till you get through to the gold-mines; and all Uncle Sam asks, is, that they shall be brought safely to his boys' headquarters in Sacramento City as soon as possible after you get into California."

Thus, by the wise forethought of our good Government, and the chivalrous management of this faithful agent, I was provided for to a sufficiency that would have looked to me, two hours before, like a fairy-dream. The programme for the afternoon was successfully carried out. Every thing was arranged for an early morning start; and, at night I lay down to sleep for the last time in the wagon that had proved such a shelter for months past. I remembered well, how dreary it had seemed, on the first night of our journey (which now looked so long ago) to have *only* a *wagon* for shelter. Now we were not going to have even that. But, never mind, if we might only reach in safety the other foot of the mountains, all these privations would in their turn look small; and the same rich Providence that had led, and was still so kindly leading us, would, in that new land, perhaps, show us better things than we had seen yet.

So, when morning came, I hailed it with cheerful hope, though with some misgivings, because I had not ridden horseback for several years, and, whenever I had, it had been with side-saddle, and all the usual equipment for lady's riding, and, certainly, with no baby to carry. Now, I was to have only a common Spanish saddle, I must have Mary in front of me, and, it turned out, that several things needed for frequent use would have to be suspended from the pommel of my saddle, in a satchel on one side and a little pail on the other. At first, I was rather awkward, and so afraid Mary would get hurt, that at uneven places in the road I would ask my husband to get up and take her, while I walked. But in a few hours this awkwardness wore off; and the second day of our new style of traveling I rode twenty-five miles, only alighting once or twice for a brief time. Our friends, the government men, had left us the morning we left our wagon; taking the road to Truckee, where they felt themselves emphatically "due," considering their orders. I have more than once since wished I could see and thank them again; for, grateful as I felt then, I was able to appreciate more highly, a thousand fold, the service they had rendered us when, only ten days after we crossed the summit, the mountains were all blocked with snow, and the stormiest winter California had known for years was fully set in.

On the 24th of October at evening we reached what in our Guide Book was called "Pleasant Valley Gold Mines"; where we found two or three tents, and a few men with their gold-washing pans. We rested ourselves and animals for two or three days, and then moved into the village of "Weaverville," of which the miners had told us. This village was made up of tents, many of them very irregularly placed; though in one part, following the trend of the principal ravine, there was, already, something like a row of these primitive dwellings, though at considerable distances apart. We added one to that row, and soon began to gather about us little comforts and conveniences, which made us feel as though we once more had a home.

And so life has rolled on, not only for the twelve years of which I was speaking, but for many years since. California as a state has rallied from numerous shocks, and is now smiling in prosperity; while her first adopted children, many of them, have passed away; and those remaining have grown old, and look back on years of wonderful experiences which they sometimes wish could be recorded along with the history of their adopted State; for their children and their children's children to read, that they might learn to love and reverence the God who through all the devious paths of life ever guides safely those who trust and obey Him.

{ 46 }

Lucy Young (1846–1944)

Lucy Young, a member of the Lassik tribe of northern California, was known in the 1930s to her friends at the Round Valley Reservation as a seer, as a woman who had answers to questions about the past, to questions about life and endurance. With her kind, round face and quick, bright manner she impressed all she met and was a wonder to her people and to the eleven grandchildren to whom she told tribal tales.

She was herself but a child when the white people came to destroy her peaceful village and her people. It is believed she was born in 1846 near present-day Alderpoint, California. She was named T'tcetsa, meaning "small one," because she was a small baby. Her father, Tiltetz, was an Alderpoint Wailaki. Her mother, Yeltas, was cousin to Chief Lassik of the Lassik tribe, who made their home in what is now the Six Rivers National Forest in southern Humboldt County.

Before the arrival of whites, her childhood was quiet and happy. Her family—a sister, a brother, and her parents—were close. They shared sparse but comfortable accommodations camping along the Eel and Mad Rivers or at the mouth of Dobbyn Creek most months of the year and moved into the cool, shaded pine and oak forests in the heat of summer. T'tcetsa and her mother gathered clover, grass seed, acorns and berries. Her father and brother hunted elk and deer, rabbits and other small game, and fished the streams. As a child, she and other Lassik children played jump rope and hopping games, made swings and ran foot races. They lived more or less in peace, although T'tcetsa remembered a conflict with a neighboring tribe, the Nai'aitci, when she was five which ended in the deaths of several of the young men in her tribe, and a retaliation as well.

T'tcetsa's tribal territory was first explored by whites in the 1840s, but because it was remote and there was no gold it was not until 1861 that the decimation of her people and takeover of tribal lands became the object of settlers and state legislators alike. In that year, after a skirmish with settlers, her whole family was rounded up and taken to Fort Seward (now the town of Fort Seward northeast of Garberville). While held there the elder women of her tribe, perhaps fearing the end of their way of life, tattooed eight vertical lines on T'tcetsa's chin and

Lucy Young (1846–1944), photograph circa 1936. Courtesy of the Held Poage Research Library, Ukiah.

two slanted lines on each cheek, a traditional rite of passage for Lassik girls at the time of puberty.

Within weeks, her people were released, but the return to their lands was shortlived. Sometime in the following year, 1862, under the command of a Colonel Lippitt, troops stormed the village and in a three-day battle killed most of the men, including T'tcetsa's father and brother. T'tcetsa ran away with her mother and sister into the mountains, facing hunger, rattlesnakes and bears—enemies much less threatening than the white men in the valleys. T'tcetsa was later captured and again taken to Fort Seward, but she again escaped to the Hayfork Valley in Trinity County, although not for long.

T'tcetsa fell prey to men engaged in the widespread practice of kidnapping Indian children and selling them as servants to white settlers. Strong children brought two or three hundred dollars each in southern communities. These sales were sanctioned by a state law that allowed for the indenture or "apprenticeship" of Indian children. Probably sometime in 1863, T'tcetsa was bartered away as a nursemaid to the wife of a man who raised hogs. As T'tcetsa later reported, the woman whipped her often, so she again ran away into the woods. She was captured again. This time she was taken south, but once again she managed an escape, walking more than fifty miles back to her territory, then to Fort Seward and her mother. Her tribespeople hid her and eventually smuggled her out, along with an aunt, by boat across the Eel River. Then they traveled by foot for several days to Cottonwood, and the house of a cousin who was under the protection of a white man named Abraham Rogers.

Several Indians lived at Rogers' quarters, and it seems they lived safely. When T'tcetsa was old enough, Rogers married her. He renamed her Lucy, and they had four children together, three girls and a boy. Whether Rogers died or Lucy left him is unknown, but it is clear that they were together for more than twenty years, and that Lucy believed Rogers was a good man.

After this, Lucy spent five miserable years with a white man named Arthur Rutledge, who she later said kept her chained at his place because she always ran away. Rutledge beat Lucy and while she was with him she endured several miscarriages. "Lots of babies dies," she reflected as an old woman. Rutledge desired a white wife and finally let Lucy go when more single white women started coming west.

In 1914, Lucy was married to Sam Young, a member of the Hayfork tribe. They lived out their lives together at the reservation in Round

Valley where Lucy lived to be about a hundred years old. She claimed to be 102, and perhaps she was: her exact date of birth is hard to establish.

In her old age Lucy became a resource for ethnographers, sociologists and botanists interested in native cultures and native plant life. When Lucy was ninety, she and Sam Young and Edith Van Allen Murphey, a botanist and friend of Lucy's, journeyed by horseback up South Fork Mountain. Stopping at streams and in the forests, at special spots where Lucy's tribe had performed ceremonies or found food or plants to use as medicine, Lucy showed Murphey the plants and herbs her people relied on for centuries, while sheets of Washington lilies nodded their heads in the wilderness breeze. Murphey also recorded Lucy's personal history word by word as Lucy told it; excerpts of that history are reprinted here.

Lucy Young was, even at ninety, an exceedingly vital woman with a natural integrity and intense, sparkling dark eyes that drew people to her. Living her last years with Sam in what many in the white community might have seen as a simple lifestyle, Lucy saw herself as rich: "We got old age pension, buy li'l place here in Round Valley, keep our horses, keep cow, keep chickens, dogs, cats too. We live good."

OUT OF THE PAST
LUCY'S STORY

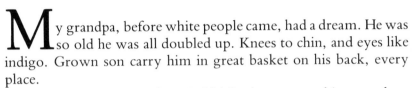

My grandpa, before white people came, had a dream. He was so old he was all doubled up. Knees to chin, and eyes like indigo. Grown son carry him in great basket on his back, every place.

My grandpa say: "White Rabbit"—he mean white people—"gonta devour our grass, our seed, our living. We won't have nothing more, this world. Big elk with straight horn come when white man bring it." I think he meant cattle. "'Nother animal, bigger than deer, but round feet, got hair on neck." This one, horse, I guess.

My aunt say: "Oh, Father, you out your head, don't say that way."

He say: "Now Daughter, I not crazy. You young people gonta see this."

People come long way, listen to him dream. He dream, then say this way, every morning.

They leave li'l children play by him. He watch good. Have big stick, wave round, scare snake away. He had good teeth. All old people had good teeth.

One time they travel, they come to big pile of brush. My grandpa stop, and look at it. He say: "This, good wood. When I die, burn my body to ashes on top of ground. Here gonta be big canoe, run around, carry white people's things. Those White Rabbit got lotsa everything."

"How canoe gonta run round on dry ground all round here?"
we askum. "Don't know," he say. "Just run that way." He mean
wagon, I guess.

I never grow much. They call me "Li'l Shorty," but I know
pretty near everything that time. My grandpa put his head on my
head, smoove my hair, and hold his hand there.

"Long time you gonta live, my child," he say. "You live long
time in this world."

Well, I live long enough. I guess 'bout ninety-five next summer,
if I living till then.

My grandpa never live to see white people, just dreaming every
night 'bout them. People come long way, listen him dream.

My grandpa move down by big spring. One day he couldn't
get up. He say: "I gonta leave you today. I used to be good hunter,
kill bear, elk, deer, feed my children. Can't feed my children no
more. Like old root, just ready for growing now. Pretty soon
dead. Speak no more."

All seem like dream to me. Long, long ago. Night-time, he die,
and in morning, all tied up in deerskin with grass rope. Sit up
knees to chin. They tie him up too soon. He roll over, and come
back. Scare everybody. He ask for water, and ask for packstrap to
basket always carry him in. He ask for li'l basket he always use
for cup. He drink lots.

"I starve for water, and want my strap," he say. "That's why I
come back."

Then he die. Our people dig big hole, put stick across. Put
brush. Put body in. Put more brush. Burn all to ashes. They put
basket and strap, too, with him, when he go where people go at last.

White people come find us. Want take us all to Fort Seward.
We all scared to dead. Inyan boy tell us: "Don't 'fraid, won't kill
you."

Tookted us to Fort Seward, had Inyan women there, all man killed. Plenty house there; any Inyan escape from Hoopa, bring to Fort Seward.

One white man come there, want take me South Fork Mountain. His woman got li'l baby. He want me stay his woman. He take me South Fork. He herd hogs, gonta takum to Weaver. I never stay long there. This Inyan woman whip me all time. Didden' talk my language. 'Bout week all I stay. Commence rain pretty hard. She tell me go get water. I go down, water muddy. I get it anyway. She ask me, make sign, "Where you get this water?" I show down to river. She think I get water in hole near house. She throw out water, commence whip me, tell me go get water.

I go down river, pretty steep go down. I throw bucket in river. I run off. Never see bucket no more. I had soldier shoes, take off, tie around neck. Water knee deep. I just had thin dress, can run good. Come up big high bank. Keep look back see if that woman follow me.

Lotsa redwood tree stand there. I see hog got killed, laying there, neck and shoulder eat up. Hog warm yet. When I put foot on it, something come up behind me. Grizzly bear growl at me. Wind blow from river. He smell me. I fall over back in tall ferns. I feel same as dead. Grizzly set there, his paw hang down. Head turn look every way. I keep eye on him. He give up listen, look, turn around, dig hole to sleep in. I keep still, just like dead. Fainty, too, and weak.

That's time I run—when he dig deep. Water up to my waist. I run through. Get to Fort Seward before I look back.

At last I come home [Fort Seward]. Before I get there, I see big fire in lotsa down timber and tree-top. Same time awfully funny smell. I think: Somebody get lotsa wood.

I go on to house. Everybody crying. Mother tell me: "All our men killed now." She say white men there, others come from Round Valley, Humboldt County too, kill our old uncle, Chief Lassik, and all our men.

Stood up about forty Inyan in a row with rope around neck.

"What this for?" Chief Lassik askum. "To hang you, dirty dogs," white men tell him. "Hanging, that's dog's death," Chief Lassik say. "We done nothing, be hung for. Must we die, shoot us."

So they shoot. All our men. Then build fire with wood and brush Inyan men been cut for days, never know their own funeral fire they fix. Build big fire, burn all them bodies. That's funny smell I smell before I get to house. Make hair raise on back of my neck. Make sick stomach, too.

That man what herd hogs, his Inyan boy speak my language. He say: "Why you come back?"

"That woman whip me every day," I say.

"What for she whip you?"

"Everything, little or big, she whip me."

Boy say: "White man say he gonta take all you folks over there, build you house."

White man got me, took to his house. I half cry, all time for my mother. After while, bald-headed man talk women long time. Gonta have big gamble over there, they say. Men got up and left. First, they give women grub, hog backbone, ribs.

These women say: "In four days you go stay old couple close by us." One um say: "I got white man, I come see you."

They leave for home. Little ridge, over hill. I hear Inyan talking, li'l way. I stand there and think. Only show for me to run off, now. Nobody there. I run in house. Match box on shelf. I put it in dress pocket. In kitchen, I find flour sacks. Take loaf bread, take boiling meat. Take big blanket from my bed.

I went out so quick, I never shut door. Then I went out to barn, open door, let all horses out.

All day I travel on edge of valley. I forgot I gonta have to swim Eel River. Then I see white man house, and lotta Inyan house, all smoke even—good sign. I go towards white man house. I go upstream, look for foot-log. Brush thick, too. I found big trail. 'Fraid then. Stop and listen, every li'l while. Pretty soon find footbridge. Just getting dark good. Star coming up. 'Nother big stream, shallow water.

Lotsa people there. Lotsa bell. Talk. Laugh. Pack-train stop there. I cross above camp. Water knee-deep. Go up long hill. Pretty near daylight, come out on mountain. Come out in big open country where Billy Dobbins' mother lived.

Owl commence holler, coming daylight. Way this side, great big rock. Big live-oak. Hollow place. I lay blanket down. Sleep all day; dark, I wake up.

Night come. I pack shoes one shoulder, blanket, 'nother shoulder, pack grub in hand. Lotsa snow that time, Bell Springs Mountain. There I put on shoes.

Saw big mountain, went over it. I back-track li'l way. I see white man hunt for me on white horse. I lay still long time, travel all night.

Went down in canyon, find big log all dry underneath. I sleep right there all day. Had to cross two li'l creek, went barefoot there. When I cross those two li'l creek, I home to old stamping ground, not far from Alder Point.

Again I lay down in sun to sleep. Three days I stay there, 'fraid go down to Fort Seward. Good weather. Think 'bout mother all time. Half-time cry. Two nights I stay alone, then I go to Fort Seward.

That white man told Inyan boys watch for me come home. Lotsa women there, man all killed.

I go where they get water, two-three places there where make buckeye soup. It ain't done yet. Nobody there. I taste buckeye, all bitter yet. I drink water, outa basket setting there. After awhile I see woman coming. I step behind brush. She never see me. She pour water in buckeye. Talk to self 'bout being bitter. It was my mother! Then I step in plain sight. She stir soup with hand, shake drops off. Look round. "Who's you," she say. "That you, my daughter?" I say: "Yes." She hug me and cry. Poor mother!

"Inyan boy watching," she whisper. "You come in 'bout morning, 'bout midnight?" "No," I told her. "Got grub, got blanket, I sleep down here, some place."

"Shall I bring buckeye soup tonight?" "No," I tell her. "Don't fetch grub out, might they follow you, find me."

Two nights I hide out. I go way down creek down under big tree roots. Sleep dry. Then I go to house. All time I never leave no sign. Mother and li'l sister hunt me. Make believe gather wood, never find me.

My uncle hunt me the last night. I see him. Then I show up on open ground. He say: "Poor li'l thing, hunted, starving. 'Bout midnight I put you 'cross river in boat." I say: "Tell mother meet me out there."

He say them two li'l girl been take away from that 'nother woman. Cry all time.

Midnight, I go in, meetum. Watch stars for time. I eat. Mother give me 'nother blanket, food too. Them two men don't make no track—walk in leaves and river. Had big boat. Put my aunt and me 'cross river. If mother let li'l sister go, white men would kill mother.

We travel all night, sleep all day till sundown. Had lotsa dry meat. Left most of my white-man grub with mother. Found some of our people at Poison Rock, pretty near sundown. I see old man pack wood. He been on look-out. He go in big bark house. I look in door, big fire in middle of house.

Man say: "Li'l girl look in door." They get up, bring me in. Young girl lay there, sick, my half sister. That night she die. Snowing, raining hard. They dig hole right by house, put body in. All went out. Tore all house down, set it afire. Midnight, snow whirl, wind howl. Then we went over to 'nother house; all left there next day, went over to Soldier Basin.

We stay there awhile, went to Cottonwood. Some of our people there. We went to head of Mad River, next day to South Fork of Trinity River. We stay all night. Tired. No horses. Next day to Cottonwood.

My cousin, Ellen, Wylackie Tom's woman, was there. We found her right away. Then I stay at Cottonwood all summer. After awhile, my cousin living with white man, he want kill her, she leave him. I stay with her and li'l boy.

Ellen's cousin-brother say to me: "Take care my li'l boy, cause I gonta Hayfork. Maybe white folks kill me," he say. "Take care my boy, takum way off."

White man name Rogers come after this. Ellen my cousin's man, went to work for him. I go with her to Hayfork, and take li'l boy too.

Rogers, my white man, took me then to take care of, that summer. Marry me bimeby when get old enough. I stay there at Hayfork long time.

My cousin, Ellen, younger than me but she got man first. We didn't neither one know much. Man told us cook beans. We cook green coffee for beans. Man cook long time for us.

Li'l sister, white man took her away. Never see her no more. If see her, maybe wouldn't know her. That's last young one tooken away. Mother lost her at Fort Seward.

I hear it, I went back, got mother, brought her to Hayfork. Lotsa Inyan there, lotsa different language, all different. Mother stay with me until she die.

You ask 'bout father. He got killed and brother in soldier war, before soldiers captured us. Three days fight. Three days running. Just blood, blood, blood. Young woman cousin, run from soldier, run into our camp. Three of us girls run. I lose buckskin blanket. Cousin run back, pick it up. I roll it up, put under arm—run more better that way.

We had young man cousin, got shot side of head, crease him, all covered his blood, everything. We helpum to water. Wash off. No die. That night all our women come to camp. I ask mother: "You see my father, big brother?" "Yes," she say, "both two of um dead." I want go see. Mother say "No."

Young woman been stole by white people, come back. Shot through lights and liver. Front skin hang down like apron. She tie up with cotton dress. Never die, neither. Little boy, knee-pan shot off. Young man shot through thigh. Only two man of all our tribe left—that battle.

White people want our land, want destroy us. Break and burn all our basket, break our pounding rock. Destroy our ropes. No snares, no deerskin, flint knife, nothing.

Some old lady wear moss blanket, peel off rock good.

All long, long ago. My white man die. My children all die but one. Oldest girl, she married, went way off. Flu take restum. Oldest girl die few years ago, left girl, she married now, got li'l girl, come see me sometimes. All I got left, my descendants.

'But twenty-five years ago I marry Sam. Marry him by preacher. Sam, he's good man. Hayfork Inyan. Talk li'l bit different to us people, but can understand him. We get old age pension, buy li'l place here in Round Valley, keep our horses, keep cow, keep chickens, dogs, cats too. We live good.

I hear people tell 'bout what Inyan do early days to white man. Nobody ever tell what white man do to Inyan. That's reason I tell it. That's history. That's truth. I seen it myself.

Dame Shirley (1819–1906)
(Louisa Amelia Knapp Smith Clapp)

Little was known about the mysterious woman who signed the name of Dame Shirley to the letters she wrote from the Indian Bar and Rich Bar mining camps to her sister "back in the states." Even historian Josiah Royce, who called Dame Shirley's narrative the "best account of an early mining camp," knew little about the author. It was not until her writings were collected in *The Shirley Letters,* and Rodman Wilson Paul wrote his 1964 essay "In Search of Dame Shirley," that the author's own story came to light. Paul's research, and that of a student of Dame Shirley's, Mary Viola Tingley Lawrence, unmasked the "Dame" of the Feather River Hills.

She was born Louisa Amelia Knapp Smith, on July 28, 1819, to Moses and Lois (Lee) Smith of Elizabeth, New Jersey. The Smiths were considered to be people of substance and position, counting among their relatives the suffragist and reformer Julia Ward Howe. Louisa's father was the local Academy master.

Louisa was one of seven children, all left orphans at the early deaths of their parents. Osmyn Baker, an attorney from Amherst, Massachusetts (the original home of Louisa's parents), became her guardian, and saw to it that she and her sister, Molly, were given a good education at the Female Seminary at Charlestown, Massachusetts, and later at Amherst Academy.

For some years, Louisa was under the affectionate tutelage of Alexander Hill Everett, a diplomat, author, editor, and admirer of the arts, especially literature. A man twice her age, he introduced himself to the fair-haired, frail-looking young woman in the course of a stagecoach ride. He was out of the country much of the time, but the two maintained a regular correspondence, often exchanging several pages of literary criticism and intellectual examinings. But Everett wasn't above offering personal advice, and in many of the letters his courtly interest in Louisa is thinly masked. His last letters to her in 1848 exhibit obvious annoyance at her decision to marry Fayette Clapp, a young medical student five years her junior and possibly a distant cousin, who Everett and others believed to be unequal to her in station and promise.

But with or without her mentor's endorsement, Louisa married Dr. Clapp. Both newlyweds were adventurers—both were slightly impractical. Both suffered from physical weakness and ill-health. Louisa was described as small, delicate, not physically strong, and Dr. Clapp was a slight man with upper respiratory problems. Still, they didn't hesitate to travel around the Horn in 1849 to San Francisco, then on to Marysville and later to Rich Bar and Indian Bar mining camps. There Dr. Clapp reported that the clean mountain air had improved his health miraculously, and Louisa reported that she was "perfectly enchanted" by her new mountain home, seldom mentioning her health except in positive terms.

Dame Shirley's letters—twenty-three in all—were written to her sister Molly in Massachusetts between September 1851 and November 1852. They are alive with the wild, impulsive, impractical fever that was the California Gold Rush. Her prose immediately involves readers in the action, and at the same time provides a meditative, assessing stance. The clarity of her thoughts and observations is startling and refreshing.

Before and after her trip to the mining camps, Dame Shirley's prose and poetry was often erudite and sometimes spoiled by her tendency to a flowery style. This style may be the main reason she published little, other than the letters. And although her student, Charles Warren Stoddard, charged that Bret Harte jealously refused to publish any of her work in the years following her trip to the mines, others agree that the letters stood markedly above any other writing she did.

But another charge hinted at by Charles Warren Stoddard and openly levied by Hubert Bancroft and others was that Bret Harte borrowed heavily from Shirley's descriptions of mining life. Two of his classic stories, "The Outcasts of Poker Flat" and "The Luck of Roaring Camp," were said to be taken directly from incidents portrayed in the letters. This may be true; some of Harte's stories have the plots and characters seen first in Shirley's letters from the mines. The letters were published in *The Pioneer,* in San Francisco, from January 1854 to December 1855, long before Bret Harte's short stories were written. But Harte always denied the charges, and even Shirley defended him to some degree, stating that his were "Unconscious Plagiarisms."

What became of Dame Shirley once she rode her mule back down the mountainside and dismounted in San Francisco is unclear. Passages in some of the Shirley Letters contain episodes which are not always flattering to her husband. Perhaps a strain had developed in their marriage either during their life in the camps or just following. This seems probable, as upon leaving the mines in 1852, Fayette Clapp left for the Sandwich Islands, then later for the eastern United States. In 1857 Dame Shirley was granted a divorce from Dr. Clapp and in that year he remarried.

By the mid 1850s, now known as Mrs. Louisa Clapp, Dame Shirley had established herself as a teacher in the San Francisco school system, where she remained for more than twenty years. Upon her retirement, students and colleagues presented her with a $2,000 farewell gift, which suggests that she was more than an ordinary teacher. After retirement, she returned to her first home, New Jersey, where she died in 1906 at the age of 87.

Historians and literati alike generally agree that the Shirley Letters are not only excellent models of sagebrush realism, California's own frontier literary genre, but fine pieces of literature by any standard. Included here are her fifth, tenth, and eleventh letters, written in 1851, which were first published in *The Pioneer* in 1854 and 1855.

A Trip Into The Mines
Letter Fifth

Rich Bar,
East Branch of the North Fork of Feather River,
September 22, 1851

It seems indeed awful, dear M., to be compelled to announce to you the death of one of the four women forming the female population of this Bar. I have just returned from the funeral of poor Mrs. B., who died of peritonitis, (a common disease of this place) after an illness of four days only. Our hostess herself heard of her sickness but two days since. On her return from a visit which she had paid to the invalid, she told me that although Mrs. B.'s family did not seem alarmed about her, in her opinion she would not survive but a few hours. Last night we were startled by the frightful news of her decease. Confess, that without being egotistical, the death of one out of a community of four women, might well alarm the remainder.

Her funeral took place at ten this morning. The family reside in a log-cabin at the head of the Bar; and, although it had no window—all the light admitted, entering through an aperture where there *will* be a door when it becomes cold enough for such a luxury—yet I am told, and can easily believe that it is one of the most *comfortable* residences in the place. I observed it, particularly, for it was the first log-cabin that I had ever seen. Everything in the room, though of the humblest description, was exceedingly clean and neat. On a board, supported by two butter-tubs, was extended the body of the dead woman, covered with a sheet; by its side stood the coffin of unstained pine, lined with white cambric. You, who have alternately laughed and scolded at my provoking and inconvenient deficiency in the power of observing, will, perhaps, wonder at the minuteness of my descriptions; but I know how deeply you are interested in everything relating to California, and therefore I take pains to describe things exactly as I *see* them, hoping that thus you will obtain an idea of life in the mines, *as it is.*

The bereaved husband held in his arms a sickly babe ten months old, which was moaning piteously for its mother. The other child, a handsome, bold-looking little girl six years of age, was running gaily around the room, perfectly unconscious of her great bereavement. A sickening horror came over me, to see her every few moments, run up to her dead mother, and peep laughingly under the handkerchief, that covered her moveless face. Poor little thing! It was evident that her baby-toilet had been made by men; she had on a new calico dress, which, having no tucks in it, trailed to the floor, and gave her a most singular and dwarf-womanly appearance.

About twenty men, with the three women of the place, had assembled at the funeral. An *extempore* prayer was made, filled with all the peculiarities usual to that style of petition. Ah! how different from the soothing verses of the glorious burial service of the church.

As the procession started for the hill-side grave-yard—a dark cloth cover, borrowed from a neighboring monte-table, was flung over the coffin. Do not think that I mention any of these circumstances in a spirit of mockery; far from it. Every observance, usual on such occasions, that was *procurable,* surrounded this funeral. All the gold on Rich Bar could do no more; and should I die to-morrow, I should be marshaled to my mountain grave beneath the same monte-table cover pall, which shrouded the coffin of poor Mrs. B.

I almost forgot to tell you, how painfully the feelings of the assembly were shocked by the sound of the nails—there being no screws at any of the shops—driven with a hammer into the coffin, while closing it. It seemed as if it *must* disturb the pale sleeper within.

To-day I called at the residence of Mrs. R. It is a canvas house, containing a suite of three "apartments,"—as Dick Swiveller would say—which, considering that they were all on the ground floor, are kept surprisingly neat. There is a bar-room, blushing all over with red calico, a dining-room, kitchen and a small bed-closet. The little sixty-eight-pounder woman is queen of the establishment. By the way, a man who walked home with us, was enthusiastic in her praise. "Magnificent woman that, sir," he said, addressing my husband; "a wife of the right sort, *she* is. Why," he added, absolutely rising into eloquence as he spoke, "she earnt her *old man*," (said individual twenty-one years of age, perhaps,) "nine hundred dollars in nine weeks, clear of all expenses, by washing! Such women ain't common, I tell *you*; if they were, a man might marry, and make money by the operation." I looked at this person with somewhat the same kind of *inverted* admiration, wherewith Leigh Hunt was wont to gaze upon that friend of his, "who used to elevate the common-place to a pitch of the sublime;" and he looked at *me* as if to say, that, though by no means gloriously arrayed, I was a mere cumberer of the ground; inasmuch as I toiled not, neither did I wash. Alas! I hung my diminished head; particularly when I remembered the eight dollars a dozen, which I had been in the habit of paying for the washing of linen-cambric pocket-handkerchiefs while in San Francisco. But a lucky thought came into my mind. As all men cannot be Napoleon Bonapartes, so all women cannot be *manglers*; the majority of the sex must be satisfied with simply being *mangled*. Re-assured by this idea, I determined to meekly and humbly pay the amount per dozen required to enable this really worthy and agreeable little woman "to lay up her hundred dollars a week, clear of expenses." But is it not wonderful, what femininity is capable of? To look at the tiny hands of Mrs. R., you would not think it possible, that they could wring out anything larger than a doll's night-cap. But, as is often said, nothing is strange in California. I have known of sacrifices, requiring, it would seem, superhuman efforts, made by women in this country, who at home were nurtured in the extreme of elegance and delicacy.

Mr. B. called on us to-day with little Mary. I tried to make her, at least, look sad, as I talked about her mother; but although she had seen the grave closed over her coffin—for a friend of her father's had carried her in his arms to the burial—she seemed laughingly indifferent to her loss. Being myself an ophan, my heart contracted painfully at her careless gaiety, when speaking of her dead parent, and I said to our hostess, "what a cold-blooded little wretch it is!" But immediately my conscience struck me with remorse. Poor orphaned one! Poor bereaved darling! Why should I so cruelly wish to darken her young life with that knowledge, which a few years experience will so painfully teach her? "All *my* mother came into my eyes," as I bent down and kissed the white lids, which shrouded her beautiful dark orbs; and, taking her fat little hand in mine, I led her to my room, where, in the penitence of my heart, I gave her everything that she desired. The little chatterer was enchanted, not having had any new playthings for a long while. It was beautiful to hear her pretty exclamations of ecstasy, at the sight of some tiny scent bottles, about an inch in length, which she called baby decanters.

Mr. B. intends, in a day or two, to take his children to their grandmother, who resides somewhere near Marysville, I believe. This is an awful place for children; and nervous mothers would "die daily," if they could see little Mary running fearlessly to the very edge of, and looking down into these holes—many of them sixty feet in depth—which have been excavated in the hope of finding gold, and of course left open.

LETTER TENTH

—— ❧·❦ ——

From our Log Cabin, Indian Bar,
November 25, 1851

Nothing of importance has happened since I last wrote you, except that I have become a *mineress*; that is, if the having washed a pan of dirt with my own hands, and procured therefrom three dollars and twenty-five cents in gold dust, (which I shall inclose in this letter), will entitle me to the name. I can truly say, with the blacksmith's apprentice at the close of his first day's work at the anvil, that "I am sorry I learned the trade;" for I wet my feet, tore my dress, spoilt a pair of new gloves, nearly froze my fingers, got an awful headache, took cold and lost a valuable breast-pin, in this my labor of love. After such melancholy self-sacrifice on my part, I trust you will duly prize my gift. I can assure you that it is the last golden handiwork you will ever receive from "Dame Shirley."

Apropos, of lady gold-washers in general—it is a common habit with people residing in towns in the vicinity of the "Diggings," to make up pleasure parties to those places. Each woman of the company will exhibit on her return, at least twenty dollars of the *oro,* which she will gravely inform you she has just "panned out" from a single basinful of the soil. This, of course, gives strangers a very erroneous idea of the average richness of auriferous dirt. I myself thought, (now don't laugh,) that one had but to saunter gracefully along romantic streamlets, on sunny afternoons, with a parasol and white kid gloves, perhaps, and to stop now and then to admire the scenery, and carelessly rinse out a small panful of yellow sand, (without detriment to the white kids, however, so easy did I fancy the whole process to be), in order to fill one's workbag with the most beautiful and rare specimens of the precious mineral. Since I have been here, I have discovered my mistake, and also the secret of the brilliant success of former gold-washeresses.

The miners are in the habit of flattering the vanity of their fair visitors, by scattering a handful of "salt" (which, strange to say, is *exactly* the color of gold dust, and has the remarkable property of often bringing to light very curious lumps of the ore) through the dirt before the dainty fingers touch it; and the dear creatures go home with their treasures firmly believing that mining is the prettiest pastime in the world.

I had no idea of permitting such a costly joke to be played upon me; so I said but little of my desire to "go through the motions" of gold washing, until one day, when, as I passed a deep hole in which several men were at work, my companion requested the owner to fill a small pan, which I had in my hand, with dirt from the bedrock. This request was, of course, granted, and, the treasure having been conveyed to the edge of the river, I succeeded, after much awkward maneuvering on my own part, and considerable assistance from friend H., an experienced miner, in gathering to-gether the above specified sum. All the diggers of our acquaintance say that it is an excellent "prospect," even to come from the bed-rock, where, naturally, the richest dirt is found. To be sure, there are now and then "lucky strikes"; such, for instance, as that mentioned in a former letter, where a person took out of a single basinful of soil, two hundred and fifty-six dollars. But such luck is as rare as the winning of a hundred thousand dollar prize in a lottery. We are acquainted with many here whose gains have *never* amounted to much more than "wages"; that is, from six to eight dollars a day. And a "claim" which yields a steady income of ten dollars *per diem,* is considered as very valuable.

I received an immense fright the other morning. I was sitting by the fire, quietly reading "Lewis Arundal," which had just fallen into my hands, when a great shout and trampling of feet outside attracted my attention. Naturally enough my first impulse was to run to the door; but scarcely had I risen to my feet for that purpose, when a mighty crash against the side of the cabin, shaking it to the foundation, threw me suddenly upon my knees. So violent was the shock, that for a moment I thought the staunch old logs, mossed with the pale verdure of ages, were falling in confusion around me. As soon as I could collect my scattered senses, I looked about to see what had happened. Several stones had fallen from the back of the chimney, mortar from the latter covered the hearth, the cloth overhead was twisted into the funniest possible wrinkles, the couch had jumped two feet from the side of the house, the little table lay on its back holding up *four* legs instead of *one,* the chessmen were rolling merrily about in every direction, the dishes had all left their usual places, the door, which ever since has obstinately refused to let itself be shut, was thrown violently open, while an odd looking pile of articles lay in the middle of the room, which, upon investigation, was found to consist of a pail, a broom, a bell, some candlesticks, a pack of cards, a loaf of bread, a pair of boots, a bunch of cigars, and some clay pipes—the only things, by the way, rendered utterly *hors de combat* in the assault. But one piece of furniture retained its attitude, and that was the elephantine bedstead, which nothing short of an earthquake could move. Almost at the same moment several acquaintances rushed in, begging me not to be alarmed, as the danger was past.

"But what has happened?" I eagerly inquired.

"Oh, a large tree which was felled this morning, has rolled down from the brow of the hill," and its having struck a rock a few feet from the house, losing thereby the most of its force, had alone saved us from utter destruction.

I grew sick with terror when I understood the awful fate from which Providence had preserved me; and even now my heart leaps painfully with mingled fear and gratitude, when I think how closely that pale death shadow glided by me, and of the loving care which forbade it to linger upon our threshold.

Every one who saw the forest giant descending the hill with the force of a mighty torrent, expected to see the cabin instantly prostrated to the earth. As it was, they all say that it swayed from the perpendicular more than six inches.

Poor W.—whom you may remember my having mentioned in a former letter as having had a leg amputated, a few weeks ago, and who was visiting us at the time, (he had been brought from the Empire in a rocking chair), looked like a marble statue of resignation. He possesses a face of uncommon beauty, and his large, dark eyes have always, I fancy, a sorrowful expression. Although he knew from the first shout what was about to happen, and was sitting on the couch which stood at the side of the cabin where the log must necessarily strike, and in his mutilated condition, had, as he has since said, not the faintest hope of escape, yet the rich color, for which he is remarkable, paled not a shade during the whole affair.

The woodman, who came so near causing a catastrophe, was, I believe, infinitely more frightened than his might-have-been victims. He is a good natured, stupid creature, and did not dare to descend the hill until some time after the excitement had subsided. The ludicrous expression of terror which his countenance wore, when he came in to see what damage he had done, and to ask pardon for his carelessness, made us all laugh heartily.

W. related the almost miraculous escape of two persons from a similar danger last winter. The cabin, which was on Smith's Bar, was crushed into a mass of ruins almost in an instant; while an old man and his daughter, who were at dinner within its walls, remained sitting in the midst of the fallen logs, entirely unhurt. The father immediately seized a gun and ran after the careless woodman, swearing that he would shoot him. Fortunately for the latter (for there is no doubt that in the first moments of his rage the old man would have slain him) his younger legs enabled him to make his escape, and he did not dare to return to the settlement for some days.

It has heretofore been a source of great interest to me to listen to the ringing sound of the axe, and the solemn crash of those majestic sentinels of the hills, as they bow their green foreheads to the dust; but now I fear that I shall always hear them with a feeling of apprehension, mingling with my former awe, although every one tells us that there is no danger of a repetition of the accident.

Last week there was a *post mortem* examination of two men who died very suddenly in the neighborhood. Perhaps it will sound rather barbarous, when I tell you that, as there was no building upon the Bar which admitted light enough for the purpose, it was found necessary to conduct the examination in the open air, to the intense interest of the Kanakas, Indians, French, Spanish, English, Irish and Yankees, who had gathered eagerly about the spot. Paganini Ned, with an anxious desire that Mrs. —— should be *amused* as much as possible in her mountain home, rushed up from the kitchen, his dusky face radiant with excitement, to inform me "that I could see both the bodies by just looking out the window!" I really frightened the poor fellow by the abrupt and vehement manner in which I declined to take advantage of his kindly hint.

One of the deceased, was the husband of an American lady-lecturess of the most intense description, and a strong-minded "Bloomer" on the broadest principles.

Apropos, how *can* women—many of whom, I am told, are *really* interesting and intelligent, how *can* they spoil their pretty mouths and ruin their beautiful complexions, by demanding with Xantippean *fervor,* in the presence often, of a vulgar, irreverent mob, what the gentle creatures, are pleased to call their "rights?" How *can* they wish to soil the delicate texture of their airy fancies, by pondering over the wearying stupidities of Presidential elections, or the bewildering mystifications of rabid metaphysicians? And, above all, how *can* they so far forget the sweet, shy coquetries of shrinking womanhood, as to don those horrid "Bloomers?" As for me, although a *wife,* I never wear the ——, well you know what they call them, when they wish to quiz henpecked husbands— even in the strictest privacy of life. I confess to an almost religious veneration for trailing drapery, and I pin my vestural faith with unflinching obstinacy to sweeping petticoats.

I know a "strong-minded Bloomer," at home, of some talent, and who was possessed, in a certain sense, of an excellent education. One day, after having flatteringly informed me, that I really *had* a "soul above buttons" and the nursery, she gravely proposed that I should improve my *mind,* by poring six hours a day over the metaphysical subtleties of Kant, Cousin, & c; and I remember, that she called me a "piece of fashionable insipidity," and taunted me with not daring to go out of the beaten track, because I *truly* thought, (for in those days I was a humble little thing enough, and sincerely desirous of walking in the right path as straightly as my feeble judgment would permit,) that there were other authors, more congenial to the flower-like delicacy of the feminine intellect than her pet writers.

When will our sex appreciate the exquisite philosophy and truth of Lowell's remark upon the habits of Lady Red-Breast and her *sposa* Robin, as illustrating the beautifully-varied spheres of man and woman:

> "He sings to the wide world, she to her nest;
> In the nice ear of Nature, which song is the best?"

Speaking of birds, reminds me of a misfortune that I have lately experienced, which, in a life where there is so little to amuse and interest one, has been to me a subject of real grief. About three weeks ago, F. saw on the hill, a California pheasant, which he chased into a coyote hole and captured. Knowing how fond I am of pets, he brought it home and proposed that I should try to tame it. Now from earliest childhood, I have resolutely refused to keep *wild* birds, and when I have had them given to me—which has happened several times in this country—young bluebirds, etc.,—I have invariably set them free; and I proposed doing the same with the pretty pheasant; but as they are the most delicately exquisite in flavor of all game, F. said "that if I did not wish to keep it, he would wring its neck and have it served up for dinner." With the cruelty of kindness, often more disastrous than that of real malice, I shrank from having it killed, and consented to let it run about the cabin.

It was a beautiful bird, a little larger than the domestic hen. Its slender neck, which it curved with haughty elegance, was tinted with various shades of a shining steel color. The large, bright eye glanced with the prettiest shyness at its captors, and the clusters of feathers forming its tail, drooped with the rare grace of an ostrich-plume. The colors of the body were of a subdued brilliancy, reminding one of a rich but somber mosaic.

As it seemed very quiet, I really believed that in time we should be able to tame it—still it *would* remain constantly under the sofa or bedstead; so F. concluded to place it in a cage, for a few hours of each day, in order that it might become gradually accustomed to our presence. This was done, the bird appearing as well as ever; and after closing the door of its temporary prison one day, I left it and returned to my seat by the fire. In less than two minutes afterwards, a slight struggle in the cage, attracted my attention. I ran hastily back, and you may imagine my distress, when I found the beautiful pheasant lying lifeless upon the ground. It never breathed or showed the faintest sign of life afterward.

You may laugh at me, if you please, but I firmly believe that it died of home-sickness. What wonder that the free, beautiful, happy creature of God, torn from the sight of the broad, blue sky, the smiling river and the fresh, fragrant fir trees of its mountain home, and shut up in a dark, gloomy cabin, should have broken in twain its haughty, little heart? Yes, you may laugh, call me sentimental, etc., but I shall never forgive myself for having killed, by inches, in my selfish and cruel kindness, that pretty creature.

Many people here call this bird a grouse; and those who have crossed the plains say that it is very much like a prairie hen. The Spanish name is *gallina del campo,* literally, "hen of the field." Since the death of my poor, little victim, I have been told that it is utterly impossible to tame one of these birds; and it is said, that if you put their eggs under a domestic fowl, the young, almost as soon as hatched, will instinctively run away to the beloved solitudes of their congenial homes; so passionately beats for liberty, each pulse of their free and wild natures.

Among the noteworthy events which have occurred since my last, I don't know how I came to forget, until the close of my letter, two smart shocks of an earthquake, to which we were treated a week ago. They were awe-inspiring, but after all were nothing in comparison to the timber-quake, an account of which I have given you above. But as F. is about to leave for the top of the Butte Mountains with a party of Rich Barians, and as I have much to do to prepare him for the journey, I must close.

LETTER ELEVENTH

— ❧·❦ —

From our Log Cabin, Indian Bar,
December 15, 1851

I little thought, dear M., that here, with the "green watching hills" as witnesses, amid a solitude so grand and lofty that it seems as if the faintest whisper of passion must be hushed by its holy stillness, I should have to relate the perpetration of one of those fearful deeds, which, were it for no other peculiarity than its startling suddenness—so utterly at variance with all *civilized* law—must make our beautiful California appear to strangers rather as a hideous phantom, than the flower-wreathed reality which she is.

Whether the life, which a few men, in the impertinent intoxication of power, have dared to crush out, was worth that of a fly, I do not know—perhaps not; though God alone, methinks, can judge of the value of the soul upon which he has breathed. But certainly the effect upon the hearts of those who played the principal parts in the revolting scene referred to—a tragedy, in my simple judgment, so utterly useless—must be demoralizing in the extreme.

The facts in this sad case are as follows: Last fall, two men were arrested by their partners, on suspicion of having stolen from them eighteen hundred dollars in gold dust. The evidence was not sufficient to convict them, and they were acquitted. They were tried before a meeting of the miners—as at that time the law did not even *pretend* to wave its scepter over the place.

The prosecutors still believed them guilty, and fancied that the gold was hidden in a "coyote hole," near the camp from which it had been taken. They therefore watched the place narrowly while the suspected men remained on the Bar. They made no discoveries, however; and soon after the trial, the acquitted persons left the mountains for Marysville.

A few weeks ago, one of these men returned, and has spent most of the time since his arrival in loafing about the different bar-rooms upon the river. He is said to have been constantly intoxicated. As soon as the losers of the gold heard of his return, they bethought themselves of the "coyote hole," and placed about its entrance some brushwood and stones, in such a manner that no one could go into it without disturbing the arrangement of them. In the meanwhile the thief settled at Rich Bar, and pretended that he was in search of some gravel ground for mining purposes.

A few mornings ago, he returned to his boarding place—which he had left some hour earlier—with a spade in his hand, and as he laid it down, carelessly observed that he had "been out prospecting." The losers of the gold went, immediately after breakfast, as they had been in the habit of doing, to see if all was right at the "coyote hole." On this fatal day, they saw that the entrance had been disturbed, and going in, they found upon the ground, a money belt which had apparently just been cut open. Armed with this evidence of guilt, they confronted the suspected person and sternly accused him of having the gold in his possession. Singularly enough, he did not attempt a denial, but said that if they would not bring him to a trial, (which of course they promised) he would give it up immediately. He then informed them that they would find it beneath the blankets of his *bunk*—as those queer shelves on which miners sleep, ranged one above another, somewhat like the berths of the ship, are generally called. There, sure enough, were six hundred dollars of the missing money, and the unfortunate wretch declared that his partner had taken the remainder to the States.

By this time the exciting news had spread all over the Bar. A meeting of the miners was immediately convened, the unhappy man taken into custody, a jury chosen, and a judge, lawyer, etc., appointed. Whether the men, who had just regained a portion of their missing property, made any objections to the proceedings which followed, I know not; if they had done so, however, it would have made no difference, as the *people* had taken the matter entirely out of their hands.

At one o'clock, so rapidly was the trial conducted, the judge charged the jury, and gently insinuated that they could do no less than to bring in with their verdict of guilty, a sentence of *death!* Perhaps you know that when a trial is conducted without the majesty of the law, the jury are compelled to decide, not only upon the guilt of the prisoner, but the mode of his punishment also. After a few minutes' absence, the twelve men who had consented to burden their souls with a responsibility so fearful, returned, and the foreman handed to the judge a paper, from which he read the will of the *people,* as follows: "That William Brown, convicted of stealing, etc., should, in *one hour* from that time, be hung by the neck until he was dead."

By the persuasions of some men more mildly disposed, they granted him a respite of *three hours,* to prepare for his sudden entrance into eternity. He employed the time in writing in his native language (he is a Swede) to some friends in Stockholm; God help them when that fatal post shall arrive; for no doubt *he,* also, although a criminal, was fondly garnered in many a loving heart.

He had exhibited during the trial, the utmost recklessness and *nonchalance,* had drank many times in the course of the day, and when the rope was placed about his neck, was evidently much intoxicated. All at once, however, he seemed startled into a consciousness of the awful reality of his position, and requested a few moments for prayer.

The execution was conducted by the jury, and was performed by throwing the cord, one end of which was attached to the neck of the prisoner, across the limb of a tree standing outside of the Rich Bar grave-yard; when all, who felt disposed to engage in so revolting a task, lifted the poor wretch from the ground, in the most awkward manner possible. The whole affair, indeed, was a piece of cruel butchery, though *that* was not intentional, but arose from the ignorance of those who made the preparations. In truth, life was only crushed out of him, by hauling the writhing body up and down several times in succession, by the rope which was wound round a large bough of his green-leafed gallows. Almost everybody was surprised at the severity of the sentence; and many, with their hands on the cord, did not believe even *then,* that it would be carried into effect, but thought that at the last moment, the jury would release the prisoner and substitute a milder punishment.

It is said that the crowd generally, seemed to feel the solemnity of the occasion; but many of the drunkards, who form a large part of the community on these Bars, laughed and shouted, as if it were a spectacle got up for their particular amusement. A disgusting specimen of intoxicated humanity, struck with one of those luminous ideas peculiar to his class, staggered up to the victim, who was praying at the moment, and crowding a dirty rag into his almost unconscious hand, in a voice broken by a drunken hiccough, tearfully implored him to take his "handercher," and if he were *innocent,* (the man had not denied his guilt since first accused), to drop it as soon as he was drawn up into the air, but if *guilty,* not to let it fall on any account.

The body of the criminal was allowed to hang for some hours after the execution. It had commenced storming in the earlier part of the evening; and when those, whose business it was to inter the remains, arrived at the spot, they found them enwrapped in a soft, white shroud of feathery snow-flakes, as if pitying Nature had tried to hide from the offended face of heaven, the cruel deed which her mountain children had committed.

I have heard no one approve of this affair. It seems to have been carried on entirely by the more reckless part of the community. There is no doubt, however, that they seriously *thought* they were doing right, for many of them are kind and sensible men. They firmly believed that such an example was absolutely necessary for the protection of this community. Probably the recent case of "Little John," rendered this last sentence more severe than it otherwise would have been. The "Squire," of course, could do nothing (as in criminal cases the *people* utterly refuse to acknowledge his authority) but protest against the whole of the proceedings, which he did, in the usual legal manner.

If William Brown had committed a murder, or had even attacked a man for his money—if he had been a quarrelsome, fighting character, endangering lives in his excitement, it would have been a very different affair. But with the exception of the crime for which he perished, (he *said* it was his first, and there is no reason to doubt the truth of his assertion), he was a harmless, quiet, inoffensive person.

You must not confound this miner's judgment with the doings of the noble *Vigilance Committee* of San Francisco. They are almost totally different in their organization and manner of proceeding. The Vigilance Committee had become absolutely necessary for the protection of society. It was composed of the best and wisest men in the city. They used their powers with a moderation unexampled in history, and they laid it down with a calm and quiet readiness which was absolutely sublime, when they found that legal justice had again resumed that course of stern, unflinching duty which should always be its characteristic. They took ample time for a thorough investigation of all the circumstances relating to the criminals who fell into their hands; and in *no* case have they hung a man, who had not been proved beyond the shadow of a doubt, to have committed at least *one* robbery in which life had been endangered, if not absolutely taken.

But by this time, dear M., you must be tired of the melancholy subject; and yet if I keep my promise of relating to you all that interests *us* in our new and strange life, I shall have to finish my letter with a catastrophe, in many respects more sad than that which I have just recounted.

At the commencement of our first storm, a hard working, industrious laborer, who had accumulated about eight hundred dollars, concluded to return to the States. As the snow had been falling but a few hours, when he, with two acquaintances, started from

Rich Bar, no one doubted that they would not reach Marysville in perfect safety. They went on foot themselves, taking with them one mule to carry their blankets. For some unexplained reason, they took an unfrequented route. When the express man came in, he said that he met the two companions of R. eight miles beyond Buck's Rancho, which is the first house one finds after leaving Rich Bar, and is only fourteen miles distant from here.

These men had camped at an uninhabited cabin called the "Frenchman's," where they had built a fire, and were making themselves both merry and comfortable. They informed the express man, that they had left their *friend*(?) three miles back, in a dying state. That the cold had been too much for him, and that no doubt he was already dead. They had brought away the money, and even the *blankets* of the expiring wretch! They said that if they had stopped with him, they would have been frozen themselves. But even if their story is true, they must be the most brutal of creatures, not to have made him as comfortable as possible, with *all* the blankets, and after they had built their fire and got warm, to have returned and ascertained if he were really dead.

On hearing the express man's report, several men who had been acquainted with the deceased, started out to try and discover his remains. They found his violin, broken into several pieces, but all traces of the poor fellow himself had disappeared, probably forever.

In the meanwhile, some travelers had carried the same news to Burke's Rancho, when several of the residents of that place, followed the two men and overtook them to Bidwell's Bar, where they had them arrested on suspicion of murder. They protested their innocence, of course, and one of them said that he would lead a party to the spot where they had left the dying man. On arriving in the vicinity of the place, he at first stated that it was under one tree, then another, and another, and at last ended by declaring that it was utterly impossible for him to remember where they were camped at the time of R.'s death.

In this state of things nothing was to be done but to return to B.'s. When the excitement having somewhat subsided, they were allowed to proceed on their journey, the money—which they both swore R. had willed in his dying moments, to a near relation of one of these very men—having been taken from them in order to be sent by express to the friends of the deceased in the States.

Although they have been acquitted, many shake their heads doubtfully at the whole transaction. It seems very improbable, that a man, accustomed all his life to hard labor and exposure, even although slightly unwell, as it is said he was, at the time, should have sunk under the cold during a walk of less than twenty miles, amid a gentle fall of snow and rain, when, as it is well known, the air is comparatively mild. It is to be hoped, however, that the companions of R. were brutal rather than criminal; though the desertion of a dying friend under such circumstances, even to the last unfeeling and selfish act, of removing from the expiring creature his blankets, is in truth almost as bad as actual murder.

I hope in my next, that I shall have something more cheerful than the above chapter of horrors, to relate. In the meanwhile, *adios,* and think as kindly as you can of the dear California, even though her lustrous skies gaze upon such barbarous deeds.

Helen McCowen Carpenter (1839–1917)

"Ho for California!" is the celebratory pronouncement that begins the 1857 diary of Helen McCowen Carpenter as she, her husband of four months, and her parents say farewell to Kansas and begin the five month trek to California. Though her cry was just an enthusiastic expression after months of preparation and anticipation, it is telling of the vivacious spirit of this young bride of eighteen.

Filled with the myth that drew hundreds of thousands to the west coast to explore their dreams, she begins her journey somewhat naive about life's hardships and inequalities. She is not burdened in the beginning with the worries often voiced by older women about to begin this arduous trek—worries about Indian attacks, having enough food, or the rumors of cholera—but is instead laudatory, almost boastful, in her remarks about her circumstance: "Our wagon gives promise of more comfort than any of the others. That, I suppose, is as it should be, for a bride should have more detail to her outfit than an ordinary emigrant." Hers is the world of youth and romance, and what she sees ahead is the glory of challenge conquered and a smiling, setting California sun. But in the process of westering to California, Helen Carpenter matures into a seasoned frontier woman—her heart goes out to starving Pawnees begging along the trail, she collects "buffalo chips" for firewood, manages days with little water, endures Indian attack, and travels, parched, across the great desert. By the time she reaches the mining camps she is keen to the dangers and difficulties of this new western territory, hardened and prepared to meet any challenge.

When Helen and her new husband, Aurelius Ormando Carpenter (known to his friends as Reel), reached California, they tried their hands at mining, but soon bought Hill's Ranch in Grass Valley. Trained as a typesetter in Kansas, Reel also found work with the local newspaper. They had fairly settled in by March of 1858 when Helen delivered their daughter, May. However, as soon as they felt the baby could travel, they headed two hundred miles northwest, to Potter Valley in Mendocino County. They spent a decade there, building a home, planting crops, laying the cornerstones for a growing community. They attended barn raisings and quilting parties, and dances where the orchestra consisted of one rusty fiddle player. Helen taught at the first

Helen McCowen Carpenter (1839–1917). Courtesy of the Edward E. Ayer Collection, the Newberry Library, Chicago.

Potter Valley school, riding her horse several miles to and from school each day in the spring and summer—school met when children weren't needed for the harvest or kept away by rain and mud.

Almost as soon as she arrived Helen went to work recording the lives and traditions of the Pomo people who lived in her area. Her essays and short stories were published for three decades in *The Golden Era, The Overland Monthly,* and other California and national periodicals. In them she championed the cause of California's Native Americans and chided the white community for its cruel treatment of the native people she had come to respect in Potter Valley. She also recorded, from oral recitings, the myths and tales of Mendocino County Indians, mainly Pomo.

In late 1864 Helen gave up her post at the school because she was once again pregnant, and in February of 1865 she gave birth to twins, a boy and a girl, Grant and Grace. Then sometime before 1870, she and Reel moved to Ukiah, where Reel managed a photographic studio with Helen's help. In 1870 she delivered their last child, a son whom they named Frank.

As a mature woman, busy with family and practical matters, Helen found far too little time for her artistic interests—writing and painting. She nonetheless managed to sketch images of early California life, of Indians, of children caught in the web of frontier history. She made goodhearted attempts to educate Indians to Anglo ways, and to improve Anglo treatment of California Indians. She initiated a tradition of artistic response to the natural environment and native cultures, which she passed on to her daughter, Grace Hudson, known now to many Californians as the Painter Lady.

Carpenter is best known for her diary, her essays and short stories. She also wrote children's stories and plays. "The Mitchells," originally published in the *Overland Monthly* in September 1895, is but one example of the many prose pieces she wrote about the "settling" period. Although she exhibits some of the prevalent attitudes of white settlers toward blacks and Indians, she also rises above the prejudices of her time by allowing her characters a full measure of humanity.

Helen Carpenter lived in Ukiah until her death in 1917. Her writings are housed at the Held Poage Research Library, and her artistic influence is easily seen in Ukiah's handsome Grace Hudson Museum.

THE MITCHELLS

Tucked away among the foot-hills of the Sierra Nevada, where
the dark pines nod familiarly to each passing breeze, is a
picturesque spot known as Penn Valley. The greater part of the
valley, is a succession of low, rocky hills, covered with chaparral
and clusters of small pines, while dotted here and there on the low
lands are numerous springs of pure cold water, with adjacent fertile
spots covered with orchards, vineyards, and green fields of alfalfa.
Owing to the heavy growth of brush and pines, there is no extended
view of the valley, but from an eminence within its limits, can be
seen an ocean of waving grain fields, and beyond the mist that
overhangs the Sacramento River, the Marysville Buttes outlined
against the sky in all their somber grandeur, while far, far away,
where the sun suddenly drops from view, is the dimly outlined,
misty blue of the Coast Range.

Taking a serpentine course through the valley, is a clear cold
stream, called Squirrel Creek, which lies here and there, in deep,
silent pools, and again rushes headlong over rocky falls, where
but a ray of sunshine finds its way through the wide spreading
boughs of the pine trees.

At the extreme lower end of the valley, on a rocky upland,
stands a little cabin, looking out upon a brush-covered opening,
with only here and there a tree to intercept the first rays of morning
light. On the north and west, a forest of pines protects it from
the chilling winds of winter, and the warm afternoon sunshine in
summer. A few rods to the south, lies a rocky road, over which
the Marysville stage bumps its passengers every day in the year;

and beyond this lies a half board, half ditch fence, enclosing the pasture lands of a thrifty farmer. The cabin was built by an old negro, named Jim Mitchell, and the quarter-section on which it stands he took as a homestead, and there with his squaw wife spent many peaceful years, esteemed by all who knew him, for truthfulness and strict integrity.

As is characteristic of his race, he loved companionship, and there were many hard struggles before poverty and ill health forced him to settle in this quiet spot. The ranch was of no value, aside from the timber and a small amount of pasturage, so he made no attempt at farming, but did odd jobs for the neighbors, and occasionally a full day's work, when the state of his health would permit.

His greatest solace in his isolation was an old fiddle. Ellen, the squaw, sat near, stroking her dog, "Cully," and looking upon her liege lord with love and admiration, as he played on long winter's evenings. The other dogs stretched themselves at full length on the hearth, to enjoy the warmth of the open fireplace. The instrument was not in the hands of a novice, and as the lively strains rose and fell in quick succession upon the ears of the uncritical listeners, a vigorous pat, pat, kept the time perfect, while an air of enchantment pervaded the humble dwelling. The poor old face, suffused with smiles, looked again youthful in the fire-light glow. In an intoxication of fond memories aroused, aches and pains were forgotten,—the old rheumatic leg was, "First upon the heel tap, then upon the toe;"—and before Jim came back to the realities of life and his infirmities, he made a futile attempt to leave his chair, and "jump Jim Crow."

Ellen kept the house in order, had the frugal meals on time, and otherwise busied herself, in piecing quilts of scraps given by the neighbors, and weaving beautifully designed baskets. The quilts kept the bed neat and made Mitchell comfortable, while the baskets were for her own people. Although very happy and contented with Mitchell, she still loved her tribe, and when a death occurred among the Indians, none contributed baskets more generously for the funeral fire than Ellen. It is doubtful if she could have broken her relations with the tribe, even had she wished to do so, for they settled down on Mitchell like a lot of vultures, ready to eat every sack of flour and side of bacon that found its way into the scanty larder.

Friends remonstrated with such arguments as, "They are more able to work than you, let them rustle for themselves."

"Couldn't tell em dat, boss, dey's her people, 'n she's good to me. What 'ud I do without dat ooman, I's a mighty sight to be thankful for."

By and by, Ellen got very little time for her patchwork and basket-making, as Mitchell's failing health made it necessary for her to seek employment at the neighboring farmhouses. Much of her time was spent on the ranch adjoining their homestead, where she made herself useful at the wash-tub and mending baskets, humming the while a mournful dirge that contrasted strangely with her beaming countenance and childlike simplicity. The little dog was her constant companion, and the invalid, too, accompanied her, as long as he retained the strength to do so; for "Boss and Madam," as he called them, were generous to a fault, and the trio were sure of a good meal and a package to carry home, if they only made a call, "up to de house."

They were in the habit of calling frequently, on their friends, and were made very welcome at more than one home in the valley. Sometimes the three came, bringing along the old fiddle; this was for pleasure only,—and Madam was entertained with the artist's very best selections. At other times, the calls were of a business nature, such as "dischargin' a settin' of aigs, to get some of Madam's percochins," or to get some "distructions 'bout making sof' soap."

A family to whom they paid regular visits, moved away, and in the course of time, the lady sent her "love and kind remembrances to Mitchell and Ellen." When the message was delivered, Ellen as usual had nothing to say, but Mitchell beamed with delight and volubly enumerated the many gifts to "me 'n Ellen," and with emphasis declared, "Madam Hyte's a squar up and down lady to think uv an ole nigger." This little token of regard was a lasting memory, kept fresh in the minds of his friends by frequent repetition, and reference to the lady, as "a mighty good ooman."

Ellen was very quiet and unobtrusive, seldom speaking unless spoken to, and not always then, but when Mitchell entertained his friends with some highly embellished narrative of past adventures, she would blink her eyes and smile, and blink again, before she made the explanation, "Jes' a talkin' now."

The neighbors were unanimous in the verdict, that "Mitchell was no common nigger." Without any education beyond reading and spelling a little, he spoke French, Spanish, English, and Indian. Although old, infirm, and destitute, he cheerfully acknowledged there was "so much to be thankful for." He had the politeness and suavity of a Frenchman, the good-natured improvidence of his own race, the hopeful simplicity of a child, and the love of a true gentleman for his wife, although she was only a Digger Indian.

In conversation with Madam, he said: "I was borned a slave, in Loosyanny. Mars Bruce he borned same day, 'n ole boss he give me t' Mars Bruce for his 'n,—'n mighty good times did me 'n Mars Bruce have ridin' the hosses. We rid when we's no taller 'n yan table, 'n 'f anybody'd cuff my years, Mars Bruce 'ud rave, 'n tell 'um he 'spex he can cuff Jim 'f 'e needs 'busin' dat way. Mars Bruce 'ud never sole my Jinsy down de Massassipy,—ole boss dun dat. Me 'n Mars Bruce done come to Californy over a plains, 'n jist at the Sabeen River, we met up with Dave Terry, a chum of our'n, 'n right there Mars Bruce give my free papers, 'n I dun been my own man ever since. We wuz forty-niners 'n made a sight o' money,—I dun made six dollars a day, jes' a washin', an' sich,— 'pears like I can't say what mine's gawn to. I never got drunk, 'n I never smoked, 'n I never chawed,—so 't ain't drunk up, nor 't ain't smoked up, nor 't ain't chawed up,—but it's gawn up de flume somehow, dat am a fac', but I'se a mighty sight to be thankful for, anyways."

Sometimes the cabin was shut up for a few days, while the Mitchells on their old horse, Suzy, went off to a Digger fandango.

Suzy had a special habit of always holding her mouth open,—Mitchell said she was "a laffin'," but from appearances, the poor animal found living a rather serious matter, with but little to excite her risibles. "Laffin' " Suzy with Mitchell and Ellen on her back, and Cully in Ellen's lap, set off at a deliberate gait,—while Ponto and Sally, with tails erect, trotted ahead, as if to encourage Suzy to quicken her pace. All together they made an interesting group on the highway.

"We allus takes our own grub," Mitchell explained apologetically, "fer I don't want none uv their truck, 'pears like it's little uv everything."

At one time Madam missed the social call of the Mitchells. Month after month went by, without a sight of their friendly faces. She was puzzled to ascribe a cause for their absence. They were not gone, for with great regularity Cully came as usual for food that was always awaiting her. One day after she had finished her lunch and licked her mongrel chops, Madam tied a bit of gay ribbon on the dog's neck, and saw her trot off home.

Mitchell espied the ribbon at once, and with tears in his eyes exclaimed: "Madam dun dat. She want us to come."

If there had been any ill feeling, it was all gone now; that bit of ribbon bridged the chasm. Visits were at once resumed, without any reference to the past, and Cully became a greater favorite than ever with Madam, who enjoyed making life a little easier for her poor neighbors.

More and more feeble the invalid became, until a stroke of paralysis rendered him helpless. For three months Ellen gave him loving care, and when the burden became too heavy, some of her tribe assisted in ministering to his wants. Madam and the friends kept a better supply of provisions than had ever before rested on Ellen's "fall leaf table," in which she had especial pride.

One morning Tanaka came with a message "up to the house,"—but Indian like, he leaned on the fence, not offering to come in, or speak, until asked, "What do you want, Tanaka?"

"Mitchell gone," he replied, and without another word departed.

Madam with her best lace pillow-cases and whitest sheets, and minor articles for Ellen, was admitted to the cabin, and led by the widow to the bed, where lay the body of her husband, covered entirely over with the best patchwork quilt. She removed the quilt from the face, and putting a hand on either side, knelt beside the bed and wept. All was done that could be for the respect of the dead and comfort of the living.

A few months later, Ellen sold the land for $600, with permission to occupy the cabin as long as she chose. Money now began to be spent freely,—not by Ellen, but her Indian friends, who came and put up a cabin conveniently near, and lived entirely on her bounty, begging the money by tens and twenties from the kind-hearted creature, who could not refuse her improvident brothers.

With a bright golden twenty, Bob was sent to Smartsville for supplies. It was late before he returned, and then beastly drunk, and the money all gone. Some dissatisfaction was expressed, and Bob became furious, vowing vengeance on everybody in general. In a frenzy, he discharged a loaded Winchester, and accidently ended his spree in a very few minutes. Ellen's face wore a pained expression when she saw the bloodstains on her patchwork quilt. No doubt she thought of the peaceful days that were past, but no word escaped her lips.

Soon after this Ellen and her friends set off for a fandango, sixteen miles away, over toward San Juan,—Ellen on "Laffin' Suzy," with numerous bundles of bedding and clothing, and the rest on foot, each with a basket or bundle. Ellen locked her cabin securely, but in the other house was left an old blind squaw, named Catum, who was too old to enjoy the fandango, and too feeble for the journey. Provisions were placed in the chimney corner near her blankets, and Cully was left for company.

Two days later the boss was passing by, and saw the cabin door standing wide open. Aware of Ellen's absence, he went to close it and beheld a scene of destruction that made his heart ache for the helpless owner. In the center of the room was heaped every article of dress and furniture the cabin contained, hopelessly chopped into bits. There lay the "fall leaf table" and dish safe, split into kindling, the cooking-stove, dishes, and chairs, a mass of debris, and over all, was emptied sugar, salt, and flour. The feathers that Ellen had been so long in collecting for pillows, were floating about unrestrained, while on top of the heap, resting snugly in its box, was Mitchell's fiddle, not one string amiss, and the only thing in the house that was not broken beyond the possibility of any future use. Before reaching the other cabin, the boss threw up his hands in horror; for there before him lay poor old Catum, stone dead. The shriveled old body was burned to a crisp, a band around the waist was all that was left of the clothing, and there, close by her side, sat faithful little Cully. She greeted boss with a growl, although the little eyes wore a pleased expression at the approach of a friend.

Out across the pine forest, not far from the big bend of Squirrel Creek, lived an ill-tempered, revengeful negro. Ineffectual attempts to convince the neighbors that he was not a gentleman of color, also added to the surly disposition. Two weeks after Mitchell's death, this person was anxious to take charge of the homestead, and fill the void in Ellen's affections,—but in both he was disappointed, and the destruction of her property was the result. Whether the death of Catum is attributable to accident while preparing her frugal meal, or a crime to be laid at the door of the same demon, will forever be a mystery.

Lack of sufficient proof was all that prevented boss and Madam, from seeing justice done their poor neighbor. Ellen was sent for, and Madam accompanied her, to be a support in her grief. She gazed long and earnestly on the ruins in her once comfortable and happy home. Silently she made her way to the little storeroom, where her beautiful baskets lay scattered about over the floor, cut up into bits. Mitchell's ax had been used for their demolition, and was lying near with the handle broken. Madam knew these were her dearest treasures, that year after year, she had worked on them, stitch by stitch, that Mitchell with his violin sat near, and watched the busy fingers weaving in and out, and praised the ever-varying designs. With such recollections, her eyes were brimming with sympathetic tears, while Ellen, with clasped hands, and a half audible "Oh!" gazed on, shedding no tear and giving no further evidence of emotion. How keenly the loss was felt, is a secret in her own bosom.

As Madam and boss were returning from Rough and Ready the next day, they met a small company of Indians, with their customary budgets and bundles, presumably all their worldly effects. It was nothing unusual to see them en route, so they were scarcely given a second glance, still it was remembered that one squaw, with muffled head and averted face, kept to the farther side of the road. It was afterwards learned that this was Ellen, fulfilling the promise made to Mitchell, of "going back to camp,"—going back to her tribe, as poor as she left it years ago, going back to certain hardship and penury, going without one word of goodby, even to Madam, her very best friend.

Frances Fuller Victor (1826–1902). Courtesy of the Society of California Pioneers.

Frances Fuller Victor (1826–1902)

Perhaps the most scholarly of the women writers collected here, Frances Fuller Victor was the only one to make her entire living by writing. She was uniquely able to do this because she could cross literary genres. She wrote estimable fiction, was sought after as a columnist and essay writer for newspapers and periodicals, and also enjoyed research and historical prose. Her flexibility enabled her to endure the ebb and flow of California literary trends.

As a young woman in New York, Frances Fuller received good reviews for a book of poetry she wrote with her sister, Metta Fuller. The two Fuller sisters then married the two Victor brothers. Metta remained in New York, writing rather sensational novels, and Frances came to San Francisco to write moving editorials, poetry, short stories and novels.

Arriving in California in 1863 with her husband, who was a naval engineer, Frances sometimes used the pseudonym Florence Fane as byline for the columns she wrote for the *Evening Herald* and the *Golden Era*. The slight but sprightly, assertive woman was highly praised for her attention to detail and powerful imagery. She was just beginning to feel comfortable as a member of San Francisco's sagebrush school of literature, publishing regularly in the *Overland Monthly* and the *Golden Era*, when her husband was transferred to Oregon.

While in Oregon she wrote historical novels: *Atlantis Arisen, All Over Oregon and Washington,* and *The River of the West,* a biography of frontiersman Joe Meek. And in 1877 she published *The New Penelope and Other Stories,* a collection of poems and short stories set in California, Oregon and Washington. *The New Penelope,* a novella, parallels the life of a western boarding house proprietress with that of Homer's Penelope, wife of Odysseus.

When her husband died in 1878, Frances Fuller Victor returned to San Francisco. Although she had always written fiction and found an audience for most of what she produced, upon her return she found it difficult to publish fictional sketches. The market for women's fiction, so open on her earlier stay in California, had dried up. But she was not easily dismissed. It was common knowledge in San Francisco that along with her kind countenance and sparkling, compassionate eyes she had the ability to hold her own in almost any conversation, and especially liked to embark on tête-à-têtes with intellectual men. One man with whom she enjoyed many such conversations was Hubert Bancroft. He realized the talent of the highly educated Frances Victor, a lover of books and history, and immediately employed her to research and draft three complete volumes of his *Bancroft's History*. She still wrote fiction when she could, but published only occasionally. The pay she received working for Bancroft was modest, and like Henry Oak and others who worked on the *Bancroft History* project, she received no credit for her work—although he wrote only ten percent of the material he published, Bancroft insisted on exclusive billing as author.

In "How Jack Hastings Sold His Mine," Victor presents a woman strong and true, caught in the snares of tradition and patriarchal expectation. Most of her women characters faced similar dilemmas between social convention and personal growth. The extent to which some of these characters, especially Alice Hastings in "How Jack Hastings Sold His Mine," resemble Frances Victor herself is speculative, but similarities of disposition are apparent. This story, first published in *The New Penelope and Other Stories* in 1877, challenges similar pieces by Bret Harte, Prentice Mulford and Ambrose Bierce. Ironically, even in her own lifetime, Frances Victor's fiction was sometimes credited to others, and several of her short stories were later attributed to Bret Harte.

In 1891 she published her last collection, *Atlantis Arisen, or Talks of a Tourist About Washington and Oregon*. In it she continued to reflect the images of the western landscape and the people who coped with it, with special attention to the lives of women. She continued to write after her retirement and died, unknown and in debt, in 1902.

Frances Fuller Victor was unique in that she survived in a profession dominated by men. She wasn't able to write what she wanted as often as she would have liked, but her sketches of westerners, especially women, are historically illuminating, well drawn, fresh and relevant even to this day.

HOW JACK HASTINGS
SOLD HIS MINE

———— ❧•❦ ————

T he passenger train from the East came thundering down the
head of the Humboldt Valley, just as morning brightened
over the earth—refreshing eyes wearied with yesterday's mountains and cañons, by a vision of green willows and ash trees, a
stream that was not a torrent, and a stretch of grassy country.

Among the faces oftenest turned to the flitting views was that
of a young, gracefully-formed, neatly-dressed, delicate-looking
woman. The large brown eyes often returned from gazing at the
landscape, to scan with seriousness some memoranda she held in
her hand. "Arrive at Elko at eight o'clock A.M." said the memoran-
dum. Consulting a tiny watch, whose hands pointed to ten minutes
of eight, the lady began making those little preparations which
betoken the journey's end at hand.

"What a strange looking place it is!" she thought, as the motley
collection of board shanties and canvas houses came in sight;—for
the famous Chloride District had been discovered but a few months
before, and the Pacific Railroad was only four weeks open. "I wish
Jack had come to meet me! I'm sure I don't see how I am to find
the stage agent to give him Jack's letter. What a number of people!"

This mental ejaculation was called forth by the sight of the long
platform in front of the eating-house, crowded with a surging
mass of humanity just issuing from the dining-room. They were
the passengers of the eastward-bound train, ready to rush headlong
for the cars when the momently-expected "All aboard" should be

shouted at them by the conductor. Into this crowd the freshly-arrived passengers of the westward-bound train were a moment after ejected—each eyeing the other with a natural and pardonable interest.

The brown-eyed, graceful young lady conducted herself in a very business-like manner—presenting the checks for her baggage; inquiring out the office of Wells, Fargo & Co., and handing in her letter, all in the briefest possible time. Having secured a seat in a coach to Chloride Hill, with the promise of the agent to call for her when the time for departure arrived, the lady repaired to the dining-room just in time to see her acquaintances of the train departing. Sitting down alone to a hastily-cooked and underdone repast, she was about finishing a cup of bitter black coffee with a little shudder of disgust, when a gentleman seated himself opposite her at table. The glance the stranger cast in her direction was rather a lingering one; then he ordered his breakfast and ate it. Meanwhile the lady retired to the ladies' sitting-room.

After an hour of waiting, one, two, three, coaches rolled past the door, and the lady began to fear she had been forgotten, when the polite agent appeared to notify "Mrs. Hastings" that "the stage was ready." This was Mrs. Alice Hastings, then—wife of Mr. Jack Hastings, of Deep Cañon, Chloride District. The agent thought Mr. Hastings had a very pretty wife, and expressed his opinion in his manner, as men will.

When, just before starting, there entered three of the roughest-looking men she had ever encountered, Mrs. Hastings began to fear that in his zeal to obey instructions, the agent had exceeded them, and in packing the first three coaches with first-comers, had left this one to catch up the fag end of travel. If the first impression, gained from sight, had made her shrink a little, what was her dismay when, at the end of ten minutes, one of her fellow-travelers— the only American of the three—produced a bottle of brandy, which, having offered it first to her, he passed to the bullet-headed Irishman and very shabby Jew: repeating the courtesy once in twenty minutes for several times.

Mrs. Hastings was a brave sort of woman, where courage was needful; and she now began to consider the case in hand with what coolness she could command. One hundred and thirty miles— eighteen or twenty hours of such companionship—with no chance of change or intermission; a wilderness country to travel over, and all the other coaches a long way ahead. The dainty denizen of a city home, shuddering inwardly, showed outwardly a serene countenance. Her American friend, with wicked black eyes and a jolly and reckless style of carrying himself, continued to offer brandy at short intervals.

"Best take some, Madame," said he; "this dust will choke you if you don't."

"Thanks," returned the lady, with her sweetest smile, "I could not drink brandy. I have wine in my traveling-basket, should I need it; but much prefer water."

At the next station, although hardly four minutes were lost in changing horses, the men procured for her a cup of water. Mrs. Hastings' thanks were frank and cordial. She even carefully opened a conversation about the country they were passing over, and contrived to get them to ask a question or two about herself. When they learned that she had come all the way from New York on the newly-opened railroad, their interest was at its height; and when they heard that she was going to join her husband in the Chloride District, their sympathy was thoroughly enlisted.

"Wonderful—such a journey! How she could be six days on the cars, and yet able to take such a stage-ride as this, is astonishing."

Such were the American's comments. The Jew thought of the waiting husband—for your Israelite is a man of domestic and family affections. "Her husband looking for her, and she behind time! How troubled he must be! Didn't *he* know how it was? Wasn't his wife gone away on a visit once, and didn't write; and he a running to the express office every morning and evening for a letter, and getting so anxious as to telegraph? Such an expense and loss of time!—and all because he felt so uneasy about his wife!"

The bullet-headed young Irishman said nothing. He was about

half asleep from brandy, and last night's travel; too stupid to know that his hat had flown out of the window, and was bowling along in the wind and dust half a mile behind—all the better for his head, which looked at a red heat now.

The lady had lifted the rude men up to her level, when directly they were ashamed of their brandy and other vices, and began to show instinctive traits of gentlemen. By the time they arrived at the dinner station, where half an hour was allowed for food and rest out of the eighteen or twenty, she had at least two humble servitors, who showed great concern for her comfort.

The day began to wane. They had traveled continuously over a long stretch of plain between two mountain ranges, over a country entirely uninhabited except by the stage company's employees, who kept the stations and tended the stock. This lone woman had seen but one other woman on the road. Plenty of teams—great "prairie schooners," loaded with every conceivable thing for sup-plying the wants of an isolated non-producing community, and drawn by ten or fourteen mules—had been passed through the day.

As night fell, Mrs. Hastings saw what she had never before seen or imagined—the camps of these teamsters by the roadside; horses and mules staked, or tied to the wagons; the men lying prone upon the earth, wrapped in blankets, their dust-blackened faces turned up to the frosty twinkling stars. Did people really live in that way?—how many superfluous things were there in a city!

The night was moonless and clear, and cold as at that altitude they always are. Sleep, from the roughness of the road, was impos-sible. Her companions dozed, and woke with exclamations when the heavy lurchings of the coach disturbed them too roughly. Mrs. Hastings never closed her eyes. When morning dawned, they were on the top of a range of mountains, like those that had been in sight all the day before. Down these heights they rattled away, and at four in the morning entered the streets of Chloride Hill—a city of board and canvas houses. Arrived at the stage office, the lady looked penetratingly into the crowd of men always waiting for the stages, but saw no face she recognized. Yes, one—and that the face of the gentleman who sat down opposite her at table in Elko.

"Permit me," he said; "I think you inquired for Mr. Hastings?"

"I did; he is my husband. I expected to find him here," she replied, feeling that sense of injury and desire to cry which tired women feel, jostled about in a crowd of men.

Leaving her a moment to say something to an employee of the office, the stranger returned immediately, saying to the man: "Take this lady to Mrs. Robb's boarding-house." Then to her: "I will inquire for your husband, and send him to you if he is in town. The hack does not go over to Deep Cañon for several hours yet. Meanwhile you had better take some rest. You must be greatly fatigued."

Fatigued! her head swam round and round; and she really was too much exhausted to feel as disappointed as she might at Jack's non-appearance. Much relieved by the prospect of a place to rest in, she followed the man summoned to escort her, and fifteen minutes after was sound asleep on a sofa of the boarding-house.

Three hours of sleep and a partial bath did much to restore tired nature's equilibrium; and, although her head still felt absurdly light, Mrs. Hastings enjoyed the really excellent breakfast provided for her, wondering how such delicacies ever got to Chloride Hill. Breakfast over, and no news of Jack, the time began to drag wearily. She was more than half inclined to be angry—only relenting when she remembered that she was two or three days behind time, and of course Jack could not know when to expect her. She had very full directions, and if she could not find her way to Deep Cañon she was a goose, that was all!

So she sent for the driver of the hack, told him to get her baggage from the express office; and started for Deep Cañon. Who should she find in the hack but her friend of the morning!

"I could not hear of your husband," said he; "but you are sure to find him at home."

Mrs. Hastings smiled faintly, and hoped she should. Then she gave her thoughts to the peculiar scenery of the country, and to the sharpness of the descent, as they whirled rapidly down the four miles of cañon at the bottom of which was the town of that name—another one of those places which had "come up as a flower" in a morning. She longed to ask about her husband and his "home"; but as there were several persons in the stage, she restrained her anxiety, and said never a word until they stopped before the door of a saloon where all the other passengers alighted. Then she told the driver she wanted to be taken to Mr. Hastings' house.

He didn't know where that was, he said, but would inquire. Did he know Dr. Earle?

"That's him, ma'am"; pointing out her friend of the morning.

"How can I serve you?" he asked, raising his hat politely.

Mrs. Hastings blushed rosily, between vexation at Jack's invisibility and confusion at being so suddenly confronted with Dr. Earle.

"Mr. Hastings instructed me to inquire of you, if I had any difficulty in finding him," she said, apologetically.

"I will show you his place with pleasure," returned the Doctor pleasantly; and, jumping on the box, proceeded to direct the driver.

Had ladies of Mrs. Hastings' style been as plenty in Deep Cañon as in New York, the driver would have grumbled at the no road he had to follow along the stony side of a hill and among the stumps of mahogany trees. But there were few like her in that mountain town, and his chivalry compelled him to go out of his way with every appearance of cheerfulness. Presently the stage stopped where the sloping ground made it very uncertain how long it could maintain its balance in that position; and the voice of Dr. Earle was heard saying "This is the place."

Mrs. Hastings, who had been looking out for some sign of home, was seized with a doubt of the credibility of her senses. It was on the tip of her tongue to say "This must be the house of some other Mr. Hastings," when she remembered prudence, and said nothing. Getting out and going toward the house to inquire, the door opened, and a man in a rough mining suit came quickly forward to meet her.

"Alice!"

"Jack!"

Dr. Earle and the driver studiously looked the other way while salutations were exchanged between Mr. and Mrs. Hastings. When they again ventured a look, the lady had disappeared within the cabin, the first glimpse of which had so dismayed her.

"If I could sell my mine," he then often said, "I could fix things up."

"If you sold your mine, Jack, you would go back to New York, and then there would be no need of fixing up this place." Alice wanted to say "horrid" place, but refrained.

At length, from uncongenial air, water, food, and circumstances in general, the transplanted flower began to droop. The great heat and rarified mountain air caused frantic headaches, aggravated by the glare which came through the white canvas roof. Then came the sudden mountain tempests, when the rain deluged everything, and it was hard to find a spot to stand in where the water did not drip through. She grew wild, looking forever at bare mountain sides simmering in the sun by day, and at night over their tops up to the piercing stars. A constant anxious fever burnt in her blood, that the cold night air could not quench, though she often left her couch to let it blow chilly over her, in her loose night robes. Then she fell really ill.

Sitting by her bedside, Jack said: "If I could sell my mine!" And she had answered, "Let the mine go, Jack, and let us go home. Nothing is gained by stopping in this dreadful place."

Then Mr. Hastings had replied to her, "I have no money, Alice, to go home with, not a cent. I borrowed ten dollars of Earle to-day to buy some fruit for you."

That was the last straw that broke the camel's back. By night Mrs. Hastings was delirious, and Dr. Earle was called.

"She has a nervous fever," he said, "and needs the carefullest nursing."

"Which she cannot have in this d——d place," Mr. Hastings replied, profanely.

"Why don't you try to get something to do?" asked Earle of the sad-visaged husband, a day or two after.

"What is there to do? Everything is flat; there is neither business nor money in this cursed country. I've stayed here trying to sell my mine, until I'm dead broke; nothing to live on here, and nothing to get out with. What I'm to do with my wife there, I don't know. Let her die, perhaps, and throw her bones up that ravine to bleach in the sun. God! What a position to be in!"

"But you certainly must propose to do something, and that speedily. Couldn't you see it was half that that brought this illness on your wife; the inevitable which she saw closing down upon you?"

"If I cannot sell my mine soon, I'll blow out my brains, as that poor German did last week. Alice heard the report of the shot which killed him, and I think it hastened on her sickness."

"And so you propose to treat her to another such scene, and put an end to her?" said Earle, savagely.

"Better so than to let her starve," Jack returned, growing pale with the burden of possibilities which oppressed him. "How the devil I am to save her from that last, I don't know. There is neither business, money, nor credit in this infernal town. I've been everywhere in this district, asking for a situation at something, and cannot get anything better than digging ground on the new road."

"Even that might be better than starving," said Dr. Earle.

Jack was a faithful nurse; Dr. Earle an attentive physician; young people with elastic constitutions die hard: so Alice began to mend, and in a fortnight was convalescent. Jack got a situation in a quartz mill where the Doctor was part owner.

Left all day alone in the cabin, Alice began staring again at the dreary mountains whose walls inclosed her on every side. The bright scarlet and yellow flowers which grew out of their parched soil sometimes tempted her to a brief walk; but the lightness of the air fatigued her, and she did not care to clamber after them.

One day, being lonely, she thought to please Jack by dressing in something pretty and going to the mill to see him. So, laying aside the wrapper which she had worn almost constantly lately, she robed herself in a delicate linen lawn, donned a coquettish little hat and parasol, and set out for the mill, a mile away. Something in the thought of the pleasant surprise it would be to Jack gave her strength and animation; and though she arrived somewhat out of breath, she looked as dainty and fresh as a rose, and Jack was immensely proud and flattered. He introduced her to the head of the firm, showed her over the mill, pointed out to her the mule-train packing wood for the engine fires, got the amalgamator to give her specimens, and in every way showed his delight.

After an hour or so she thought about going home; but the walk home looked in prospect very much longer than the walk to the mill. In truth, it was harder by reason of being up-hill. But opportunely, as it seemed, just as Jack was seeing her off the door-stone of the office, Dr. Earle drove up and, comprehending the situation, offered to take Mrs. Hastings to her own door in his carriage, if she would graciously allow him five minutes to see the head man in.

When they were seated in the carriage, a rare luxury in Deep Cañon, and had driven a half mile in embarrassed silence—for Mrs. Hastings somehow felt ashamed of her husband's dependence upon this man—the Doctor spoke, and what he said was this:

"Your life is very uncongenial to you; you wish to escape from it, don't you?"

"Yes, I wish to escape; that is the word which suits my feeling—a very strange feeling it is."

"Describe it," said the Doctor, almost eagerly.

"Ever since I left the railroad, in the midst of a wilderness and was borne for so many hours away into the heart of a still more desert wilderness, my consciousness of things has been very much confused. I can only with difficulty realize that there is any such place as New York; and San Francisco is a fable. The world seems a great bare mountain plane; and I am hanging on to its edge by my fingertips, ready to drop away into space. Can you account for such impressions?"

"Easily, if I chose. May I tell you something?"

"What is it?"

"I've half a mind to run away with you."

Now, as Dr. Earle was a rather young and a very handsome man, had been very kind, and was now looking at her with eyes actually moistened with tears, a sudden sense of being on the edge of a pitfall overcame Mrs. Hastings; and she turned pale and red alternately. Yet, with the instinct of a pure woman, to avoid recognizing an ugly thought, she answered with a laugh as gay as she could make it.

"If you were a witch, and offered me half of your broomstick to New York, I don't know but I should take it—that is, if there was room on it anywhere for Jack."

"There wouldn't be," said the Doctor, and said no more.

The old fever seemed to have returned that afternoon. The hills glared so that Mrs. Hastings closed the cabin door to shut out the burning vision. The ground-squirrels, thinking from the silence that no one was within, ran up the mahogany tree at the side, and scampered over the canvas roof in glee. One, more intent on gain than the rest, invaded Jack's outside kitchen, knocking down the tin dishes with a clang, and scattering the dirt from the turf roof over the flour-sack and the two white plates. Every sound made her heart beat faster. Afraid of the silence and loneliness at last, she reopened the door; and then a rough-looking man came to the entrance, to inquire if there were any silver leads up the ravine.

Leads? she could not say: prospectors in plenty there were.

Then he went his way, having satisfied his curiosity; and the door was closed again. Some straggling donkeys wandered near, which were mistaken for "Diggers"; and dreading their glittering eyes, the nervous prisoner drew the curtain over the one little sliding window. There was nothing to read, nothing to sew, no housekeeping duties, because no house to keep; she was glad when the hour arrived for preparing the late afternoon meal.

That night she dreamed that she was a skeleton lying up the cañon—the sunshine parching her naked bones; that Dr. Earle came along with a pack-train going to the mill, and picking her up carefully, laid her on top of a bundle of wood; that the Mexican driver covered her up with a blanket, which so smothered her that she awakened, and started up gasping for breath. The feeling of suffocation continuing, she stole softly to the door, and opening it, let the chilly night air blow over her. Most persons would have found Mr. Hastings' house freely ventilated, but some way poor Alice found it hard to breathe in it.

The summer was passing; times grew, if possible, harder than before. The prospectors, who had found plenty of "leads," had spent their "bottom dollar" in opening them up and in waiting for purchasers, and were going back to California any way they could. The capitalists were holding off, satisfied that in the end all the valuable mines would fall into their hands, and caring nothing how fared the brave but unlucky discoverers. In fact, they overshot themselves, and made hard times for their own mills, the miners having to stop getting out rock.

Then Jack lost his situation. Very soon food began to be scarce in the cabin of Mr. Hastings. Scanty as it was, it was more than Alice craved; or rather, it was not what she craved. If she ate for a day or two, for the next two or three days she suffered with nausea and aversion to anything which the outside kitchen afforded. Jack seldom mentioned his mine now, and looked haggard and hopeless. The conversation between her husband and Dr. Earle, recorded elsewhere, had been overheard by Alice, lying half conscious; and she had never forgotten the threat about blowing out his brains in case he failed to sell his mine. Trifling as such an apprehension may appear to another, it is not unlikely that it had its effect to keep up her nervous condition. The summer was going—was gone. Mrs. Hastings had not met Dr. Earle for several weeks; and, despite herself, when the worst fears oppressed her, her first impulse was to turn to him. It had always seemed so easy for him to do what he liked!

Perhaps *he* was growing anxious to know if he could give the thumb-screw another turn. At all events, he directed his steps toward Mr. Hastings' house on the afternoon of the last day in August. Mrs. Hastings received him at the threshold and offered him the camp-stool—the only chair she had—in the shade outside the door; at the same time seating herself upon the door-step with the same grace as if it had been a silken sofa.

She was not daintily dressed this afternoon; for that luxury, like others, calls for the expenditure of a certain amount of money, and money Alice had not—not even enough to pay a Chinaman for "doing up" one of her pretty muslins. Neither had she the facilities for doing them herself, had she been skilled in that sort of labor; for even to do your own washing and ironing pre- supposes the usual conveniences of a laundry, and these did not belong to the furniture of the outside kitchen. She had not worn her linen lawn since the visit to the mill. The dust which blew freely through every crack of the shrunken boards precluded such extravagance. Thus it happened that a soiled cashmere wrapper was her afternoon wear. She had faded a good deal since her coming to Deep Cañon; but still looked pretty and graceful, and rather too *spirituelle*.

The Doctor held in his hand, on the point of a knife, the flower of a cactus very common in the mountains, which he presented her, warning her at the same time against its needle-like thorns.

"It makes me sick," said Alice hastily, throwing it away. "It is the color of gold, which I want so much; and of the sunshine, which I hate so."

"I brought it to you to show you the little emerald bee that is always to be found in one: it is wondrously beautiful,—a living gem, is it not?"

"Yes, I know," Alice said, "I admired the first one I saw; but I admire nothing any longer—nothing at least which surrounds me here."

"I understand that, of course," returned the Doctor. "It is because your health is failing you—because the air disagrees with you."

"And because my husband is so unfortunate. If he could only

get away from here—and I!" The vanity of such a supposition, in their present circumstances, brought the tears to her eyes and a quiver about her mouth.

"Why did you ever come here! Why did he ever ask you to come—how *dared* he?" demanded the Doctor, setting his teeth together.

"That is a strange question, Doctor!" Mrs. Hastings answered with dignity, lifting her head like an antelope. "My husband was deceived by the same hopes which have ruined others. If I suffer, it is because we are both unfortunate."

"What will he do next?" questioned the Doctor curtly. The cruel meaning caused the blood to forsake her cheeks.

"I cannot tell what he will do"—her brief answer rounded by an expressive silence.

"You might help him: shall I point out the way to you?"—watching her intently.

"Can you? *can* I help him?—her whole form suddenly inspired with fresh life.

Dr. Earle looked into her eager face with a passion of jealous inquiry that made her cast down her eyes:

"Alice, do you *love* this Hastings?"

He called her Alice; he used a tone and asked a question which could not be misunderstood. Mrs. Hastings dropped her face into her hands, her hands upon her knees. She felt like a wild creature which the dogs hold at bay. She knew now what the man meant, and the temptation he used.

"Alice," he said again, "this man, your husband, possesses a prize he does not value; or does not know how to care for. Shall you stay here and starve with him? Is he worth it?"

"He is my husband," she answered simply, lifting up her face, calm, if mortally pale.

"And I might be your husband, after a brief interval," he said quickly. "There would have to be a divorce—it could be conducted quietly. I do not ask you to commit yourself to dishonor. I will shield you; no care shall fall upon you, nor any reproach. Consider this well, dearest darling Alice! and what will be your fate if you depend upon him."

"Will it help *him* then, to desert him?" she asked faintly.

"Yes, unless by remaining with him you can insure his support. Maintain you he cannot. Suppose his mine were sold, he would waste that money as he wasted what he brought here. I don't want his mine, yet I will buy it to-morrow if that will satisfy you, and I have your promise to go with me. I told you once that I wanted to run away with you, and now I mean to. Shall I tell you my plan?"

"No, not to-day," Mrs. Hastings answered, struggling with her pain and embarrassment; "I could not bear it to-day, I think."

"How cruel I am while meaning to be kind! You are agitated as you ought not to be in your weak state. Shall I see you to-morrow— a professional visit, you know?"

"You will buy the mine?"—faintly, with something like a blush.

"Certainly; I swear I will—on what conditions, you know."

"On none other?"

"Shall I rob myself, not of money only, but of what is far dearer?—On *none other*." He rose, took her cold hand, clasped it fervently, and went away.

When Jack came home to his very meagre dinner, he brought a can of peaches, which, being opened, looked so deliciously cool and tempting that Alice could not refrain from volubly exulting over them. "But how did you get them, Jack?" she asked; "not by going into debt, I hope."

"No. I was in Scott's store, and Earle, happening to come in just as Scott was selling some, and praising them highly, paid for a can, and asked me to take them to you and get your opinion. They are splendid, by Jove!"

"I do not fancy them," said Alice, setting down her plate; "but don't tell the Doctor," she added hastily.

"You don't fancy anything, lately, Alice," Mr. Hastings replied, rather crossly.

"Never mind, Jack; my appetite will come when you have sold

your mine;" and upon that the unreasonably fastidious woman burst into tears.

"As if my position is not trying enough without seeing you cry!" said Jack, pausing from eating long enough to look injured. Plastic Jack! your surroundings were having their effect on you.

The *Mining News* of the second of September had a notice of the sale of Mr. Hastings' mine, the "Sybil," bearing chloride of silver, to Dr. Eustace Earle, all of Deep Cañon. The papers to be handed over and cash paid down at Chloride Hill on the seventh; at which time Dr. Earle would start for San Francisco on the business of the mining firm to which he belonged. Mr Hastings, it was understood, would go east about the same time.

All the parties were at Chloride Hill on the morning of the seventh, promptly. By eleven o'clock, the above-mentioned trans-action was completed. Shortly after, one of the Opposition Line's stages stopped at Mrs. Robb's boarding-house, and a lady, dressed for traveling, stepped quickly into it. Having few acquaintances, and being closely veiled, the lady passed unrecognized at the stage-office, where the other passengers got in.

Half an hour afterwards Mr. Jack Hastings received the following note:

> DEAR JACK: I sold your mine for you. Dr. Earle is running away with me, per agreement: but if you take the express this afternoon, you will reach Elko before the train leaves for San Francisco to-morrow. There is nothing worth going back for at Deep Cañon. If you love me, save me.
>
> Devotedly,
>
> ALICE.

It is superfluous to state that Jack took the express, which, arriving at Elko before the Opposition, made him master of the situation. Not that he felt very masterful: he didn't. He was thinking of many things that it hurt him to remember; but he was meaning to do differently in future. He had at last sold his mine—no, he'd be d——d if *he* had sold it; but—Hallo! there's a big dust out on the road there!—it must be the other stage. Think what you'll do and say, Jack Hastings!

What he did say was: "Ah, Doctor! you here? It was lucky for my wife, wasn't it, since I got left, to have you to look after her? Thanks, old fellow; you are just in time for the train. Alice and I will stop over a day to rest. A thousand times obliged: good-bye! Alice, say good-bye to Doctor Earle! you will not see him again."

Their hands and eyes met. He was pale as marble: she flushed one instant, paled the next, with a curious expression in her eyes which the Doctor never forgot and never quite understood. It was enough to know that the game was up. He had another mine on his hands, and an ugly pain in his heart which he told himself bitterly would be obstinate of cure. If he only could be sure what that look in her eyes had meant!

Josephine Clifford McCrackin (1839–1920)

The daughter of a German baroness and a Prussian army officer, Josephine Wompner Clifford McCrackin is best known for advocating the preservation of coastal redwoods and the creation of sanctuaries for native wildlife. As she put it, "I claim to have done more for the preservation of the Redwoods of California, for the conservation of birds and game, than any Native Daughter of California." But while her conservation efforts took much of her time during the last half of her life, her youthful years were largely dedicated to fictionalizing the true histories of ordinary people caught in extraordinary times on the frontiers of Arizona and California.

Born in Prussia and brought to America as an infant, she spent her childhood in St. Louis. Like her mother before her, she married a career army officer. With Lieutenant Clifford, she moved to Washington, D.C., where she met General Grant, General Sherman, and President Lincoln. At the close of the Civil War, her husband was assigned to the Southwest Territory to fight the Indian wars. There the young couple met Kit Carson and others prominent in the history of the Southwest.

As an officer's wife, Josephine heard the stories of pioneers and the sometimes gruesome tales of interaction between the Navajo people and settlers. Through the mid-1860s she fictionalized these stories, which were later published in 1877 in an anthology called *Overland Tales*.

In 1867, perhaps stained by the bloody nature of Navajo suppression wars, Lieutenant Clifford suffered a complete mental and physical breakdown and died within a couple of weeks. Suddenly a widow, with little time to grieve and no means of support, Josephine Clifford made her way to San Francisco to try to make her living as a professional writer, if, as she said, she could "stop crying long enough."

Within weeks of her arrival she was secretary to Bret Harte at the *Overland Monthly* office. Like Ina Coolbrith, she was for years reluctant to share her tragic past. Harte was respectful enough not to urge it, offering instead a safe environment in which she could grow, and encouraging her to write for both the *Overland* and the *Golden Era*. Josephine took full advantage of Harte's support and the relationships she soon developed with Ina Coolbrith—which would last a lifetime—

*Josephine Clifford McCrackin (1839–1920). Courtesy of the
Bancroft Library.*

and others of the sagebrush school, including Charles Warren Stoddard and Joaquin Miller.

In San Francisco she wrote extensively for several years, developing a dedicated readership and the respect of editors across town. Possessed of a stately and noble presence, especially as a young woman, she impressed San Franciscans with her hip-length, wavy chestnut hair and her piercing dark eyes. She was slim and although a little shy, she was richly competent at intellectual and social discourse. Businessmen and artists alike pursued her as a prospective wife, but she dedicated herself to her writing. She completed a partly autobiographical novel, *The Woman Who Lost Him,* and her short stories were published regularly. Then, rather suddenly, her stories ceased to appear. She had met and married a rancher from Santa Cruz, Jackson McCrackin, and turned another page in her life history.

Josephine had taken a chance trusting her heart again, but this time her trust paid off. The McCrackins were happily married for decades, and established a ranch oasis in the Santa Cruz mountains aptly named Monte Paraiso, a sanctuary in the redwoods for family and friends. Away from the influence of the *Overland* and her sagebrush writer friends, Josephine McCrackin shifted her emphasis to writing on environmental issues and became just as successful as she had been in fiction. This pursuit consumed much of her mature years, but she also eventually edited and managed her own news publication, the *Santa Cruz Sentinel,* which survives to this day.

Her declining years were not comfortable or particularly happy; a forest fire destroyed Monte Paraiso not long after the death of her husband. She struggled financially, forced to work up to the day of her death at age 81, writing for the *Sentinel* almost totally blind. She wrote to Ina Coolbrith just before she died: "The world has not used us well, Ina; California has been ungrateful to us. Of all the hundred thousands the state pays out in pensions of one kind and another, don't you think you should be at the head of the pensioners, and I somewhere down below?"

Her works included *Overland Tales,* a collection of stories published in 1877 from which "La Graciosa" is taken; *The Woman Who Lost Him*; and numerous uncollected short stories that appeared in Bay Area periodicals. Her sketches of Navajo and military life are compelling, in part because they are based on true histories: "There is little fiction, even in the stories; and the sketches, I flatter myself, are true to life—as I saw it, at the time I visited the places."

Her youthful years in San Francisco were productive and creative, and the legacy of her later efforts for the conservation of forests and game in California lives on.

LA GRACIOSA

———— ❧·❦ ————

I t was a stolid Indian face, at the first casual glance, but lighting up
wonderfully with intelligence and a genial smile, when the little
dark man, with the Spanish bearing, was spoken to. Particularly
when addressed by one of the fairer sex, did a certain native grace
of demeanor, an air of chivalrous gallantry, distinguish him from
the more cold-blooded, though, perhaps, more fluent-spoken,
Saxon people surrounding him.

Among the many different eyes fixed upon him now and again,
in the crowded railroad-car, was one pair, of dark luminous gray,
that dwelt there longer, and returned oftener, than its owner chose
to have the man of the olive skin know. Still, he must have felt
the magnetism of those eyes; for, conversing with this, disputing
with that, and greeting the third man, he advanced, slowly but
surely, to where a female figure, shrouded in sombre black, sat
close by the open window. There was something touching in the
young face that looked from out the heavy widow's veil, which
covered her small hat, and almost completely enveloped the slender
form. The face was transparently pale, the faintest flush of pink
tinging the cheeks when any emotion swayed the breast; the lips
were full, fresh, and cherry-red in color, and the hair, dark-brown
and wavy, was brushed lightly back from the temples.

The breeze at the open window was quite fresh, for the train
in its flight was nearing the spot where the chill air from the ocean
draws through the Salinas Valley. Vainly the slender fingers tried
to move the obstinate spring that held aloft the upper part of the
window. The color crept faintly into the lady's cheeks, for suddenly

a hand, hardly larger than hers, though looking brown beside it, gently displaced her fingers and lowered the window without the least trouble. The lady's gloves had dropped; her handkerchief had fluttered to the floor; a small basket was displaced; all these things were remedied and attended to by the Spaniard, who had surely well-earned the thanks she graciously bestowed.

"Excuse me," he said, with unmistakable Spanish pronunciation; "but you do not live in our Valley—do you?"

"This is my first visit," she replied; "but I shall probably live here for the future."

"Ah! that makes me so happy," he said, earnestly, laying his hand on his heart.

The lady looked at him in silent astonishment. "Perhaps that is the way of the Spanish people," she said to herself. "At any rate, he has very fine eyes, and—it may be tedious living in Salinas."

Half an hour's conversation brought out the fact that a married sister's house was to be the home of the lady for a while; that the sister did not know of her coming just to-day, and that her ankle was so badly sprained that walking was very painful to her.

From the other side it was shown that his home was in the neighborhood of the town ("one of those wealthy Spanish rancheros," she thought); that he was slightly acquainted with her brother-in-law; that he was a widower, and that his two sons would be at the depot to receive him. These sons would bring with them, probably, a light spring-wagon from the ranch, but could easily be sent back for the comfortable carriage, if the lady would allow him the pleasure of seeing her safely under her sister's roof. She said she would accept a seat in the spring-wagon, and Señor Don Pedro Lopez withdrew, with a deep bow, to look after his luggage.

"Poor lady!" he explained to a group of his inquiring friends, "poor lady! She is deep in mourning, and she has much sorrow in her heart." And he left them quickly, to assist his *protégé* with her wraps. Then the train came to a halt, and Don Pedro's new acquaintance, leaning on his arm, approached the light vehicle, at either side of which stood the two sons, bending courteously, in acknowledgment of the lady's greeting. When Don Pedro himself was about to mount to the seat beside her, she waved him back, with a charmingly impetuous motion of the hand. "I am safe enough with your sons," she laughed pleasantly. "Do you stop at my brother-in-law's office, pray, and tell him I have come."

Sister Anna was well pleased to greet the new arrival—"without an attachment." Her sister Nora's "unhappy marriage" had been a source of constant trouble and worry to her; and here she came at last—alone. Brother-in-law Ben soon joined them, and Nora's first evening passed without her growing seriously lonesome or depressed. Sister Anna, to be sure, dreaded the following days. Her sister's unhappy marriage, she confided to her nearest neighbor, had so tried the poor girl's nerves, that she should not wonder if she sank into a profound melancholy. She did all she could to make the days pass pleasantly; but what can you do in a small town when you have neither carriage nor horses?

Fortunately, Don Pedro came to the rescue. He owned many fine horses and a number of vehicles—from an airy, open buggy to a comfortably-cushioned carriage. He made his appearance a day or two after Nora's arrival, mounted on a prancing black steed, to whose every step jingled and clashed the heavy silver-mounted trappings, which the older Spaniards are fond of decking out their horses with. He came only, like a well-bred man, to inquire after the sprained ankle; but before he left he had made an engagement to call the very next morning, with his easiest carriage, to take both ladies out to drive.

And he appeared, punctual to the minute, sitting stiffly in the barouche-built carriage, on the front seat beside the driver, who, to Nora's unpractised eye, seemed a full Indian, though hardly darker than his master. True, the people of pure Spanish descent did say that this same master had a slight admixture of Indian blood in his veins, too; but Don Pedro always denied it. He was from Mexico, he said, but his parents had come from Spain. However this might be, Nora stood in mute dismay a moment, when the outfit drew up at the door; and she cast a questioning glance at her sister, even after they were seated in the carriage; but Sister Anna's eyes seemed repeating an old admonition to Nora—"Be patient, poor child; be still." And Nora, passing her hand across her face, heeded the admonition, gathered courage, and gave herself up to the perfect enjoyment of the scene and the novelty of the expedition.

It was a late spring day—the Valley still verdant with the growing grain, the mountains mottled with spots of brown where the rain of the whole winter had failed to make good the ravages of thousands of sheep, or where, perhaps, a streak of undiscovered mineral lay sleeping in the earth. Scant groups of trees dotted the Valley at far intervals, ranged themselves in rows where a little river ran at the foot of the Gabilan, and stood in lonely grandeur on the highest ridge of the mountain. Where the mountain sloped it grew covered with redwood, and where the hills shrank away they left a wide gap for the ocean breeze and the ocean fog to roll in.

Across the Valley was another mountain, dark and grand, with flecks of black growing *chemasal* in clefts and crevices, and sunny slopes and green fields lying at its base. And oh! the charm of these mountains. In the Valley there might be the fog and the chill of the North, but on the mountains lay the warmth and the dreaminess of the South.

Keenly the dark eyes of the Spaniard studied the lovely face, flushed, as it seemed, with the pleasure derived from the drive in the pure air and the golden sunshine.

"You like our Valley?" he asked, as eagerly as though she were a capitalist to whom he intended selling the most worthless portion of his ranch at the highest possible figure.

"Not the Valley so much as the mountains," she returned. "We have had fogs two days out of the week I have spent here, and I fancy I could escape that if I could get to the top of the mountains."

"Ah! you like the sunshine and the warm air. You must go farther South then—far South. I have thought a great deal of going there myself. There is a beautiful rancho which I can buy—you would like it, I know,—far down and close by the sea. And the sea is so blue there—just like the heavens. Oh! you would like it, I know, if you could only see it," he concluded, enthusiastically, as though this were another ranch he was trying to sell her.

But the thought of traffic or gain was very far from his heart just then, though Don Pedro was known to be an exceptionally good business man and a close financier. Many of his Spanish compeers looked up to him with a certain awe on this account. Most of them had parted with their broad acres, their countless herds, all too easily, to gratify their taste for lavish display and easy living, with its attendant cost under the new American *régime*; or had lost them through confiding, with their generous heart, their guileless nature, to the people whose thoughts were bent on securing, by usury and knaves' tricks, the possessions of the very men whose hospitable roof afforded them shelter. "He can cope with any American," they would say proudly, speaking of Don Pedro; and Don Pedro would show his appreciation of the compliment by exercising his business qualifications towards them, as well as towards "los Americanos."

But the haughty Don was well-mannered and agreeable; and after securing from Nora an indefinite promise that she would some time, when her ankle got strong, ride his own saddle-horse, he left the ladies safely at their door and retired, his heart and brain filled with a thousand happy dreams. He had only once during the ride pointed carelessly across the valley to where his ranch lay; but Nora had gained no definite idea of its extent.

One pleasant afternoon the two sons of Don Pedro stopped at the door. Their father had encouraged them to call, they said; perhaps the lady and her sister would bestow upon them the honor of driving out with them for an hour. Both lads spoke English with elegance and fluency (let the good fathers of the Santa Clara College alone for that), but among themselves their mother-tongue still asserted itself; and in their behavior a touch of the Spanish punctilio distinguished them favorably from the uncouth flippancy of some of their young American neighbors.

Nora cheerfully assented, and in a few minutes the whole party was bowling along—the eldest brother driving, the younger explaining and describing the country and its peculiarities. Pablo and Roberto had both been born on their ranch, though not in the large white house they saw in the distance. That had been finished only a little while when their mother died. The *adobe* which had been their birthplace stood several miles farther back, and could not be seen from here.

"It is not on this ranch, then?" queried Nora.

"Pardon, yes; on this ranch, but several miles nearer the foothills; in that direction—there."

"And is the land we are passing over all one ranch?" Nora continued, persistently.

"We have been driving over our own land almost since we left town," replied Pablo, a little proudly. "San Jacinto is one of the largest ranchos in the county, and the Americans have not yet succeeded in cutting it up into building-lots and homestead blocks," he added, laughing a frank, boyish laugh, which seemed to say, "you are as one of us, and will not take it amiss."

Sister Anna looked stealthily at Nora, but her eyes, with a strange light in them, were fixed on the horizon, far off, where they seemed to read something that made her brow contract and lower a little while, and then clear off, as, with an effort, she turned to the boy and brought up some other topic of conversation. But her heart was not in what she said, and Sister Anna exerted herself to cover the deficiencies that Nora's drooping spirits left in the entertainment.

It was sunset when they reached home, and standing on the rose-covered veranda of the little cottage a moment, Nora looked across to where the lingering gleams of the sun were kissing the black-looming crown of the Loma Prieta, with floods of pink and soft violet, and covering all its base with shades of dark purple and heavy gray. She raised her clasped hands to the mountain top.

"How glad, how thankful I could be, if from the wreck and the ruins I could gather light and warmth enough to cover my past life and its miseries, as the pink and the purple of the sunset cover the black dreariness of yon mountain."

"Come in, Nora, it is getting cold," interrupted Sister Anna; "or the next thing after having your nerves wrought up so will be a fit of hysterics."

"Which, you will say, is one more of the bad effects of Nora's unhappy marriage."

If Nora's unwillingness and Nora's unhappy marriage had been ever so deeply deplored by her, the loss of Sister Anna's love, or Anna's sisterly kindness, could not be counted among its many bad effects. Brother-in-law Ben, too, was whole-souled and affectionate; more practical, and a trifle more far-seeing than Anna; but he never said, "I told you so." He quietly did all he could to bind up bleeding wounds.

It soon came to be looked upon as quite a matter of course that Don Pedro should be seen in his carriage with the two sisters; or, that his black steed should be led up and down before the cottage door, by one of his servants, dark of skin, fiery-eyed, and of quiet demeanor, like his master. Then, again, the sons were seen at the cottage, always courteous, attentive, and scrupulously polite. If in the privacy of their most secret communings the "Gringa" was ever spoken of *as* the Gringa, it was only in the strictest privacy. Neither to Nora, nor to any of their servants, did ever look or word betray but that in the fair young American they saw all that their widowed father desired they should see.

The retinue of the Whitehead family consisted of but a single Chinaman, who was cook, laundress, maid-of-all-work; but during Nora's stay she was never aware but that she had half-a-dozen slaves to do her bidding, so careful, yet so delicate was Don Pedro in bestowing his attentions. He soon hovered about the whole family like one of the *genii*. If Nora just breathed to herself, "How pleasant the day is—if we only had carriage and horses"—before the hour was over the Don, with his carriage, or Don Pedro's boys, or an invitation to ride from the Don, was at hand. Before she had quite concluded that fruits were not so abundant or fine in the country as in the city markets, the Don had contracted a pleasant habit of sending his servants with the choicest of all his fields and store-houses contained to the little cottage in town. Fish, fresh from the Bay of Monterey, and game, that plain and mountain afforded, came in the run of time, quite as a matter of course, to the kitchen and larder of Don Pedro's dear friend Whitehead. It was not to be refused. Don Pedro had a hundred points of law that he wished explained; had so much advice to ask in regard to some tracts of land he meant to purchase, that Brother-in-law Ben always seemed the one conferring the greatest favor.

It was a little singular, too, this friendship of the Don's for Lawyer Whitehead. As a general thing, the Spanish population of California look upon our lawyers with distrust, and have a wholesome horror of the law. Don Pedro, though liberal-minded and enlightened, was not backward in expressing the contempt he felt for many of our American views and opinions; but above all he abominated our most popular institution—the Divorce Court. Not as a Catholic only, was it an abomination to him, he said. He had often declared to see a divorced woman gave him the same shuddering sensation that was caused by looking upon a poisonous snake.

When her ankle had grown quite strong, Don Pedro solicited for Rosa the honor of carrying Nora for a short ride through the country. And Nora, mounted high on the shapely animal's back, had seemed in such pleasant mood when they left her sister's door, that she quite bewildered her escort by the sudden sharp tone with which she replied to the question he asked: what feature she admired most in the landscape before them?

"Those many little lakes," she said. "They have an enticing look of quiet and rest, and hold out a standing invitation to 'come and get drowned,' to weary mortals like myself."

He was too delicate to allow his shocked glance to rise to her face, but to himself he repeated, "Poor lady! she has much sorrow in her heart," and aloud he said:

"You are homesick, Leonora?" How much prettier it seemed to hear the sonorous voice frame the word "Leonora," than the stiff appellation of "Mrs. Rutherford," which the Don could hardly ever bring himself to utter. It was so long, he excused himself, and not the custom of his country—though, in direct contradiction to the first part of the excuse, he would slyly smuggle in an addition—Blanca, Graciosa, Querida—trusting for safety in her lack of acquaintance with the Spanish tongue.

"No," she answered honestly to his question, "I have no place to be homesick for. I am glad to be here; but—"

"Ah! but you must see the Southern country first," he interrupted, eagerly. "I am going South this winter to purchase a ranch, on which I shall make my home. I leave this ranch here to my two boys. Their mother died here, and the ranch will be theirs. But my ranch in the South will be very fine; the land is so fair—like a beautiful woman, almost."

"I shall miss you, if you leave us; particularly through the rainy winter months," she said.

"How happy that makes me!" he exclaimed, as once before; and he did now what had been in his heart to do then—he bent over her hand and kissed it warmly, heedless of the swarthy Mexican who rode behind his master.

All through the summer, with its dust and its fog and its glaring sun, did Don Pedro still find a pleasant hour, early after the fog had risen, or late after the sun had set, to spend, on horseback or in carriage, with "the one fair woman" who seemed to fill his whole heart. Sometimes, when returning from an expedition on which Sister Anna had not accompanied them, she would greet them on the veranda with uneasy, furtive eyes; and the Don, blind to everything but his passion for Nora, still did not observe the impatient answering glance.

Don Pedro was delicacy and chivalry itself. Bending low over her white fingers one day, he asked, "And how long was Mr. Rutherford blessed with the possession of this most sweet hand?"

"I was married but a year," she answered, with her teeth set, and quickly drawing back her hand.

On reaching home she reported to her sister. "Aha," she commented, "he wants to know how long you have been a widow, and whether it is too soon to make more decided proposals."

Then came the early rains, and for Nora fits of passionate crying, alternating with fits of gloomy depression. Don Pedro was in despair. Her varying moods did not escape him, and when, to crown all, her ankle, still weak from the sprain, began to swell with rheumatism, she took no pains to hide her fretfulness or sadness either from her sister Anna or the Don. In the midst of the gloom and the rain came Don Pedro one day to announce that he was about to set out for the South, to conclude the purchase of the ranch he had so long spoken of.

"And you are going, too?" she said, lugubriously.

"I beg you to give me permission to go. I am the slave of Leonora, La Graciosa, and will return soon. I will not go, if you grant me not permission; but I beg you to let me go for a short time." He had sunk on his knees by the couch on which she rested, and his eyes flashed fire into hers for a brief moment; but he conquered himself, and veiled them under their heavy lashes. "Let me go," he pleaded, humbly, "and give me permission to return to you, Leonora. In my absence my sons will do all your bidding. They know the will of their father."

Nora had extended her hand, and motioned him to a chair beside her couch, and listened with a smile on her lips to all the arrangements he had made for her comfort during his absence.

"Since I have allowed you your own way in everything, I must have mine in one particular. Of course, you will take a saddle-horse for yourself besides the spring-wagon. Now you shall not leave Rosa here for me, but shall take her along for your own use. It is absurd for you to insist that no one shall use her since I have ridden her; I shall not keep her here while you are struggling over heavy roads, in the wagon, or on some other horse."

It was, perhaps, the longest speech she had ever made to him, and it was all about himself too, and full of consideration for him—oh! it was delicious. With fervent gratitude he kissed her hand, called her Preciosa, Bonita, till she declared that he should not say hard things of her in Spanish any more. He desisted for the time, on her promise that she would try to be cheerful while he was away, and not get homesick, unless it were for him; and they became quite gay and sociable over a cup of tea which Sister Anna brought them into the sitting room—so sociable, that Nora said of the Don, after his departure:

"If anyone were to tell me that a church-steeple could unbend sufficiently to roll ten-pins of a Sunday afternoon, I should believe it after this."

But in a little while the fits of dejection and the fits of crying came back again. Sister Anna did her best to break them up; she rallied her on breaking her heart for the absent Don; she tried to interest her in her surroundings, so that she should see the sungleams that flashed through the winter's gloom.

"See this beautiful cala that has just opened in the garden," she would say, with an abortive attempt at making her believe that her ankle was strong and well.

"I cannot get up, miserable creature that I am," came back the dismal response.

"Oh, that lovely cloth-of-gold has grown a shoot full half a yard long since yesterday; come and see."

"I cannot."

"Yes, you can; come lean on me. Now, isn't this sunshine delightful for December?"

Nora drew a deep breath; after a week's steady rain, the sky was clear as crystal, and the sun laughed down on hill and valley, blossoming rose and budding bush.

"See how the violets are covered with blue, and the honeysuckle has just reached the farthest end of the porch. Oh, Nora, how can any one be unhappy with flowers to tend, and a home to keep?"

"Ah! yes. You are right, sister; but it is your home—not mine."

Anna laid her arm around her as though to support her. She knew her sister's proud spirit and yearning heart, and she only whispered, as she had so often done, "Be patient, poor child; be still."

But that short, passionate plaint had lightened Nora's heart; after a week's sunshine the roads were dry enough to ride out once more with Don Pedro's sons, and when steady rain set in once more after that, she tried to show her sister that she could take an interest in "home"—though it was not her own.

A month had worn away, and as long as the weather permitted the regular running of the mails, Pablo and Roberto brought greeting from their father once a week; but when the roads grew impassable, they too were left without news. Not an iota did they fail of their attention to Nora, however; whatever dainties the ranch afforded were still laid at her feet, or rather on her sister's kitchen table; and the roads were never so bad but that they paid their respects at least twice a week.

"You have no cause to complain," said Sister Anna.

"No," replied Nora, with a yawn; "but I wish the Don would come back."

And he did come back.

"I am so glad you have come," she said, frankly, meeting him on the threshold.

"I can read it in your eyes," he exclaimed, rapturously. "Oh, how happy that makes me!" And if Sister Anna's head had not appeared behind Nora's shoulder, there is no telling what might have happened.

He had brought the spring with him; mountain and valley both had clothed itself in brightest green, in which the bare brown spots on the Gabilan Range were really a relief to the satiated eye. In the deep clefts of the Loma Prieta lay the blackish shade of the *chemasal,* and only one degree less sombre appeared the foliage of the live-oak against the tender green of the fresh grass. Again did Nora all day long watch the sun lying on the mountains—a clear golden haze in the daytime; pink and violet, and purplish gray in the evening mist.

"Is it not beautiful?" she asked of Brother-in-law Ben, one evening, as he came up the street and entered the gate.

"You are just growing to like our Valley, I see; it is a pity that you should now be 'borne away to foreign climes.' "

"And who's to bear me away?" she asked, laughing, as they entered the house.

"Let me call Anna," he said; "we will have to hold family council over this."

In council he commenced: "Don Pedro has this day requested that I, his legal adviser, go South with him, to see that all papers are properly made out, all preliminaries settled, before he fairly takes possession of his land."

"Well?" queried Anna.

"Well, my dear, so much for his counsellor Whitehead. But to his friend Benjamin's family he has extended an invitation to accompany us on this trip, presuming that his friend's wife and sister-in-law would be pleased to see this much-praised Southern country."

"We'll go, of course," assented Anna, artlessly.

"Certainly, my dear—of course;" affirmed easy-going Ben. "But, my dear, I hope you both understand all the bearings of this case."

Nora's head drooped, and a flush of pain overspread her face, as she answered chokingly, "I do."

"Then, my dear, since Don Pedro has never mentioned Nora's name to me, except to send message or remembrance, had I not better tell him—"

"No, no!" cried Nora, in sudden terror. "Oh, please not; leave it all to me."

"Certainly, Mrs. Rutherford," he assented, still more slowly; "I am not the man to meddle with other people's affairs—unasked," he added, remembering, perhaps, his business and calling.

"Don't be angry with me, Ben," she pleaded; "you have always been so kind to me. What should I have done without you two? But you know how I feel about this—this miserable affair."

"All right, child," he said, pressing her hand. "I should like to give you a piece of advice, but my lawyer's instinct tells me that you will not take it, so that I am compelled to keep my mouth shut—emphatically."

They set out on their Southern trip, a grand cavalcade; Don Pedro on a charger a little taller, a little blacker than Nora's horse; in the light wagon Anna and her husband, and behind them a heavier wagon containing all that a leisurely journey through a thinly populated country made desirable. For attendance they had Domingi, the Don's favorite servant, two *vaqueros*, and an under-servant, all mounted on hardy mustangs. Never did picnic party, intent on a day's pleasuring, leave home in higher spirits. The fresh morning air brought the color to Nora's cheeks, and her musical laugh rang out through the Valley; and when they passed one of the little lakes, all placid and glistening in the bright sun, Nora turned to her companion with a smile: "I don't think those lakes were meant to drown one's self in, at all; they were made to cast reflections. See?" and she pointed to herself, graceful and erect, mirrored in the clear water.

"Oh, Graciosa," murmured the Spaniard.

How bright the world looked, to be sure; flowers covered the earth, not scattered in niggardly manner, as in the older, colder Eastern States, but covering the ground for miles, showing nothing but a sea of blue, an ocean of crimson, or a wilderness of yellow. Then came patches where all shades and colors were mixed; delicate tints of pink and mauve, of pure white and deep red, and over all floated a fragrance that was never equalled by garden-flowers or their distilled perfume.

When twilight fell, and Don Pedro informed them that they would spend the night under the hospitable roof of his friend, Don Pamfilio Rodriguez, Nora was almost sorry that, for the complete "romance of the thing," they could not camp out.

"We will come to that, too," the Don consoled her, "before the journey is over. But my friend would never forgive me, if I passed his door and did not enter."

"But so many of us," urged Nora, regarding, if the truth must be told, the small low-roofed *adobe* house with considerable disfavor.

"There would be room in my friend's house for my friends and my-self, even though my friend himself should lie across the threshold."

Nora bowed her head. She knew of the proverbial hospitality of the Spanish—a hospitality that led them to impoverish themselves for the sake of becomingly entertaining their guests.

Of course, only Don Pedro could lift Nora from her horse; but Sister Anna found herself in the hands of the host, who conducted her, with the air of a prince escorting a duchess, to the threshold, where his wife, Doña Carmel, and another aged lady, received them. Conversation was necessarily limited—neither Don Pamfilio nor Doña Carmel speaking English, and Brother Ben alone being conversant with Spanish.

The ladies were shown into a low, clean-swept room, in which a bed, draped and trimmed with a profusion of Spanish needlework and soft red calico, took up the most space. Chairs ranged along one wall, and a gay-colored print of Saint Mary of the Sacred Heart, over the fire-place, completed the furnishing. Nora pleasantly returned the salutation of the black-bearded man who entered with coals of fire on a big garden-spade. Directly after him came a woman, with a shawl over her head and fire-wood in her arms. She, too, offered the respectful *"buenos días,"* and she had hardly left when a small girl entered, with a broken-nosed pitcher containing hot-water, and after her came another dark-faced man, the *mayordomo,* with a tray of refreshments and inquiries as to whether the ladies were comfortable.

Nora dropped her arms by her side. "I have counted four servants now, and Don Pedro told me particularly that his friend, Pam—what's-his-name—was very poor."

"Spanish style," answered Anna, with a shrug of the shoulder. "But it is very comfortable. How cold it has grown out-doors, and how dark it is. I wonder if we shall be afraid?"

"Hush! Don't make me nervous," cried Nora, sharply, shivering with the sudden terror that sometimes came over her.

"Be still," said Anna, soothingly; "there is nothing to be afraid of here."

After a while they were called to supper, where, to their surprise, they found quite a little gathering. Neighbors who spoke English had been summoned to entertain them, and after supper, which was a marvel of dishes, in which onions, sugar, raisins, and red pepper were softly blended, and which was served by three more servants, they got up an *impromptu* concert, on three guitars, and later an *impromptu* ball, at which Nora chiefly danced with the Don.

In spite of the biting cold next morning, all the male members of last night's company insisted on escorting our friends over the first few miles of the road. They came to a stream which they must cross, and of which Don Pamfilio had warned them, and the Don insisted on Nora's getting into the wagon with her sister. The *vaqueros* with their horses were brought into requisition, and Nora opened her eyes wide when, dashing up, they fastened their long *riattas* to the tongue of the wagon, wound the end of the rope around the horn of the saddle, and with this improvised four-horse team got up the steep bank on the other side in the twinkling of an eye.

Reaching San Luis Obispo directly, they delayed one whole day, as Nora expressed herself charmed with what she saw of the old mission church, and what remained of the old mission garden. A group of fig-trees here and there, a palm-tree sadly out of place, in a dirty, dusty yard, an agave standing stiff and reserved among its upstart neighbors, the pea-vine and potato.

"Oh! it is pitiful," cried Nora, hardly aware of the quotation. "Even this proud avenue of olives, towering so high above all, has been cut up and laid out in building-lots."

"The advance of civilization," Brother Ben informed her; and, in reply, Nora pointed silently into a yard, where a half-grown palm-tree stood among heaps of refuse cigar-ends and broken bottles. The house to which the yard belonged was occupied as a bar-room, and one of its patrons, a son of Old Erin, to all appearances, lay stretched near the palm, sleeping off the fumes of the liquor imbibed at the bar.

They laughed at Nora's illustration, and decided to move from so untoward a spot that very afternoon, even if they should have to use their tent and camp out all night.

More flowers, and brighter they grew as our friend travelled farther South. On the plain the meadow-lark sang its song in the dew and the chill of the morning, and high on the mountain, in the still noonday, the lone cry of the hawk came down from where the bird lived in solitary grandeur. Wherever our friends went they were made welcome. Not a Spanish house dare the Don pass without stopping, at least for refreshments. He had *compadres* and *comadres* everywhere, and whether they approved of his intimate relations with the "Gringas" or not, they showed always the greatest respect, extended always the most cheerful hospitality.

At last they approached Santa Barbara, its white, sun-kissed mission gleaming below them in the valley as they descended the Santa Inez Mountains. Stately business houses and lovely country-seats, hidden in trees and vines—the wide sea guarding all. But they tarried not. Don Pedro announced that he had promised to make a stay of several weeks at his particular friend's, Don Enrico del Gada. He was proud to introduce them to this family, he said. They would become acquainted with true Castilians—would be witness to how Spanish people lived in the Southern country; rich people—that is—. They had always been rich, but through some mismanagement (through the knavery of some American, Nora interpreted it), they were greatly in danger of losing their whole estate. A small portion of their rancho had been sold to a company of land-speculators, and now they were trying to float the title to this portion over the whole of the Tappa Rancho.

"Pure Castilian blood," the Don affirmed; "fair of skin, hair lighter than Nora's tresses, and eyes blue as the sky. Such the male part of the family. The female portion—mother and daughter—were black-eyed, and just a trifle darker; but beauties, both. The daughter, Narcissa (Nora fancied that a sudden twinge distorted the Don's features as he spoke the name), was lovely and an angel; not very strong, though—a little weak in the chest."

All the evening the De Gadas formed the subject of conversation, so that it is hardly surprising that morning found Nora arrayed with more care than usual, if possible, and looking handsome enough to gratify the heart of the most fastidious lover.

A two hours' ride brought them to the immediate enclosure of the comfortable ranch house, and with a sonorous *"buenos días caballeros!"* the Don had led his party into the midst of a ring formed by the host, his son, and other invited guests. Some of them had just dismounted, and the spurs were still on their boots; some had red silk scarfs tied gracefully around the hips, and all were handsome, chivalrous, picturesque-looking men. Don Enrico advanced to assist Anna, while Don Manuel, his son, strode toward Leonora's horse and had lifted her from the saddle before Don Pedro could tell what he was about. Such clear blue eyes as he had! All the sunshine of his native Spain seemed caught in them; and his hand was so white! Nora's own could hardly vie with it.

His head was uncovered when he conducted her to the veranda, where the ladies were assembled. His mother, a beauty still, dark-eyed, full-throated, and with the haughty look and turn of the head that is found among the Spanish people; the sister a delicate, slender being, large-eyed, with hectic roses on her cheeks. Nora detected a strange glimmer in her eye and a convulsive movement of the lips as she addressed a question in a low tone to her brother, after the formal introduction was over.

"You must excuse my sister," he apologized to Nora, "she speaks no English. She wanted to know whether you had ridden Rosa. Long ago she tried to ride the horse, but could not, as she is not strong. When Don Pedro was here last she wanted to try again; but he would not consent. I suppose she is astonished at your prowess."

Nora watched the darkened, uneasy eyes of the girl; she thought she knew better than the unsuspecting brother what had prompted the question.

The Del Gada family, their house, their style of living, was all the Don had claimed for them. The first day or two were devoted mainly to out-of-doors entertainments; the orange-groves, the vineyards, the almond-plantation on the ranch were visited, and a ride to the mission of Santa Barbara, whose Moorish bell-towers haunted Nora's brain, was planned and undertaken.

The warm light of the spring-day shed a soft glimmer over crumbling remnants of the monuments that the patient labor of the mission fathers have left behind them—monuments of rock and stone, shaped by the hands of the docile aborigines into aqueducts and fountains, reservoirs and mill-house; monuments, too, of living, thriving trees, swaying gently in the March wind, many of them laden with promises of a harvest of luscious apricot or honey-flavored pear. The hands that planted them have long fallen to dust; the humble *adobe* that gave shelter to the patient toiler is empty and in ruins, but the trees he planted flourish, and bear fruit, year after year; and from the shrine where he once knelt to worship his new-found Saviour, there echoes still the Ave and the Vesper-bell, though a different race now offers its devotion.

A day or two later, winter seemed to have returned in all its fury; the rain poured ceaselessly, and swelled the creeks till their narrow banks could hold the flood no longer; the wind tore at the roses, hanging in clusters of creamy white and dark crimson, on trellises and high-growing bush, and scattered showers of snow from almond and cherry trees. The fireplaces in the Del Gada mansion were once more alive and cheerful with a sparkling fire. It made little difference to the company assembled at the ranch; it gave Nora and Sister Anna an opportunity of seeing more of the home-life of the family, and impressed them with the excellence of the haughty-looking woman at the head of the establishment. No New England matron could be a more systematic housekeeper, could be more religiously devoted to the welfare of her family and servants. "And the romance of it all," Nora often repeated. Night and morning the far-sounding bell on the little chapel in the garden called the members of the house to worship; and Doña Incarnación, kneeling, surrounded by her family and servants, read in clear tones the litanies and prayers. Once a week the priest from the neighboring mission visited the house, and then the large drawing-room was fitted up with altar and lights and flowers, and neighbors, high and low, of all degrees, attended worship.

This, however, did not prevent the family from being as jolly as Spanish people can well be, in this same drawing-room, when Mass was over, and "the things cleared away." Of cold or rainy nights the company resorted to this room, where they had music, conversation, refreshments. But everything had a dash of romance to Nora's unbounded delight. Refreshments were brought in on large trays, borne by dusk, dark-clad women; trays loaded with oranges, pomegranates, figs, the product of the orchards surrounding the house; and wine, sparkling red and clear amber, pressed from grapes gathered in the vineyard that crept close up to the door. It was not only California, but the South, of which Don Pedro had always spoken with such enthusiasm.

"And how enthusiastic he does grow sometimes," said Nora one evening, in the large drawing-room where they were all assembled.

Manuel, who performed on the piano as well as the flute, had just finished a piece of music which Nora had taken from her trunk for him to play, and she had insisted on turning the leaves for him. Don Pedro sat near, and Nora looking up, had caught his eye. "See the enthusiasm in his face," she said to Manuel. "How fond all of you Spaniards are of music."

"You are mistaken in two points, Doña Leonora," the young man replied. "Don Pedro is no Spaniard, he is a Mexican; and he has not grown enthusiastic over the music—he has seen and has been thinking only of you."

Nora's cheeks burned at something in Manuel's voice; but a grateful feeling stole into her heart. To tell the truth, she had felt a pang of something like jealousy of late, when Narcissa, who, from speaking no English, was thrown on Don Pedro's hands, seemed to take up more of his attention than necessary.

When the weather cleared off, our party began to talk of moving on; Don Pedro's new possession was only one or two days' journey from here, below San Buenaventura. There was to be a Rodeo on the Del Gada ranch, not so much for the purpose of branding young cattle, as to give the different rancheros an opportunity of selecting their own that might have strayed into the mountains and found their way into the Del Gada herds. Nora was for attending the Rodeo; she could hardly form an idea of what it was; but she was sure, as usual, that it must be something "highly romantic."

They were warned that they must get up early in the morning, and seven o'clock found them already on the ground—a little valley, shut in by mountains more or less steep. A small creek, made turbulent by the rains, ran through the valley, where an ocean of stock seemed to roll in uneasy billows. It was all as romantic as Nora's heart could wish. The countless herds of cattle gathered together and kept from dispersing by numbers of *vaqueros*, who darted here and there on their well-trained horses, leaped ditches, flew up the steep mountain-sides after an escaping steer, dashed through the foaming torrent to gather one more to the fold, and seemed so perfectly one with their horse that from here might have sprung the fable of the old Centaurs.

Eyes sharper than eagles had these people, master and man alike; out of the thousands of that moving herd could they single the mighty steer that bore their brand, or the wild-eyed cow whose yearling calf had not yet felt the searing-iron. Into the very midst of the seething mass would a *vaquero* dart, single out his victim without a moment's halt, drive the animal to the open space, and throw his lasso with unerring aim, if a close inspection was desirable— a doubt as to the brand to be set aside. If a steer proved fractious, two of the Centaurs would divide the labor; and while one dexterously threw the rope around his horns, the other's lasso had quickly caught the hind foot, and together they brought him to the earth, that he had spurned in his strength and pride but a moment before.

Manuel himself could not resist the temptation of exhibiting his skill; and when his father and one of the neighbors—of about fifty miles away—both claimed a large black bull, almost in the centre of the herd, he dashed in among the cattle, drove his prey out on a gallop, flung his lasso around the animal's hind feet, and brought him to the ground as neatly as any *vaquero* could have done.

He saw Nora clap her hands; he saw, too, how every ranchero of the county had his eyes fixed on her, as she sat proudly, yet so lightly, on the showy black horse; and sadly he owned to himself that he would risk life and limb any time, to gain the little hand that wafted him a kiss. But what was he? A beggar, perhaps, tomorrow, if the suit went against them.

Meantime the sun grew hot, and they all dismounted and left the wagons, and lunch was discussed; the *élite,* Americans and Spaniards alike, assembling around the Del Gada provision wagon, while the *vaqueros* were well satisfied with a chunk of bread, a handful of olives, and a draught of wine, as they leisurely drove the cattle separated from the Del Gada herd to their respective territory.

Then came the parting day. Doña Incarnación stood on the veranda, as on the day of their arrival, proudly erect, conscious of herself and the dignity she must maintain. Beside her stood her daughter, the spots on her cheeks larger and brighter, but a pained, restless expression in the eager eyes, and printing itself sharply in the lines about the mouth. Her mother seemed not to note the girl's evident distress.

Nora, Mr. and Mrs. Whitehead, and the Don had made their adieux; and Manuel, mounted and ready to escort them, together with some half dozen others, turned once more to the veranda to ask his sister some question. Like a flash the truth broke on him as he caught the eager, straining glance that followed Don Pedro's form, and with a little passionate cry he urged his animal close to Nora's side.

"It is not my heart alone you have left desolate behind you, Leonora. My sister's, too—oh! my poor Narcissa! Now I know why my mother said that she would not live to see spring again; now I know why she prays to the saints for a 'still heart,' night and morning. Oh, Leonora, think no more of the dagger you have planted in my breast; think of poor Narcissa, and pray for her as you would for one already dead—for the love of a Spanish girl is deep and abiding, and cannot be outweighed by gold and leagues of land and fine clothes."

It was well that Don Pedro came up; Nora was almost fainting in her saddle. He did not catch the import of Don Manuel's words, but, if never before, he recognized in him now a bold and dangerous rival. The confusion attending a general breaking-up had covered this little by-scene, and when the party escorting them turned back, it would have been impossible to discover that one or two hearts throbbed wildly at the parting words.

When they rode into San Buenaventura, with its dingy little mission church fronting on the main street, Nora was not half so much interested as she had been. They were right in the midst of the mission garden. The obtrusive frame houses of the fast-crowding American population had been set up in it; the streets had been laid out through it; the ugly, brick-built court-house stood away down in the lower part of it, where the blue ocean washed the shore, and murmured all day of times long past to the tall-growing palms, that stood desolate and alone.

It made her sad, she said to the Don, when he expressed his surprise at her silence, to see the stately olives of a century's growth spread their great branches over flimsy little shops; to see the neglected vines trailing their unpruned lengths over rubbish-piled open lots, which a paper placard announced "for sale."

When night came, she retired to her up-stairs room at the hotel, put the light out, and gazed long hours on the placid ocean.

"Let us get on as soon as possible," said Sister Anna, in confidence, to her husband the next morning. "This place seems to have a singular effect on Nora. She says she could not sleep last night, for thinking whether she had a right to barter herself away, body and soul, truth and honor, perhaps, for a grand home and a great deal of money."

So they "got on." Don Pedro was happy to gratify every wish of the ladies, and very willing to enter upon his own territory, which lay so near. The earth looked so smiling to Don Pedro when, together with Nora, a little in advance of the wagons, he crossed the border of his own domain. All the morning they had passed droves of cattle on the road, and flocks of sheep, and the *vaqueros* tending them had still saluted Don Pedro as their master. Shortly they encountered the *mayordomo* of the new ranch, and after a short parley with him, the Don turned to Nora with an apology for discussing business affairs in an unfamiliar tongue in her presence.

"Let us make a compromise," suggested Nora; "do you take me down yonder to that piece of white pebble-beach, by the gray rock, and you may come back and talk to all the *vaqueros* and *mayordomos* in the land."

The *mayordomo* wended his way to where he saw the wagons halting in a grove, and Nora and the Don pursued their own way. It was quite a distance before they had reached the exact spot that Nora said she had meant—they were out of sight of the rest. The ocean, grand and solemn, lay before them, grassy plains around them, groups of trees and sloping hills in the near distance, and far off the mountains in their never-changing rest.

Lightly Don Pedro sprang to the ground, and detaining Nora one moment in her saddle, he said, impressively: "Now you set foot upon your own land, a territory named after you, 'La Graciosa.' "

Then he lifted her tenderly to the ground, and she sprang lightly away from him, and lavishly praised the beauty of his new possession.

"And it is all like this," he continued, "for miles and miles, good and beautiful, like the one for whom I named it."

"What a flatterer you are," she said, forced at last to take notice of the name. He clasped her hand, but she uttered a little shriek, "Oh! that wicked horse of yours has bitten my poor Rosa." A snort from the black mare seemed to corroborate the accusation, and Nora had gained time—to fight her battle out, and make peace with herself.

"Please get rid of that tiresome *mayordomo* of yours, and come back to me. I want to stay here alone with Rosa and decide whether your ranch has been well named." She could not prevent the kiss he imprinted on her slender hand, but she drew it back impatiently.

"You will stay here till I return, Leonora?" he asked, earnestly.

"Yes, yes," she said, a little fretfully, and waved him off.

He had made fast her horse to the stump of a scrub-oak, that had lived its short, mistaken life here close by the sea; and Nora, when the sound of the other horse's hoofs had died away, stroked the animal's mane approvingly, and patted her neck. Then she turned and walked slowly around the abrupt gray crag, and stopped; she was alone at last. She raised her hand, and looked from under it out on the sunlit sea. The waves came up with a long, gentle swirl, till the light foam splashed against the foot of the crag, then receded, leaving a strip of white, glistening pebble exposed. She watched it silently, then turned her face to let her eyes sweep the plain, the clumps of trees, and the rolling hills.

" 'For miles and miles,' he said," she soliloquized, "and that is not all his fortune. And *he* has nothing if the suit goes against them. American cunning matched against Spanish recklessness. But what have I to do with that boy? All I have wanted and prayed for is a home and an honored name; it is within my reach now; why should I let an idle dream stand in my way?"

She stood where the ocean washed up to her feet, and when she looked down she thought she saw two deep-blue eyes, wild with suppressed passion, flashing up from there. She turned, for she thought she heard behind her, in the sighing of the wind and the shriek of the sea-mews, the cry of a tortured heart. But she banished these fancies and forced her thoughts into other channels. She thought of her past life, of the wish she had had, even as a child, to travel—to see strange lands. She thought of the Pyramids of Egypt, and that her wish to see them could now, perhaps, be gratified—in his company. Well, was it not romantic, after all, to marry the dark-eyed Don, with the haughty bearing and the enormous wealth? She had a lady friend once, a city acquaintance, who had married a wealthy Spaniard. But she had been divorced after a year's time. Divorced! what an ugly sound the word had. Was Don Pedro near? Had his ear caught the sound? No; thank God, she was alone.

And then her thoughts strayed again to the old Gada mansion, and the broken-hearted girl she had left there. "She will die," he had said; and she fell to wondering whether Father Moreno would anoint those wistful eyes with the consecrated oil, in her last hour, and mutter that "they had looked upon unholy things," and touch the little waxen ears "because they had listened to unchaste speech." What a mockery it seemed, in the case of the young innocent girl. "When *I* die—" She stooped suddenly to dip her hand into the water, and dashed it into her face and over her hair. *"Mea culpa!"* she murmured, striking her breast, *"mea culpa! mea maxima culpa!"*

And once more she pressed her hand across her face, for the gallop of approaching hoofs fell on her ear, and directly "Leonora!" rang out in sharp, uneasy tone.

She answered the call, and Don Pedro, panting, but with a happy smile, reached out his hand to draw her away from the wet sand.

"I felt as though I had lost you. What would life be without you, Graciosa?"

"You would have my god-child left," she replied, laughing.

"It would be worthless without the sponsor. I have acquired it for you. Do you accept it?"

"With you into the bargain?" she smiled gayly as she said it. She hated romance and sentimentality all at once, and when the Don kneeled at her feet to kiss both her hands, she said, with a laugh:

"There will be but one Graciosa, after all, unless you take me to my friends and the lunch-basket. I am almost starved."

"I am your slave," he avowed; "you have but to command."

He lifted her into the saddle, with trembling hands and beaming eyes. "Oh, Graciosa! Rightly named," he cried.

"Meaning me or the ranch?" asked Nora, mischievously; and, with a touch of the whip, she urged Rosa ahead, and threw a kiss over her shoulder to the Don. His eyes followed her proudly awhile, ere he spurred his horse to overtake her, and they joined Sister Anna laughing and happy as she could wish to see them.

They camped out that night, as there was no house on that part of the ranch, though there was one to be erected near the spot where they had joined Sister Anna, for Nora said she liked the view there. Early next morning they left camp, expecting to reach Los Angeles before sunset.

All day the road led along the mountain-chain, in the San Fernando Valley—a soft, warm day, made to dream and reflect. The clear blue haze hung, as ever, on the mountain-ridge, and the plain at the foot was white and odorous with the wild "Forget-me-not" of California. They looked to Nora as though passionate eyes had been raining tears on them till the color had been blanched out; and when Don Pedro gathered a handful and brought them to her, she said, "Don't, please; it hurts me to see you break them off. Throw them away."

"How strange you are," he said, but he obeyed, and did not assert his authority till some hours later, when they reached the crossing of the Los Angeles River.—Had he not said he would be her slave?

The river rushed by them muddy and wild, spread far beyond its allotted limits—an ugly, treacherous-looking piece of water. It was deep, too; and while Don Pedro was giving orders in regard to arranging the contents of the baggage wagon, Sister Anna was trying to persuade Nora to come into their wagon while fording the stream. Nora demurred; but the Don riding up decided the question at once.

"You must go in the wagon, Leonora," he announced, with somewhat pompous authority. "I will not have you exposed to such danger. The river is wide at present, and your head will get light. Mr. Whitehead and I will go on horseback, but you must go in the wagon."

A rebellious gleam shot from Nora's eye, but Sister Anna listened with flushed face, as to something new, but very pleasant to hear. It proved an ugly crossing, and while the servants were rearranging the baggage, the Don strayed a little apart with Nora, and found a seat under a clump of willows.

"It *is* hard to go down into the floods when there is so much of life and sunshine all around," and with a little nervous shiver she nestled closer to the Don's side. Impelled by a feeling of tenderness he could not control, the stately Don threw his arms around the supple form and pressed the first kiss on her pale lips.

She shrank from him; had any one seen them? There was no need to spring up; she knew he would not attempt to repeat the caress.

The City of the Angels lay before them—a dream realized.

Whatever there was unlovely about the older, *adobe* built portion of the place was toned down by the foliage of waving trees, and warmed into tropical beauty by the few isolated palms, which some blessed hand set out long years ago. Our friends did not pass through the heart of the city, but wended their way to the house of a wealthy Spanish family, which lay among the gay villas and stately residences of the modern portion of the city. Large gardens enclosed them, in many cases surrounded by evergreen hedges of supple willow and bristly osage. Tall spires arising from a sea of green, and imposing edifices, marked the places where the Lord could be worshipped in style. The American element is strong in Los Angeles.

Señor Don José María Carillo had been looking for his guests, and met them with much state and ceremony on the highway, conducting them grandly to the gate-posts of his garden, where they were received by Doña Clotilda and a retinue of servants. Even the children, with their governess, were summoned from the school-room to greet the guests, and Spanish courtesy and Californian hospitality were never better exemplified than in the case of our friends.

"Oh, Annie, only look!" exclaimed Nora, clasping her hands in admiration, and pointing through the French window at the back of the double parlors.

The house was an *adobe,* two stories high, which the father of the present inmate had built, and of which the son was properly proud. He would not have it torn down for the world, but it had been modernized to such an extent as to rival in comfort and elegance any of the newer American houses, though the Spanish features were still predominant. The particular feature that had attracted Nora so strongly as to lead her into making the hasty, unceremonious exclamation, was a *remada,* a kind of open roof built of heavy timber beams, at the back of the house, and extending over several hundred feet of the ground. It was covered with the grape, among whose shading leaves and graceful tendrils the sunlight glinted in and out, playing in a thousand colors on clustering vines with bright flowers, that clung to the pillars supporting the roof. Beyond stretched an orange-grove, where yellow fruit and snowy blossoms glanced through the glossy leaves.

"It is beautiful, is it not?" asked a voice at her side. She had stepped to the open French window, regardless of all etiquette, and Don Pedro led her across the sill into the covered garden.

"Your own home shall be like this, Leonora, only finer and grander; you shall have everything that your heart can wish."

"You are very good." It was not the conventional phrase with her; she meant what she said, for her eyes were raised to his, and tears trembled in the lashes.

It was a charming retreat. Doña Clotilda spoke English, though none of the servants did, except a ten-year old Indian girl, who was detailed to wait on the guests. There was a round of visiting and going through the city, where every one admired Nora, and looked from her to the little Don. And Don Pedro was proud and happy, and always sought new opportunities of passing through the crowded thoroughfares, on foot, on horseback, or in carriage.

"My dear," he said, one day, "I would know how handsome you are from looking at the people who meet us, even though I had never seen your face."

"Yes?" said Nora, a little absent and dispirited, as she sometimes was.

"Yes; one man, standing at the corner there, behind those boxes—you did not see him—opened his eyes very wide and looked hard at you, and then pushed his hat back till it fell to the ground. Then he saw me, and felt ashamed, and turned quick to pick up his hat."

"What a striking appearance mine must be!" laughed Nora, restored to good-humor, for the time.

It has often seemed to me that all Spanish people, of whatever degree, throughout California, are either related or intimately acquainted with each other. Thus Nora heard from the Del Gadas occasionally; nay, even from the Rodriguez, away back in the Salinas Valley, did they hear news and greeting once. Narcissa Del Gada was dying, the Don told her; and the twinge that had distorted his features when he first mentioned her name again passed over them.

But all the time of our friends was not given to pleasuring; many a long morning did Brother Ben and the Don pass together at the Court-House, the Hall of Records, and other places where titles are examined and the records kept. A ranch of twenty or thirty thousand acres is well worth securing, so that through no loophole can adverse claimant creep, or sharp-witted land-shark, with older title, spring on the unwary purchaser.

In the meantime spring was growing into summer; the sun began to burn more fierce, and Nora, always fond of out-doors, had made the *remada* her special camping-ground. She sat there one morning, after having declined to go on a shopping expedition with Sister Anna. It had seemed rather ungracious, too; but Brother Ben had come to the rescue, as usual, and had taken Nora's place. Now she sat here, pale and listless, her hands idly folded, her eyes wandering among the shadows of the orange grove.

There had been an arrival at the house, she thought, for she heard the tramp of a horse as it was led around to the stables; but she took no heed. After a while she heard the noise of one of the long windows opening, and soon she heard steps behind her. Then a low voice said "Leonora!" and Manuel, pale and haggard, stood before her.

All her listlessness vanished in an instant, and she would have flown into his arms, but for something that seemed to make him unapproachable.

"Narcissa is dead," he said monotonously, "and since coming to town I have learned that I am a beggar; we are all homeless—outcasts."

"Oh, Manuel!" she cried, laying her hand on his arm, "my poor, poor boy. Come with me into the open air—this place chokes me. And now tell me about Narcissa." She drew him out into the sunshine, and back again to the fragrant shadows of the orange grove. She sought a rustic seat for them, but he threw himself on the sod beside it.

"Wrecked and lost and lonely," he groaned, "it is well that Narcissa is dead; and yet she was our only comfort."

"Poor Manuel!" she repeated, softly; "my poor boy." Her fingers were straying among the sunny waves of his hair, and he caught her hand suddenly, and covered it with a frenzy of kisses.

"Leonora!" he cried, all the reckless fire of his nation breaking into flames, "come with me, and we will be happy. You do not love your wealthy affianced, you love me. Be mine; I will work and toil for you, and you shall be my queen. Oh, Nora, I love you—I love you—I love you."

Poor Nora! why should stern reality be so bitter? "Foolish boy," she said, disengaging her hand, "you are mad. What if Don Pedro—"

"Ah, true; I had forgotten—you are an American. Go, then, be happy with your wealthy husband; Manuel will never cross your path again."

"Manuel!" she cried, and she stretched out her arms towards the spot where he had just stood, "come back, for I love you, and you alone." But a rustling in the willow-hedge only answered to her passionate cry, and she cowered on the garden-bench, sobbing and moaning out her helpless grief.

The rustling in the willow-hedge behind her grew louder, so that even she was startled by the noise.

"Ho, Nell!" The words fell on her ears like the crack of doom, her face grew white to the very lips, and a great horror crept into her eyes. She turned as if expecting to meet the engulfing jaws of some dread monster, and her eyes fell upon the form of a man, whose slovenly dress and bloated features spoke of a life of neglect and dissipation—perhaps worse.

"Why, Nell, old girl," he continued, familiarly, "this is a pretty reception to give your husband. I'm not a ghost; don't be afraid of me."

"Wretch!" she cried, trembling with fear and excitement. "How dare you come here? Go at once, or I shall call for help."

"No, you won't. I'm not afraid. Come, you can get rid of me in a minute. The truth is, I'm d——d hard up; got into two or three little unpleasantnesses, and got out only by a scratch. I want to get away from here—it's unhealthy here for me—but I've got no money. Saw you down town with that pompous Greaser the other day; know him well; he's got lots of money; and I thought that, for love and affection, as they say in the law, and in consideration of our former relations, you might help me to some of his spare coin."

"You miserable man," she cried, beside herself, "is it not enough that you blasted my life's happiness? Must I be dragged down to the very lowest degradation with you? Oh, Charlie," she added, in changed, softened tones, "what would your mother say to all this?"

"And my daddy the parson," he laughed, hoarsely. "Yes, we know all that. But here, Nell," he went on, while a last glimmer of shame or contrition passed over his once handsome face, "I don't want to hurt you, my girl; you've always been a trump, by G——; I am willing you should become the respected wife of Don Pedro Lopez, but I must have money, or money's worth. That cluster-diamond on your finger; tell the Greaser you lost it. Or pull out your purse; I know it is full."

"Nothing," she said, slowly and determinedly, "nothing shall you have from me—a woman you have so wronged and deceived—"

"Stop, Nell; I haven't time to wait for a sermon. Give me what you've got— Oh, here's h—— to pay and no pitch hot," he interrupted himself; "there's the Don, and he's heard it all."

He spoke true; Don Pedro stood beside them, frozen into a statue. At last he breathed.

"Yes, heard all. And I would have made you my wife—you a divorced woman. Oh, Santa Maria! She divorced of such a man—

for I know you, Randal," he continued, lashing himself into a fury—"horse-thief, stage-robber, gambler. It was you who killed my friend Mariano Anzar after robbing him at cards—murderer! You shall not escape me as you escaped the officers of the law. *Hombres!* catch the murderer!" he shouted towards the house, as he made a dart at the man, who turned at bay, but halted when he saw that the Don was not armed.

"Stop your infernal shouting and don't touch me," he said, in a low, threatening voice. But the Don was brave, and his blood was up; he sprang upon the man, shouting again; they closed and struggled, and when the man heard footsteps swiftly approaching, he drew back with an effort, and hissing, "You *would* have it so, idiot," he raised his pistol and fired.

Before the smoke cleared away he had vanished, and the people who came found Don Pedro stretched on the ground. His life was almost spent, but his energy had not deserted him. He gave what information and directions were necessary for the prosecution of his murderer, and Manuel, who was among the excited throng, threw himself on his horse to head the fugitive off. The others lifted the wounded man tenderly from the ground, bore him gently into the house, and frowned with hostile eyes upon Nora; it had taken possession of their minds at once that, in some unexplained manner, the Gringa was the cause of all this woe.

Nora followed them like an automaton; she saw them carry him through the open door-window into the back parlor, and lay the helpless figure on a lounge. A messenger had already been despatched for priest and doctor, and the servants, who were not admitted into the room, lay on their knees outside.

Then the priest came, and Nora, in a strange, dazed way, could follow all his movements after he went into the room. The odor of burning incense crept faintly through the closed doors, and she wondered again—did the priest touch the white lips and say, "for they have uttered blasphemies." The fingers were stiffening, she thought; would the priest murmur now—"for with their hands do men steal;" the eyelids were fluttering over the glazed eyes; the cleansing oil was dropped upon them, for "they had looked upon unholy things."

She saw it all before her, and heard it, though her eyes were fast closed, and her ears were muffled, for she had fallen, face down, by one of the pillars supporting the *remada,* and the thick-growing tropical vine, with its bright, crimson flowers, had buried her head in its luxuriant foliage, and seemed raining drops of blood upon the wavy dark brown hair.

Thus Manuel found her when he returned from the pursuit of the fugitive. He raised her head, and looked into large, bewildered eyes. "What is it?" she asked; "have I been asleep? Or is he dead?"

"The wretched man I followed? Yes; but my hand did not lay him low. The sheriff and his men had been hunting him; he attempted to swim the river at the ford; the sheriff fired, and he went down into the flood."

Nora's eyes had closed again during the recital, and Manuel held a lifeless form in his arms, when Sister Anna and her husband came at last. They had heard of the shooting of Don Pedro in the city, and the carriage they came in bore Nora away to the hotel. Manuel did not relinquish his precious burden till he laid the drooping form gently on the bed at the hotel. Then the doctor came, and said brain-fever was imminent, and the room was darkened, and people went about on tip-toe. And when the news of the death of Don Pedro Lopez was brought down to the hotel, Nora was already raving in the wildest delirium of the fever.

Weeks have passed, and Nora has declared herself not only well, but able to return home. Manuel has been an invaluable friend to them all, during these weeks of trial, and Nora has learned to look for his coming as she looks for the day and the sunshine.

To him, too, was allotted the task to impart to Nora what it was thought necessary for her to know—the death of Don Pedro and the finding of the body of the other, caught against the stump of an old willow, where the water had washed it, covered with brush and floating *débris.* But he had glad news to impart, too;

the report of an adverse decision from Washington on the Del Gada suit had been false, and circulated by the opposing party in order to secure better terms for withdrawal.

One morning Nora expressed her wish to leave Los Angeles, and Mr. Whitehead did not hesitate to gratify her wish. An easy conveyance was secured, the trunks sent by stage, and a quick journey anticipated. Manuel went with them only as far as San Buenaventura, he said, for it was on his way home. But when they got there, he said he must go to Santa Barbara, and no one objected. At Santa Barbara Nora held out her hand to him, with a saucy smile:

"This is the place at which you were to leave us; good-by."

"Can you tolerate me no longer, Nora?"

"You said at San Buenaventura you would try my patience only till here. How long do you want me to tolerate you, then?"

"As long as I live. Why should we ever part? Be my wife, Nora," and he drew her close to him, pressing his lips on hers; and she did not shrink away from him, but threw her arm around his neck, to bend his head down for another kiss.

"But you would never have married me—a poor man," he says, bantering.

"Nor would you have married me—a divorced woman," she returns, demurely.

MAKING ROOM

Jessie Benton Frémont (1824–1902), as painted in 1856 by Thomas Buchanan Read. Courtesy of the Southwest Museum, Los Angeles.

Jessie Benton Frémont (1824–1902)

Jessie Frémont was a gifted writer and magnetic social figure in nineteenth century America. But it is difficult to write a biography of her without the shadow of Colonel John C. Frémont creeping into every paragraph; Frémont cut a striking figure, charging into Sonoma as the leader of the Bear Flag Rebellion that eventually led to California being taken into the union. It is not a complete surprise, however, that history should remember Col. Frémont more than Jessie, since this was in fact the primary goal of Jessie Benton Frémont's life.

Born in 1824, the daughter of Senator Thomas Hart Benton of Missouri, Jessie Benton grew up in the lavish surroundings of Washington, D.C., attending private schools and debutante parties with the offspring of politicians and wealthy Americans, and enjoying great freedom as her father's favorite child. She could read what she wanted and travel in realms that were usually reserved for young men. She knew few boundaries, and by fifteen had become so involved in academic pursuits that she cut off her wavy chestnut hair and demanded of her father that she be allowed to "study and be his friend and companion." Senator Benton was horrified—and from the experience Jessie learned, as she put it, that "men like their womenkind to be pretty and not of the short-haired variety." Benton learned that his daughter had a mind of her own.

In 1841 Jessie Benton eloped with the dashing Second Lieutenant John Charles Frémont, twelve years her senior, a member of the Army Topographical Corps, and reputed to be an up-and-coming figure in Washington. Her father was livid, questioning Frémont's background and potential, but Jessie was quite under his spell. For the next fifteen years the tall, willowy, impeccably-gowned Jessie spent much of her time waiting for her husband to return from four trail-blazing expeditions to the west coast, and caring for their growing family. They had four children in eight years, two of whom died in infancy. These were worrisome and lonesome years for Jessie, even amid the glamour and pomp of the nation's capital. Sometimes she would go for a year without hearing from John unless a trader or trapper who happened to meet him at some river crossing or forest encampment agreed to carry back a letter.

Twice during the frontier period, first in 1848 and later in 1858, Jessie lived in California, mainly at Las Mariposas Ranch in Bear Valley. The ranch was on seventy square miles of original Mexican land grant that John secured for $3,000 in what is now the Stanislaus National Forest, near Yosemite National Park. Jessie's biographer, Pamela Herr, noted that during her first stay the beautiful but tough frontier taught Jessie about herself: "sick, lonely, and afraid, she had not only survived but emerged far stronger." Eventually, she was captivated by the magnificent landscape of Las Mariposas and the Monterey coast and was reluctant to return to Washington, D.C. But return she did, to John's unsuccessful campaign as the first Republican candidate for the U.S. presidency.

By 1858 they were once again back at Las Mariposas, along with their three children: Lily, 15; Charley, 7; and Frank, 4; John's 18-year-old niece, Nina; and four servants. They were happier than they had ever been, and exhilarated by the bear, deer and snakes, by the miners and California Indians, and by their new wealth. The whitewashed house they built was called "the little White House" by locals, and marble-topped tables and crystal lamps, tapestry rugs and fine white linen bedclothes were soon shipped over land or sea to adorn the interior. Soon too, the stables were fitted with horses, and honeysuckle and violets, Jessie's favorite flowers, gave color to the gardens. From gold mines on the property and rents, Frémont netted around $39,000 a month, and Jessie hosted parties and social benefits and entertained guests like Horace Greeley and Richard Dana.

In the years that followed this stay at Las Mariposas, through a combination of mismanagement, questionable tactics, lawsuits and neglect, John Charles Frémont gradually slid into humiliation and bankruptcy. His Civil War military appointment was revoked by Abraham Lincoln, and his governorship of Arizona ended in a scandal of conflicting interests. Other business deals ended in disaster. Through these years Jessie stood fiercely loyal to her husband, scaffolding his reputation with all her political, social and rhetorical talents, until his death in 1890.

Because they needed cash, Jessie began writing seriously after the Civil War, and for two decades produced what she called "harmless puddings" that she knew would sell without drawing too much praise or attention. She told friends that she relished the time she spent writing and found both solace and intellectual stimulation in it, but she admitted that she never allowed herself to excel. Writing was not her primary goal. Supporting her husband was, as she wrote, "the business of my life."

From the Mariposa years, 1858–1861, Jessie Frémont drew the stories for the *Mother Lode Narratives,* which were written and published separately in the 1880s. (These, along with unpublished letters and stories, were collected in one volume, *Far West Sketches,* by Shirley Sargent in 1970.) Her sketches "My Grizzly Bear" and "Sierra Neighbors" are part of this collection and exemplify some of her best writing. In the narratives she is freely inquisitive and charmingly naive to the wonders of the new state. Her voice is light but not effusive, and her exquisite detail allows readers to participate along with her in the frontier experience. Her other publications include *Land of Sunshine, Distinguished Persons I Have Known, Souvenirs of My Time,* and *The Will and the Way Stories.*

Jessie Benton Frémont was a notable woman of the nineteenth century. But instead of challenging the system, she chose to stand behind her husband and buttress his reputation, to suffer with him the pendulum of fate that threw them back and forth from riches to poverty, from elation to depression. She was a gifted writer, but was often drawn away by the needs of her husband, who became increasingly unhappy and aloof. Altogether, she had the breeding of an aristocrat, the experience of a woman caught in the vise of history and poor fortune, and the heart of a pioneer.

She died Christmas morning of 1902, quiet and unafraid, in her home in Los Angeles.

My Grizzly Bear

— ❧·❦ —

B ear Valley was the name of the busy mining town nearest us on our mining place in the Lower Sierra. It troubled our sense of fitness to call a town a valley, but it was fixed by custom and fitness; for this had been a happy hunting-ground of the grizzlies. Acorns of the long variety, tasting like chestnuts, abounded here as well as the usual smaller varieties, while the rich oily nut of the piñon-pine made their delight. These acorns and piñones were the chief bread-supplies of the Indians also who did not give them up easily, and consequently bear-skeletons and Indian skulls remained to tell the tale to the miners, who came in to the rich "diggings" there. American rifles, then the pounding of quartz mills and strange shrieks of steam engines drove them away, and only the name remained.

To my objection of using "valley" and "town" as one and the same, I was told best let it alone or worse would follow, for there was a strong party intending to change the name of the place to "Simpkinsville," and how would I like that? The postmaster was the Simpkins—a tall, "showy" young man with an ambitious wife much older than himself; he was a London footman and she Irish, active, energetic, with a good head, and with ambition for her Simpkins. That neither of them could read or write was a trivial detail that did not seem to disturb the public. Men would swing down from horse or wagon-box, go in and select from the loose pile of letters their own and those of their neighbors, and have their drink at the bar over which Simpkins presided (they kept a tavern and the post-office was only a little detail).

But with the instinct of a man who "had seen the world" toward people of somewhat the same experience, the postmaster treated us with the largest courtesy, for everything with a capital "F" on it was laid aside for us.* Isaac, our part-Indian hunter, who generally rode in for the mail did not read either, and often had to make return-trips to give back what was not ours. It was in the time of Mr. Buchanan's administration, and had Simpkins sent in a petition signed as it would have been by the *habitues* of his bar, of course so faithful a political servant would have been granted this small favor, of change of name. You may be sure I lay low in my valley to avert this cruel address on my letters.

I had never before gone up to this property, and now it was chiefly as a summer open-air and camping-out tour to be over in three months, when we were to return to Paris where all arrangements had been made for a three-years stay.

Although the bear had long disappeared from this favorite old haunt I felt nervous about horseback excursions. Mountains are grim things at best, but all those deep clefts and thickets in ravines and horrid stony hill-slopes barred me from any but the beaten stage and wagon-roads, with our cool, brave Isaac to drive me. However, there was one view Mr. Frémont wanted me to see which we could get only on horseback, with a short climb at the peak of the mountain. From the summit we could see eighty miles off the line of the San Joaquin River, defined by its broad belt of trees, running north and south parallel to our mountains; connecting the two were many mountain rivers crossing the broad plain and glittering like steel ribbons in the afternoon sun—the Merced, the Stanislaus, the Tuolumne and others; a turn of the head showed the peaks of the Yosemite thirty miles off, and lines of blue mountains back to the everlasting snow of Carson's Peak—a stretch of a hundred and fifty miles.

It was a rough ride up, and rougher climbing after the horses could go no further and had to be left tied to trees with one man to watch them—only one other was with us; our party was only

---

* This "F" was the brand on all the tools and belongings of the works—in these countries whatever else was defied, the brand had to be respected.   —J. B. F.

myself and my daughter with her father and the two men.

We were growing more and more enthusiastic as glimpses of this rare view came to us. Mr. Frémont told us the distances, which only singularly pure mountain air could have let the eye pierce. "And the ear, too," I said. "We must be three miles from the village and yet how near sounds the barking of that dog!"

Dead silence fell on our animated people. They listened, as the rough, low bark—broader and rougher even than that of a bull-dog—rose again, sounding really close to us.

I never question any acts of some few people but I was surprised, and not too pleased, to find myself hurried back down the steep, stony peak with only, "It is too late to finish the climb—we must hurry—do not speak—keep all your breath for walking." And hurry we did. I was fairly lifted along. Mr. Burke had disappeared and was now with Lee bringing the horses to meet us—the horses refractory.

Without a word I was lifted into the saddle—Mr. Frémont gathered up my reins himself and kept close to my side—and we fairly scurried down the mountains, I shamelessly holding to the saddle as the steep grade made me dizzy. This dizziness so pre-occupied me with the fear of fainting that I felt nothing else. We gained the stage-road by the shortest cut, and then a loping gallop soon brought us home, where I was carefully lifted down and all the consideration and care which they dared not give me on the hurried ride was now lavished on me. I had been seriously ill not long before and could not understand why I was so roughly hauled along.

There was reason enough.

It was no dog, but a grizzly bear that made that warning bark, and we were very close to it.

My ignorance spared me the shock of this knowledge, but the practised mountain men knew it was not only a bear, but a she-bear with cubs. They knew she would not be likely to leave her cubs at that hour when they were settling for the night unless we came nearer or irritated her by talking and noises. Horses are terribly afraid of this powerful and dangerous animal, and one danger was that our horses would break away and run for safety leaving us to the chances of getting off on foot. There I was the weak link in the chain. My daughter was fleet of foot and so steady of nerve that she was told the truth at once, and did her part bravely in keeping me unaware of any unusual condition. Fortunately our riding horses were, each, pets and friends, and only required to be safe with their masters; Burke had got back instantly to help Lee, and once mounted we were moved by one intelligence, one will.

Very quickly our bright drawing-room filled with eager men gun in hand. Armed men rode down the glen intent on that bear—first coming to get all information of the exact locality, then to ride and raise the countryside for a general turnout against it. For every one had kept from "the Madam" the fact that a she-bear had been prowling about for some time seeking what she could devour; and that she had devoured some and mangled more of "Quigley's hogs"—Quigley having very fine and profitable hogs at a small ranch three miles from us.

Lights frighten off wild beasts. I had no shame in illuminating the house that night. Men laughed kindly over it, but they all felt glad that I had come off so safely, and next day I was early informed that the cubs were all killed. The bear went as usual to Quigley's for her raw pork supper, the digestion of a bear making this a pleasure without drawback, but the stir about the place was evident to the keen senses of the grizzly and the men watched that night in vain. Her tracks were plain all around about, and the poor thing was tracked to her return to her cubs. She had moved them—made sure they were all dead, and her instinct sent her off into close hiding.

The watch was kept up, but she was wary and kept away.

At length one dark night the Quigley people heard sounds they were sure came from the bear though the hogs in the big pen were quiet. They were stifled sounds blown away by a high wind. There was but one man in the house, and he said his wife would not let him go after them; it was so desperately dark the odds would be all against him.

The woman said she was not sure it was a bear. She half thought it was men fighting, an equally great danger in that isolated way of living. So they shut their ears and their hearts although human groans and stifled blown-away cries made them sure it was no animal.

The sounds passed on. In the morning they went to the wagon-road which ran near their enclosure and found a trail of blood. Followed up, it led to a little creek close by with steep clay banks. Dead, his face downward in the water, lay a young man in a pool of blood—shockingly mangled across the lower part of the body. His sufferings must have been great, but his will and courage had proved greater.

He had not been torn by a bear as was first thought, but by a ball from his own pistol. This was found, a perfectly new pistol, in his trousers pocket; the scorched clothing showing it had gone off while in the pocket. The trail was followed back, leading to a brook where he must have stopped to drink when the pistol, carrying a heavy ball, went off. Yet such was his courage and determination that he crawled that long way in a state plainly told by the place where he had rolled in agony—the last was where he made his vain appeal for help at the Quigley house. Perhaps he fell face downward into the shallow streams and was mercifully drowned.

His good clothing, a geologist's hammer, and some specimens of quartz wrapped in bits of a German newspaper, told of an educated, worthy sort of man. But there was nothing to identify him, and the poor fellow was never inquired after. One of the many who came from afar with high hopes, and whose life was summed up in that most pathetic of words, "Missing."

The grizzly had disappeared and was, I am told, the last ever known in that valley, which still has as postmark for the town, "Bear Valley"; it is to be presumed the succeeding post-masters have been men who knew the whole of the alphabet as well as the letter "F."

Sierra Neighbors
— ❧·❧ —

We had not easily reached this condition of orderly comfort. Our earlier housekeeping had presented difficulties which would have dismayed regular forces, but we were the kind of volunteers "who did not know when they were beaten." And by keeping on trying against all failures, we won at last, and made the domestic wheels go round with smooth regularity.

Labor was all concentrated into the one channel of mining work, and so long as canned and salted things, easily kept and easy of transportation, suited the miners, no effort was made to give them fresher food. Consequently we found some unusual conditions for housekeeping; fancy going about it with no milk, no eggs—no hens to lay them—no vegetables. And as there was no ice, the only meat, beef, had to be killed, cooked and used the same day, during summer weather. It was almost the fable of King Midas— gold everywhere, but nothing but gold.

Our garden was run wild except the unfailing cabbage patch. That had been cared for. My friend, Miss Seward, has laughed with me over this inevitable around-the-world vegetable—"we left it in fields in our own Mohawk Valley, and saw it everywhere, even in the Valley of Cachemire"; but "Thy sweet vale, Cachemire," had not sweeter roses than we found taking care of themselves and spreading over the rioting artichokes which claimed their birthright as thistles to possess the land.

Even water, that life-blood of all growths, was hard to get at. Large clear springs were many, welling up from under projecting rocks, but it was a heart-break and a back-break for the women to dip up enough of this for daily uses.

Perhaps the laundry work was our most serious question; for the two nurses had taken the kitchen and laundry, the heat made both hard for them at best, and this novel bother about water made it harder.

And no money could prevail on any of the very few women up there to work; they were too much at ease in this prospering mining community to fatigue themselves, which was good for them while it was trying for us. Whatever men could do was quickly accomplished. A big barn and stable, a fine hen-house, a duck-pond, made by leading the water of several springs to a depression and there damming it, quickly gave proper living to our animals and the load of fowls we had sent up from Stockton. But the clothes began to accumulate into an alarming mound.

At last we got a laundress. Hearing of our *carte-blanche* offers, there came a group of a man, his wife and baby and a pack-horse loaded with their traps. "He" would "let her stay" until she was strong again. Her baby was very young and she looked, as she said she was, "most beat out."

Thankfully we accepted all demands; a separate lodging, and their separate cooking establishment; provisions for all the party, and feed and pasture for the horse; and a hundred dollars a month in money. As an incident, when her health, her housekeeping and her baby permitted, she was to do the washing.

I had difficulty in suppressing my French nurse, who was fortunately not fluent in English—"*des voleurs!*" was her comment; but it was Hobson's choice.

"He" was a surly creature, holding himself high above our two colored men because he was white; but not above living off his wife's work. She looked timidly at me while the unpleasant young man dictated his terms. Her wistful look and the thin little dirty baby made all of us women close round her in protection, though the man was repelling. With good rest and nourishing food, and kindly cares from women, she regained strength fast and came so bravely in help to our people that the clothes-mountain diminished rapidly.

But before the month ended, she came to me, crying; "He" said she was well enough to go on, that she could make money now by her washing while he worked in the diggings at Walker's Creek (the last new excitement) and must come then—that day.

We could not help her any further. It had been to her a paradise of friendly helping, of care such as she never dreamed of for her baby as well as for her own young ignorant self, and now she knew the difference, while we hated to see her dragged back into the fagging tramp-life; but he strode off, gun on shoulder, leading the horse, and she trailed after him, head down, carrying the baby.

After this I boldly utilized Indian girls from their village hard by. We were warned they would carry off anything they fancied, but they never did. Punctuality was not their gift, but good-humor was, and a genuine girlish pleasure in praise and rewards. The silver piece, large or smaller, according to their merit, which closed the day was a quick education, and we had more candidates than we had places for. A competitive practical testing of steadiness and capacity winnowed out an efficient corps of washerwomen and "scrub-girls."

As water will not run uphill, we built the laundry down the hill, over a spring; lining the spring with smooth planking, and leading its gathered waters by a trough into large tubs, each a grade below the other, the water let on by a plug from above, and off by others in the bottoms of the tubs—the whole running off into a little ravine to the happiness of our ducks and geese. A discarded invention for roasting crushed ore made a capital hot-water boiler, with the advantage of standing outside under a spreading oak. The spring gave its own freshness to the large laundry-room where, after work had grown to smooth habit in her domain Rose could sit in comfort at the mending, or reading her beloved *David Copperfield* and govern her dusky crew by a shake of the head and an exhibit of the smallest coin, or an encouraging smile and *"bueno bueno"* with a large coin held up; and a bright ribbon or a string of beads equalled a gold medal reward. Extra rewards were given for personal neatness—some combs and brushes and much soap, with object-lessons by my tidy sweet natured Rose.

They looked of a different race after they had seen the advantage of cleanliness, and learned to plait their thick hair in a club. Starch in their own calico skirts was the crowning touch of finery. A clean white under garment, a bright-colored cotton skirt, with a large gay cotton handkerchief pinned across the shoulders, and the tidy club of plaited hair tied with a bright ribbon, made them into picturesque peasants.

I had grown up among slaves and could make allowance for untutored people, as I knew them of all grades, from the carefully trained and refined house-servants to the common fieldhands; and knew that with them, as with us, they must have nature's stamp of intelligence and good-humor, without which any teaching and training is not much use. As the early Mission Fathers had taught weaving and cooking to the women, and simple agriculture and the care of flocks and herds to the men, and left in the fine mission building proof of their capacity as workmen, so I experimented on these Indian women with advantage to them as well as to ourselves.

And later we had our reward from Indian men also. Often on our rides, as I have said, we would stop in the Indian village and watch them as we sat on our horses. The center of the village was their open-air work room and salon, where they seemed always cheerfully busy and useful—the women, I mean—the men went too much to the white's village; but they also went after squirrels and birds and game, and the squirrel-skins made an important feature in their clothing. They sewed these together into large capes; a woman, laughing, held up an unfinished garment huddled across her breast with a pretended shiver as she looked high up the mountains, making us see they were providing against cold weather.

We noticed one very old body, too old to pound acorns or gather sticks—she looked herself like a fagot of dried sticks—who was always peeling mushrooms, or carefully peeling the oily piñon-nut, which they grind and mix with acorn flour into a cake. Her one only garment was a scant and ragged old cloak of squirrel skins that did not meet around her. We carried her and made her put on a woolen undershirt and a warm balmoral skirt, and shortly after saw this striped skirt worn as a hussar jacket, jauntily, one bare arm and shoulder free, by a young Indian man going into our village. And he only shook his head and grinned and kept on when I tried to make him ashamed of robbing the old crone. Then I tried Prussian war-tactics and made their whole village responsible—no more presents to any one unless they all joined in keeping for the one we gave to what was his or hers. And it worked about as well as our elaborate methods of securing justice. There is no protection for age and helplessness except among really Christian communities.

Their babies had, I thought, a roughish life. You can't fondle a cradle as well as a baby, and these little ones, tight-swaddled and strapped to flat osier cradles, with a little wicker hood to them, were carried on the mother's back when she went about the country; and just hung up on trees when she was home. The flies bothered them sadly; they were not clean, but they were stoically quiet—no one ever heard an Indian baby cry.

Some of their baskets they wove so compactly that they were used to boil water in—basket-work tea-kettles; others, long and wide-mouthed cones with one flat side, were carried on the back by a strap around chest and forehead, and were of the exact shape and use of the *botte* of the French peasant. Into these they gathered and carried heavy loads of acorns, of berries and mushrooms; of these last they used great quantities, both dried and fresh.

People who of their own accord did these things, could do more when instructed, encouraged and rewarded.

The older women dearly loved their pipes and delighted in the tobacco we carried them; they added to it in small proportion the customary dried leaves and herbs in regular use. Great as was their interest in our visits and though they were sure of beads and tobacco and other treasures from us, yet they never failed in genuine politeness; never crowding, or even looking eager, but gaily welcoming us, and offering us piñon-nuts or whatever berries were in season, with native good manners.

{ 165 }

It was exactly the Bible picture of the "two women shall be grinding corn" to see them pounding acorns into meal for bread (how they did prize a real sieve), a flat stone with a vigorous woman either side squatted on the ground, lifting her pounding stone with both hands, the arms of the two rising and falling alternately in accurate time and even stroke. The younger women and girls wove baskets, sewed skins and calico skirts and made nets of twine and beads for the men, as well as for their own manes of hair—in their way they were comfortable and industrious and had useful purpose and forethought in their occupations.

Our house, ourselves and our kitchen remained of endless interest to them. They would drop in a ring on the grass near the open door of the kitchen, and follow all Meme's doings with laughing comments, she with true French good humor indulging them and by lively pantomime explaining—often following up by a portion for them to taste.

Their soft voices would chorus out the *"eh-eh-eh!"* which expressed by its intonation wonder, sorrow or pleasure. Beef-suet was to them what chocolate bonbons are to our girls—they shredded it daintily, laughing with each mouthful. The cook kept it all for them, melted into cakes, and to combine enjoyment they would flock over to the tree under which lessons generally went on, pleased and quiet unless Douglass in a boyish fit of fun recited poetry with gestures, when the *"eh-eh-eh!"* became a chorus of praise—it was a picture, the fair-haired very white English lad reciting the Morte d'Arthur with Indians and mountains for audience and theater.

They quickly saw our love of wild flowers and brought the first of each—even some of their young men brought flowers that grew in difficult places, to the amazement of the white people who met them carrying wild jasmine and larkspur and the tulip-like mariposa-flower to "Flemon" as they named us all. "I'd never have believed it of an Injun," said one man to me.

Quite our nearest white neighbors, occupying each a small "rise" by which flowed the waste-water of the mill, were on one an

Italian with his wife and baby, and on the other the family I have spoken of—a typical family of a kind now impossible, "the poor whites of the South." Deprived there by surrounding influences of all advantages, of chances, their whole pride concentrated in the fact that they were white; this, by the curious alchemy of ignorance and self-conceit, endowed them with complacent superiority. The swarthy, black-eyed, black-haired Italians they looked down upon with contempt because they were so dark, and because "that Eye-talian worked like a nigger." He worked a great deal harder. He had put a fence around his few acres, saved some of the fine trees, and was already raising cabbage and beans when I first went up to the place.

His small cabin solidly plastered and white-washed outside and in, with its door, and a glass window with a white curtain, showed their industry and neatness in contrast with the dingy log-cabin and hard bare ground of the next knoll.

The "Eye-talian" had behaved well during the mining trouble; he produced a long gun shaped like a wide-mouthed trumpet and reported for defensive duty at our house or the mill; further he would not go from his wife. Not only for prudent care of her but, he was known to be wildly jealous. She was many years younger than himself, and really beautiful. When I first saw her in her picturesque peasant dress, her own young beauty and the noble baby in her arms made a vision of artistic beauty, and Old World art-associations—a true peasant Madonna and Child. She was never let to leave their little enclosure, but her picture-like beauty attracted me often, and the baby was a little Murillo. Seeing the man so industrious and capable, I got for him from San Francisco proper implements and seeds of herbs and vegetables and some flowers, and soon he had a market garden that paid him well, and was a great luxury to us.

As for their scornful neighbors, the "Cal-hoons," my one look in upon them when they called me to help the baby through "a fit" was enough. Theirs was a hopeless case of contented ignorance of better things. There, where every one was getting rich simply by easy work, they lived for mere existence. Deer and hares and birds they could have in quantity, for hunting was not "work." The father prided himself on *not* working unless when he wanted a little more money than his fitful gold-digging gave him. He had made a short dam and collected the water running by his door, and by its aid could always wash out enough "pay-dirt" for their pork and coffee and tobacco; if he needed more he came to the mill and asked a job of wood-cutting, and always got it; the Colonel had so ordered for, he said, he "liked a man to be thorough, and Calhoun was the most thoroughly idle man he ever knew."

The climax was easy, and there was no end to the fine fuel to be had for the gathering, and with a little industry he and his boys could have gathered gold as easily, but they toiled not, nor did they care to adorn themselves even with cleanliness, though nature had fairly endowed both man and woman; both were tall, erect, and easy in motion, with good straight features, and large clear eyes. Yet their small log-cabin had an earth floor; the windows mere gaps left between the mud-chinked walls; the bedstead low stakes with a hide stretched across, and a dreadful-looking feather bed and old quilt made the bed. A wide-yawning rough chimney of stones made a fine fireplace, but furniture there was none beyond some blocks of wood for seats. *On mangeat sur la pouce★* evidently, and the "thumb" was not tidied up after meals.

They were utterly without the most simple instruction, and still this woman had some of the instincts and feminine little arts belonging to high training. Once *Cal*-hoon cut down a large group of fine oaks the Colonel specially protected for their beauty and their position near our village. Returning from San Francisco he found this harm done and for once was angry; sending for the evil-doer to come to him at the house.

In his place came Mrs. *Cal*-hoon with her following of children. Easy, unconcerned, with quite the manner of any morning visitor of society, she walked in upon me and installed herself in an arm-

★ Literal translation: "One eats from his thumb."

chair; the Colonel being out she told me I might just go on teaching my little girl—"she liked to hear me"; then tilting back her sunbonnet proceeded to nourish the baby and issue orders to the children who stuck to her: "You jest set down there, and don't scrape your feet ag'in the carpet" (down settled many little boys in high-necked tow trousers, only these and nothing more). "You," to the bigger boys, "you just go to Uncle Ike" (our Isaac) "and tell him I'll take a settin' o' the white turkey's eggs; he kin put 'em in a basket."

All obeyed her. I went on with the French reading while the cake I had sent for was being quietly eaten by the little ones and the mother, who in one lank garment of calico lay back in the chair and stretched her long limbs, showing brogans without stockings, but as simply content listening to our reading as any lady might listen at a concert.

She did not rise when the Colonel came, for the baby was asleep, but she was so natural and direct, so instinctively sure of disarming displeasure, that she carried the day and left us amused and pleased by her native tact.

"Kurnel, I heard you was mad at *Cal*-hoon for cuttin' them oaks, and I came over to tell you 'twa'n't him, 'twas *me* did it. You see he'd got a big job o' cuttin' while you was down to 'Frisco ef he could git it done up right away, and *I*" (with a little feminine toss of the head) "tole him, jest take the little grove on the stage road and you'll haul it in quick—an' he done it because *I* tole him. So it's *me,* Kurnel, you've got to be mad at."

The absurd contradiction between her looks and her falling back on the privileges of an irresponsible fine lady who feels no barrier to her caprices, fetched us, and she went off satisfied with herself, though promising for the future to keep her husband to the trees marked out for cutting.

These were our immediate neighbors. In the large town twelve miles away were, as one is sure to find in our frontier towns, an advance-guard of exceptional men strong in heart and purpose, and some fine, patient, hoping women who tell well in forming the community.

Among those connected with our own works were men of education and travel, and already travelers came up with letters of introduction to visit the mines and works, and from us go on to the Yosemite region near by. In this way we had a charming visit from Richard Dana—"Two Years Before the Mast" Dana. He and the Colonel met as two Selkirks might, revisiting their once desert island and finding it a busy seaport. And a visit from Horace Greeley who could not sufficiently praise my "executive ability" as he called it—for to him any well-ordered household was the acme of woman's genius, and now after his overland-stage experience he was surprised by this evolution of elegance and comfort in such remote surroundings.

But months of isolation from such women as one needs for human nature's daily food, made the long visit of our friend Hannah [Lawrence] beyond telling precious. With her Quaker name and complexion she had their sweet even domestic nature, and a happy overflowing wit and gayety of heart, all her own. Like Charles Lamb's Hester,

> "Her parents held the Quaker rule
> Which doth the passions train and cool;
>   It could not Hester,
> For she was trained in Nature's school
>   And Nature blest her."

With all, she had the gift of song and a musical organization, which with high training and the best associations in music made of her the most complete, the most enjoyable musical person I have ever known. We had met often in the usual society ways in New York and our mutual love of music brought us together at many intimate musicales, but now in this odd framing her talent came out resplendent. And in all ways it became a friendship for life. The delightful long days in the open air, the charming evenings of music, the appreciative zest with which she entered into the novel interests of the work on the place, were helping and refreshing to the Colonel, while I was in a long good dream of content.

We would make an early start, Hannah driving the light strong mountain-wagon, a man following on horseback, in case of need, and go wherever wheels could carry us, making unexpected finds of isolated houses or little settlements where we gave a bit of pleasure to some lonely woman and always met the most cordial, real hospitality and welcome. At some places where I saw it would be a joy, I asked Hannah to sing, and never did a glorious gift do more gracious and lovely duty than when she sang to them the songs they knew of, and other music which was a revelation.

We came once on a place that looked as though a woman's care had shaped things; the grass was cut short, and a clean path led up to a side porch with seats and a table, and the great oaks all around and overhanging the house and corral were very different from the usual stumps which make our national frontier decoration—and behold! there was not a woman around there. Only men—but Frenchmen. And a "hard lot" as we learned afterwards. Isaac, who knew every one, was not with us that day, only a man we had brought up from San Francisco. But the "hard lot" came forward and offered milk and spring water, or if we would do them the honor to descend they asked to offer us an omelet and some claret—which we had to decline, as it was late and we were nearly fourteen miles from home.

Hipolita Orendain de Medina (1847–1922). Courtesy of the California Historical Society, San Francisco. FN-29127.

Hipolita Orendain de Medina (1847–1922)

The few short poems and philosophic ruminations penned by Hipolita Orendain de Medina help us remember that California was not always an American state. Between 1822 and 1846 it was under Mexican rule, and before that it was part of the Spanish empire. Even after California became part of the United States, its links with Mexico remained strong.

Born in Mexico, probably in 1847, Hipolita Orendain de Medina was the daughter of a silver mine owner, Jesús Orendain, who died sometime around 1850. His widow, Francisca Tejada de Orendain, brought her two daughters, Hipolita and Virginia, to San Francisco. With the wealth she took with her, Hipolita's mother invested in Oakland waterfront property and assimilated into Bay Area society. Before long she had remarried lawyer Humphrey Marshall, who in 1861 left San Francisco to defend his home state of Virginia in the Civil War. He died in Virginia, and Hipolita's twice-widowed mother educated her daughters with private tutoring, making sure both were bilingual and conversant in literature, music and art. But through the unscrupulous dealings of opportunists and her own naivete, and later the heavy contributions to the cause of ridding Mexico of the French-supported Maximilian, Francisca de Orendain lost her wealth. Her daughters had to make their living in a dressmaking business, but still remained, at least socially, members of upper class San Francisco society. Letters from friends in Sonora, Sacramento, Guadalajara, Acapulco, and Mazatlán written in 1867 talk of parties for "worthy president Juarez," and of Hipolita being "happy surrounded by so many handsome fellows."

Hipolita Orendain was said to have been playful, intelligent and introspective—a woman of nobility who looked the part. Tall, gowned in flowing crinoline and lace, shy in public behind her fan, but talkative and teasing among people she knew, she had a crowd of friends— Americans too, but mainly Mexican-Americans.

In October of 1869, Hipolita married Emilio Medina, a musician, diplomat and later editor of *La República,* a Spanish language newspaper he established in San Francisco as counterpoint to his land investment company. Their family eventually included four daughters, Josefina (1869), Virginia (1871), Zarina (1873), and finally Mercedes (1876). But by 1880 the census reported that Hipolita was living apart from her husband, although he was very active in San Francisco political and business circles. In 1887, Hipolita listed herself as a widow. Still, up through 1908 Hipolita Orendain de Medina followed an active social calendar, suspended only for a time after the 1893 death of her daughter, Zarina. Her cultural and social roots ran deep. She and her sister were always close, and she worked at keeping family ties strong, even with cousins far away in Mexico.

Hipolita's exact date of death is uncertain. She was buried in a Los Angeles cemetery, probably in 1922. Her granddaughter, Francisca Brigante, donated her papers to the California Historical Society in San Francisco.

Through the years, Hipolita Orendain maintained a "spirit journal," a log to which she alone was privy, wherein she could reflect on Catholic services she attended, and on her own spiritual fluctuations and intentions and those of her family. It is from this "libro íntimo," or intimate book, that the following selection is drawn.

Delirium

—✦·✦—

I

Delirium
a delirium is trapped in my mind
it is two o'clock in the morning and the night
    dew shivers my chest
under the moonlight a heart
inflamed with love vibrates

II

And everything quiets down the world sleeps
in the middle of a sacred silence
a voice is heard—a song is heard
that demands a memory flower
that demands a memory of love.

III

Archangel of mine
goodness of my life
do not doubt of my passion.

Georgiana Bruce Kirby (1818–1887). Courtesy of the Society of California Pioneers.

Georgiana Bruce Kirby (1818–1887)

What the reader notices about Georgiana Kirby's writings, whether it is her diary or fiction, is her range of intellect and emotion.

Born in 1818 in Bristol, England, Georgiana Bruce came to Canada at sixteen, to work as a governess. Later, in Boston, she joined abolitionist and Unitarian organizations and worked for the suffrage of women, for prison reform and for programs for inner-city factory workers. Georgiana was also a school teacher in Georgia, a matron at Sing Sing Prison in New York, where she worked to rehabilitate women prisoners, and a free-lance author.

At eighteen she moved to Brook Farm, the famous experimental community in Massachusetts, where she and her half-brother Charles followed the philosophy of the transcendentalists. Nathaniel Hawthorne and Margaret Fuller were among Brook Farm's inhabitants.

In 1848, the tall, stately, rather prim looking Georgiana Bruce, her dark, thick hair pulled back in a braided bun, was booked on a steamer for California with her brother. The two were settled in their stateroom on the day of departure, and were bidding good-bye to friends on the dock, when they were notified that their stateroom had been vandalized and that their entire California stake had been stolen—luggage, provisions, money.

Despondent, they returned to Brook Farm, where they redoubled their efforts to save money for passage to California. But before the money could be gathered, Charles died. In 1850, Georgiana Bruce departed alone for California, "to become a sharer in the general prosperity." This time she had the financial aid of Margaret Fuller, a gift of money Fuller insisted was the result of her own good fortune, meant to be shared with friends. Unfortunately, Fuller died just a few years later, and Brook Farm as a way of life also came to an end.

When she arrived by steamship in San Francisco, Georgiana Bruce joined the company of a longtime friend, Eliza Farnham, with whom she had worked at Sing Sing. Farnham's husband had died just weeks before his wife sailed into Monterey Bay to join him. He left her a select piece of property and when Georgiana Bruce arrived a year later, the two women began to work the farm, turning it into a profitable enterprise. They shared an interest in books and social and political issues, and even considered establishing a school together near the old Franciscan mission at Santa Cruz.

But by early 1852, Georgiana Bruce had married Richard Kirby, a local tanner and orchardist. In her diary which begins in this period, on December 14, 1852, Georgiana chronicles her experiences with Kirby as homesteaders. The Kirbys lived several miles inland from Santa Cruz, which was only a mission at that time, and in her diary Georgiana describes her sense of isolation. Pregnant, and jubilant about the impending birth of her first child, she nevertheless must cope daily with loneliness and a lack of intellectual stimulation. Later, as the homesteading does not go well, more physical needs such as safety, food and shelter surface, and she slips into a mood of distress, frustration and melancholy. In her frank personal notes we can witness the tremendous power the raw frontier had over pioneers.

Details about Kirby's mature years in Santa Cruz are sketchy. In 1869 she organized the first local chapter of suffragists. For a number of years she taught music and French, generally to young women, and for several decades she counseled local young people who sought her out. Throughout the '60s she published a number of polished short stories in the *Overland Monthly,* generally reflecting themes relevant to women in early California. She also contributed essays to the *Santa Cruz Sentinel.* Later she published two reflective works: *Transmission,* thoughts on the "natural laws of life"; and her autobiography, *Years of Experience,* which was published in 1887, the year of her death. These memoirs, however, do not offer the immediacy we experience in her diary, excerpted here, or the images of early California women we see in her short stories. In "A Tale of the Redwoods," first published in the *Overland Monthly* in 1874, we can once again feel the remoteness and isolation Kirby refers to in her diary.

JOURNAL OF
GEORGIANA KIRBY

——— ❧•❦ ———

December 14, 1852

T he day is blustering and rainy and cold but I feel in better health and spirits, especially the latter, than for some time. This morning immediately after breakfast I rode my good old Rosea over into the "off hollow" and onto the hills beyond, wishing "Tom" had hauled the new fencing stuff.

It always puts me in good spirits to gallop up the hills and view the wild mountain scenery so on my return after taking in the clothes and all the wood that we chopped as the clouds looked ominous, I concluded that today for the first time in my life I would commence a journal. I think that perhaps I may die and my baby may live, in which case it would be pleasant for the latter to have some record of my external and spiritual life during these important months; or should I survive this great trial of my physical powers and live to see my child grow up it will be interesting to me to see how far and in what manner my present and succeeding states of mind may have had influence in forming the character and consequently the external appearance of my child.

Since I was a girl of eighteen I have been ever conscious of the most intense desire to become a mother. The thought (in anticipation) on the condition in which I now find myself used to fill my whole being with joy. Often and often when alone with nature my soul has been lifted up as it were to higher spheres and so filled with a sense of harmony and melody that I was obliged to relieve myself by a long recitative, not, owing to my inferior vocal organs, at all worthy of the emotions that gave rise to it.

It is not that I am especially fond of little babies, for I am not though I doubt not that this instinct will in due time become developed in me, but I do so earnestly love to watch the unfolding of character and intellect. I love so much to influence youth right, to arouse moral ambition, to instill by precept and example a thorough respect for labor that my own child, be it boy or girl, may have some prominent noble trait, some beautiful spiritual gift, like music, for instance, and no mean streak or fatal weakness. I desire that my child have a generous nature, good common sense and industry, at the very least.

My husband has so many excellent qualities that I am deficient in, and also so excellent a temperament that unless other causes have force enough to counteract the good I feel we have every reason to hope for the best.

For more than two months I have been suffering from the ordinary ailments of such a condition and they are such as do not conduce to healthy intellectual action by any means. Mr. K., kind and active and ever cheerful, gets up and prepares breakfast, brings me chocolate and toast or whatnot to bed, kills and dresses a chicken for my dinner or saddles the horse for me to take a short ride—then hurries off to the tan yard, two miles or so.

At night he often goes to the mission after closing the yard and is then sure to bring home a variety of articles with which to tempt my appetite or in some way contribute to my comfort.

Our rancho, with its hollows and gulches and noble sweep of hills, exactly suits me, but I have been used to mixing in pretty large circles and miss the pleasant and healthy excitement caused by the friction of mind on mind. I long for flowers and fruits and music too but cannot expect every good in the present state of society. I have many as it is—unsurpassed beauty of scenery and climate, good health, neither poverty or riches, and the most devoted friend in my husband.

The other day Mr. K. brought home a balm of gilead tree about four and a half feet high and planted it just opposite the kitchen window. It really gladdened my heart and I watched it constantly during the day as I would a child. It was the first step in the way of refined cultivation and gives me faith in future roses, lilies, dahlias and antwerp raspberries and luscious English gooseberries in our own garden on our own Rancho a La Salud near Santa Cruz, California.

The day before yesterday (Sunday) we went to see Mr. and Mrs. Sawin, who live up the coast maybe two miles from the mission. Owing to the first rains which lasted pretty much for three weeks, and to K's being so busy that he had to raise sheds and stables on Sunday instead of taking me on a "pasear" for more than three months previous to this, I had not been off the rancho or seen a woman, and the Sawins are so friendly that I enjoyed this visit very much.

It is three miles from here to the mission and those women who have side saddles and horses at their command are yet so occupied by their housekeeping cares that they are unable excepting at distant intervals to leave home for a day. There are no sisters or aunts or grown-up daughters to take their places while absent and if it should happen that any such sisters, aunts or grown-up daughters did exist, then before you could turn around they would be certainly snatched up and themselves immediately in the same plights as the rest of the women and quite as hardly as before.

When I came down here a little more than two years ago, there were scarcely any buildings in the mission but the old adobe ones, no fences up the coast or down with the exception of a bit of Spanish fencing by Rodriguez or Majors, which had to be rebuilt every year. Now from the mission fully up to Moore's the land is taken up and fenced well as a general thing. Several families raise a variety of vegetables but as yet no orchard or nursery has been planted in this region. There is no wild fruit but the strawberries twelve miles up the coast. The pears in the mission orchard are tasteless things and the apples from San Juan a slight improvement on the crab, and yet this will one day be the finest fruit region in California.

In coming to Santa Cruz it was my intention to teach school. There were many girls belonging to these western families of sufficient promise to interest me in them. I could and desired not only to instruct them in books but in their personal habits of cleanliness, neatness, order, courtesy—how to make and mend their clothes—but the fierce young villain who was then keeping the mixed school—one of the cloth who frequently exhorted in the meeting (Methodist Methodism)—reigned supreme. The regular local minister, Mr. Briar, a self-conceited, bawling brute without a spark of tenderness, used all his influence against me and this, added to the unpopularity of Mrs. Farnham, at whose house I was staying, rendered the entire plan abortive. This teacher afterwards seduced some of the young girls and had to leave in the night, went onto the boards in San Francisco and afterwards joined the filibustering expedition to the Sandwich Islands.

After giving up the school I took to gardening much to the benefit of my health and impoverishment of my pocket. The soil proved too sandy for onions. For more than a year I did not make one cent. Then I went down with Bryant Hill to the Pajaro Valley to cook for his men. He was the first American that settled there and I remained there six months in a house without a chair or bedstead or table, with the exception of the boards on tressels that we and the men eat off of. For three months we had no windows, the light came through the door which was left open, no looking glass, no flat irons.

I ironed the bosoms and collars of two white shirts with a half pint tin tumbler kept constantly half full of boiling water. I worked very hard indeed. My only comfort was a game of whist after eight o'clock. Mrs. Thrift, a young New England woman who had married an illiterate young southern man, I had with me. She was avowedly an abolitionist and I respected her for this and hoped to find in her a companion and friend, but I found her selfish in the extreme, without a shadow of aspiration, self-willed and wholly wanting in the common traits of New England women—

judgement, skill in the various domestic departments, economy and so forth. I was very sorry to give her up but she obliged me to.

December 15, 1852
Last night there was ice on the pools a quarter of an inch thick and about 10 this a.m. there was quite a brisk shower of snow which lasted some five minutes and then changed to rain. I believe myself incapable of experiencing pleasures excepting through association, so this snow reminding me of happy days in Canada and Massachusetts fairly made my heart merry.

Last evening I was reading the closing scene in Browning's *Paracelsus.* What wonderful power and yet what fineness, what delicacy, in this man's experiences! Somehow I was led to compare the philosophy of Paracelsus with that of the manly James, especially in their enlightened acceptance of the past, their just interpretation of it as the necessary prelude to the future. I have the most intimate sympathy with the views advanced by Henry James. The subjects, being so comprehensive, are necessarily treated very imperfectly but still what he gives you is clean, sound wheat, fit to be assimilated with the inmost of the blood.

How heartily I agree with him in his contempt of the teachings of the modern church—mean, cringing, self blaspheming!

I am happy in remembering that notwithstanding the soul searching religious experience I went through in my youth, lasting indeed through years, I never for the moment believed that God regarded me in any other light than a friendly one. I never knew what remorse meant. I never believed that God would bless me for Christ's sake, for I felt intuitively that our primal relation was a good and harmonious one. I never would thank him for goods I enjoyed which were withheld from others. To entertain any of these sentiments struck me as degrading the character of the deity below that of inferior men.

With what for a child were superhuman efforts I made confession of stealing plums from a dish, a humming top from a shop, and of sundry less heinous crimes, feeling that in doing so I must resign all hopes of the world's respect, but I know no other emotions than courage, love of truth, a desire to stand honestly with myself. I had much reverence, much love of the being loved, steady aspiration after inmost truths. How could I with my moderate intellectual powers build a harmonious system out of the savage and discordant material around me? I was interested always in theological questions and yet theology would by no means cling to me. God be thanked, for it was all false and would have made me less loving and less intelligent than I am. Chaning's mild moralities, Carlyle's indignant ravings, Parker's bold analysis of the religious sentiments, dreams of immediate perfection of society by association, satisfactory working at "fragmentary" reforms! Now James fits the keystone, which authenticates all of these.

December 22, 1852

The rain of ten days and nights and the winds that have sent seven vessels on shore have at length, so appearances would argue, passed away. The earth is green and the sky fair. Bryant Hill, who had $25,000 worth of produce on board of two of the vessels and who supposes his rancho with $25,000 worth more in bags and heaps of potatoes and cetera is for the most part under water and the house blown into the river, left here to return this morning. He came up with his two partners a week ago and owing to the rise in the San Lorenzo and the Soquel creek he could not cross to return. I pray that his affairs be not so desperate as he apprehends for I long to see Eleanor and the child, and she must be very weary of waiting to join him. I wish also that he may keep the 2,000 acres in the Pajaro that so satisfy his farming aspirations.

I am out of reading matter and have neither the health or energy to attempt to study as a means of occupying my time and mind. Once in two weeks the mail brings the Tribune, A. S. Standard and Freeman. When these are read, first hurriedly, then carefully, I am in the same position as before. The last Tribune contained Parker's discourse on Webster. It is a just verdict which the future will attest. I'm glad these three worthy idols of the American people, Clay, Calhoun and Webster, are dead. It may be that better men will gradually fill their places in the public estimation.

When I think of Mann and Sumner, Giddings, Phillips and Garrison, I agree with Dickens that "If this were a republic of intellect and worth instead of vaporing and jobbing they would not want the lever to keep it in motion," but the great mass of the people in all classes are so wholly wanting in integrity of character, are so shallow and at the same time so self-conceited that one is almost tempted to despair of their ever making radical progress toward the really good and noble.

Whenever any crisis comes to try their metal you hear the ring of brass, nothing better. The nation has no great heart, as the German or English people. Material gain is its one sole object. As a people they have no sentiment—nothing that makes it impossible for them to do the meanest or wickedest thing conceivable.

January 7, 1853

The remnants of this remarkable rain storm still hang about us. There can not have less than two and a half feet of water fallen during these last six weeks. Farming operations are thus put back— no ploughing done as yet. In former years wheat was sowed in November and December. The upper country must be flooded and all planting necessarily stopped for the present.

There must be great suffering in the mines. Provisions, especially the staples flour and pork, were so high that traders waited for a fall before purchasing their winter stock and now the long rain has cut off communication. A few speculators buy up all the flour and pork and hold it at $35, $40 and $47 the barrel. If the railroads were built between California and Missouri it would equalize the market; the rich valleys on the route would help supply this land of non-producers. Potatoes have risen to eight cents and ere long will be ten cents a pound, I doubt not, so what Bryant Hill loses by the rot and extra freight will be made up.

Two weeks ago tonight John Bowen, a Quaker farmer from Byberry, Pa., arrived. He had been determined a week in the Santa

Clara valley by the rain and had a great time crossing the mountains. It was well that he had a cheerful heart and good horse or it might have fared worse with him. He was soaking wet and sand to his knees when he reached here but in fine spirits as if he had got home at last. He had spent his last month in Pennsylvania at the house of my beloved friend Robert Purvis, and brought me letters, "Uncle Tom" and a beautiful daguerreotype of our sweet young friend Tacie Townsend.

John Bowman had lived some twenty years in Byberry and I was glad to hear all the news, though I thought it an uncommonly stupid place the eighteen months I spent there. Purvis is the beautiful star that gives the place any character at all and there are a few pretty fair women but all hampered by their miserly dolts of fathers and their poverty.

The second day of Mr. B's visit was devoted to the gossip of his neighborhood and Mr. P's particular family. His wife's relations treated him very meanly and I'm glad he has come out here where his industry, strength and skill will in a few years secure him an independent fortune. His nasal tones and too great enthusiasm at first made me very nervous and irritable but before he left on Sunday to fetch his trunks from San Francisco I had become used to his voice and ways and was really glad to look forward to his return.

He will plant the first nursery in Santa Cruz on our land and besides makes us a family garden. After March he will work in the tan yard and may live with us many years. When Mr. K. returned from escorting him by a nearer road to Major's rancho at the foot of the mountains (he goes to San F. to fetch his things) he brought with him some young pine trees and set them around the house. The cattle nibble them and rub against their slender stems. It's such a pity.

It is so delightful here when the rain does stop, we have the most glorious summer weather at once. The birds sing, and the Bay is covered with a haze of glory, the earth is green as emerald.

January 12, 1853

My health begins to mend. My mind returns to its old picture-making, conversation-holding (imaginary) habits. I regret that I find the exertion of walking much disagreeably fatiguing. The various forms of measure (rhythm) that so constantly used to repeat themselves in my mind come back again and also the same vivid conceptions of persons and events as I lie awake at night. Occasionally, too, I have a beautiful dream—of being indeed asleep and the spirit leaving the body finds itself overlooking a noble city, examining its architecture, plans, etc., it being cold and solemn and clear at night. Oh, that my best dream nights may be reproduced!

I have nearly done what sewing I have to do and next week I shall help them cut potatoes for planting and hope to be strong enough to drop for a few days. Such work seems more of work, more productive, than puttering in the house.

Daubentisch's dam was so deranged by the flood that it has to be repaired. Flour is $35 and $40 a barrel in San Francisco and few can afford that price and pay freight ($3 a barrel) down. I've heard of the miners at the nearest mining region back of Sacramento eating barley at $1 the pound and of those who were packing provisions on their backs from the city being frozen to death. As yet no news from the more distant settlements.

January 17, 1853

Three days ago a young friend from Fairfield County, Pennsylvania, by name Albert Brown passed the night with us. He with hundreds of others was driven from the mines by the snow and want of provisions. He had a brother of seventeen with him. He is only nineteen himself but possesses the energy, firmness and self-respect of a much older person.

He very wisely considered that he would be more likely to obtain work in the country than in the crowd at San F. and so walked to San Jose and across the mountains. He has engaged with Meader for $60 a month and will send for his brother who will also readily find employment as the fine weather lasts and the farmers are in a hurry to get their crops in.

I do hope we can build a kitchen in which the men can have their meals and sit, and we have quiet home times in the dining room.

January 20, 1853

I have been reading the Atkinson and Martmean book and find it very suggestive and consoling, just as James is. Work based on false sentiment, the outgrowth of a false morality, unless indeed they have the direct power to help renovate society, as "Uncle Tom," are very stupid things. One thing constantly forces itself on the free soul—the danger of attending thorough freedom of speech or action. (One does not wish to die and to a well balanced mind the love of their fellows is necessary. If one is faithful to one's convictions of what is right you are not only an outlaw yourself but you involve the well being of those of your friends who may not be so well able to cope with the difficulties as yourself.)

I am in better health from taking arsenic but still the least indiscretion with regard to the nature of my food causes wearisome relapses. To be occupied solely with the sense of pain in the stomach is such sad waste of time and I am so desirous of being cheerful and thoughtful.

Mr. Bowman had brought down a few strawberry roots, asparagus, and one little peach tree. I wish he were more quick and had some sufficient satisfaction with his own labors, great and small, so as to avoid the necessity of telling of every little thing he does and every movement he makes. It detracts so much from a man's manliness, the constantly asking the suffrage of his fellows. He talks and explains in one endless nasal monotone with the most tedious prolixity about all sorts of unimportant and common-place things, never seeming to think that the people he is talking to may be as well informed on the subject as himself or that the trifling incident he so minutely describes may be thoroughly uninteresting to his auditors, who for civility's sake are obliged to listen against their will and respond occasionally. It is a thousand pities that no one warned him of the disagreeable habit when he was a young man. It serves to alienate many who would otherwise be his warm friends, I doubt not. By talking one quarter as much he would have twenty times the influence.

January 27, 1853

We planted our first potatoes on the 25th. There was so great a press of work (as is usually the case in a California spring) that I volunteered to drop potatoes. I was so anxious to have Mr. Bowman go on with the garden fence. The first day I got along pretty well but yesterday at noon I completely gave out and went straight to bed dreading a miscarriage after all I had endured for the sake of a future blessing. Today I am rested somewhat but do not like the symptoms at all—regret that I have no arnica★ to take. Today it rains a little with a prospect of more behind. It is good for our uphill barley only I pray that it stops in seasonable time.

February 1, 1853

The weather continues fair and mild with the farming proceeding briskly. I am still very unwell, consumed by heartburn (so-called). My work is a burden to me and the constant pain and consequent weakness keep my mind heavy. I suffer from intolerable thirst and avoid drinking until my tongue is parched because the liquid increases the heartburn.

I have seen the face of but one woman (Mrs. Sawin) in four months and a half and it is likely to be two months more before any one will have time to visit. No bright and beautiful thoughts and at the same time no fretfulness or anxiety. K. is so thoroughly kind that he has a tranquilizing effect on me, who am as a general thing inclined to be apprehensive of evil and sensitive to the influence of others.

★ a homeopathic remedy

February 3, 1853

Sowing barley below the road. Bryant stayed over night with us, in fine spirits because of the calmness of the weather which enables him to get off all his produce from Castro's. It is well that he has an excess of hope in his composition, for he has had enough trouble to crush one ordinary person. Success makes such a difference, too, in his looks. When under the influence of hope he is handsome; when oppressed with care, decidedly homely.

I am not sure that anything whatever could relieve or comfort me under my present very depressing condition of health, but if any thing could it would be a congenial female companion with whom I could chat and be merry, sympathize and advise. The being alone all day from eight in the morning to seven at night ensures too great a seriousness. There is nothing to call out any other faculties of the mind, fancy, imagination, affection, mirthfulness, nothing in fact to kindle or excite a worthy spirit life. I regret this more than I can express, dreading the effects on the little one.

Every good woman needs a companion of her own sex. No matter how numerous or valuable her male acquaintances, no matter how close the union between herself and husband, if she have a genial, loving nature, the want of a female friend is felt as a sad void. I have a fixed habit also of living nearly altogether in the future. Not that I am in the least discontented with my present circumstances; it is a habit that if I remember rightly grew out of my desire for knowledge when a young girl. I always hoped something would "happen" in a few years to enable me to attain the intellectual culture I so earnestly desired and which I found myself utterly unable in my cramped circumstances to arrive at.

Benevolence and affection always came in to interfere with the fulfillment of aspiration and so the years wore away in ceaseless yearning and this habit became fixed of looking far far away, even to the future of death when social duties and individual aspirations would never conflict.

Wednesday, February 9, 1853

Fine weather still lasts. I rode to the mission last Sunday, took tea at the Whitings and then went to pass the night at Mrs. Dryden's, the wife of the M. minister. She is in the like case with myself and as her husband was at San F. we slept together and had quite a cheerful time of it. The next day I saw at her house one or two other pleasant women. Mrs. W. is to come up this evening to pass a few days with me. I enjoyed the visit exceedingly and feel better in consequence. On the 6th sowed cauliflower, asparagus, rhubarb and onions and set out the strawberry plants.

February 13, 1853

We sowed celery, sea kale and set out the first little peach tree up by the house and the rose bushes around. I am better and had a two days visit from Mrs. Whiting which made me quite forget myself and my ailments. She also is about to become a mother as are many other women in the mission and for the first time after being married many years. The place has become proverbial for its 'fruitfulness.' We are all in a state of partial anxiety about doctors and nurses. Those here, of the former class, are briefless, giving calomel to a confined woman and losing healthy patients frequently, and most of the latter being filled more or less with old women's superstitions as regards the treatment of newborn babes.

I am reading "Reveries of a Bachelor" to Mr. K. It is good to read just enough to stimulate thought.

February 23, 1853

Last night the much needed rain came. Tom had given up further ploughing for want of it and only yesterday. It is a gentle and not cold rain. They have finished this side of the garden fence and today make a large gate in the place of bars. Last week the mare foaled; I am sorry it is not a horse colt. I am very busy sewing sacs and shirts. The transplanted rose bushes are putting out their leaves and the rhubarb is getting quite green.

Two months is a long time to await the answer to a letter. If there were a weekly mail from the east it would help the matter.

February 27, 1853

I am 34 years old and my husband either one or two years older. My mother was not married till her thirtieth year. I was her second child, born three years afterward. My sister, two years my senior, is thoroughly superficial and selfish—one of those persons who are mature as they will be at the age of fifteen.

March 14, 1853

I spent yesterday afternoon at the Meader's, galloped there and felt invigorated by the exercise and change. Today Mr. and Mrs. Sawin came to see me and on returning were, I fear, caught in the rain which has come again heavily this afternoon. Last week Mrs. Meader sent me four or five pounds of her good butter which is a great present here in these days, being a dollar a pound and not to be had at that.

April 7, 1853

I spent part of Sunday and Monday at the Whiting's. Whiting is a shallow, conceited, dogmatic, insolent, pro-slavery braggert and I came home quite sad and hopeless about the progress of truth and justice in this country.

April 16, 1853

There is now a weekly mail from the Atlantic states. K. has gone to the Pajaro. Our garden begins to look ship shape.

May 1, 1853

I sprained my ankle pretty badly stepping off the piazza. I hobbled in, mixed some bread and fed the youngest chickens so that matters might not stand quite so bad when K. and Tom returned with the cow which they did shortly. The Brown brothers spent the day with us. Health quite well since K. supplies me so well with candy of which I am extravagantly fond.

May 3, 1853

K. planted melons and many other things. Last night it showered a little. The opinion among intelligent persons is that the general cultivation of the soil is fast changing the climate.

May 15, 1853

K. gone again to Pajaro to make more certain of a nurse for me and to bring home the American cow he bought of Bryant. Our new Spanish cow, Abumblah, is quite good, giving six or seven quarts of the most excellent milk per diem. Yesterday I got letter from Moses and May Atwood, Alton, Ill., containing seeds, hop, althea, china aster, and others.

May 19, 1853

Rain threatening again. Yesterday I did a very large washing that I had been putting off for months. The little fawn and the numerous broods of young chickens are a great trouble to me.

Instead of a cow and the certainty of a nurse K. came home with a plan for selling out here and buying a large rancho in the Pajaro. I earnestly hope he may succeed in doing so for I like the idea of a large landed estate and especially in the neighborhood of Bryant and Eleanor. I have made the best of acquaintances here but alas for friends. I shall feel more settled down there.

May 21, 1853

Six visitors from the mission to dinner and tea. In the afternoon most of us turned out blackberrying. The berries we ate for supper with cream and sugar. I got my arms poisoned by the ivy pretty badly. They want me to return the compliment by passing Saturday and Sunday in town but I feel that it would be imprudent to risk the fatigue of horseback riding and as yet we have no buggy.

May 29, 1853

Mr. K. gone again to the Pajaro. I do not like the being left alone. Everything grows very fast though we have showers every week and coolish weather. On the 27th we sent off 40 bags of ripe potatoes and shall continue to dig more largely every week. A sort of caterpiller is making sad work of the potatoes, onions, etc., in most places, especially on the bottom lands near the mission. They cut them off clean at the root. As yet they have done us little damage.

June 15, 1853

All goes well. Two weeks ago we sent up our first ripe potatoes, which brought .10 and .09 cents. Last week more and they brought .08 cents. Five hands are digging ready for tomorrow's steamer. The few debts will be paid and a piece of desirable land for a new tan yard in the "village" bought; a team; also a kitchen and barn put up. I can hardly hope for a buggy and yet without one and with our infant I shall be sadly isolated.

I have read Thackery's "Pendennis" and can see that there is great talent in the book but it does not excite in me the least emotion; does not strengthen or enlighten me in any way. I can see how it may be popular with those who have no interest in progress. The flowers that are blossoming quite cheer me, the great sun flowers, African marigolds, poppies and princes' feathers and the nasturtiums, too. Yellow for some reason always pleases me and in my rides a patch of yellow flowers in a green field rivets my attention till I have quite passed it by.

Besides the chickens, turkeys, dog (Nep), cat and other livestock, K. has just had the present of a couple of English terriers, little cunning things. The female will sit on her haunches and beg. He has such a hearty, boyish love of animals that although I am sometimes inclined to rebel against the size of the family I am reconciled again by a consideration of the beauty of such simple affections.

July 29, 1853

Exactly two weeks after the preceding entry (June 29) my little girl was born. K. had gone to the tan yard and I was expecting Mr. and Mrs. Meader to spend the day. They had been up the coast to try and engage someone and were now to report progress. It was fortunate the Meaders came for there was no woman nearer than the mission and when I should have sent off Tom to fetch Mr. K. I should have been entirely alone.

Mrs. Meader remained until the babe was born and Mrs. Frick, the school master's wife, was persuaded to come and stay with me for a week. She is a conscientious, gentle, thoughtful person with many practical ideas but weakly inefficient and untidy. In ten days she was bound to go home.

There is considerable excitement just now about the discovery of gold at Siant and the Rincon and other places in the neighborhood. It has never been found in sufficient quantities as yet to pay for all the digging but now they say they can get $5 a day and that is fair wages. However, we do not feel at all certain as to the truth of the case.

September 10, 1853

It is some time now since I heard from Byberry and I begin to feel deserted and lonely. Besides our pecuniary affairs are in no flourishing condition. The rapid decline in the price of potatoes made the last two shipments a loss and now the worms, a species of maggot, have got at all the late crop, both in the near and off hollows, and these potatoes will not sell at all and indeed will soon be eaten hollow. The potato crop through the valleys and on the coast is a total failure through this worm. It throws us back so—no ready money and various bills for labor due. These considerations keep me in a state of unrest.

November 5, 1853

The winter rains are delayed. Mr. K. goes to San F. tomorrow to sell leather. Tom Purdy, a nice English lad, has come to live with us. Baby is as well as it is possible for a child to be and has been so for the last two months. She is remarkably strong, especially in the back, and so is very happy in her existence that I quite envy her, wishing I myself were a child and so cared for. She scarcely ever cries and usually smiles gleefully whenever I look at her. She observes much for her age, loves to be out of doors early in the morning when the deer and other animals are about. Dr. McLean has done me a good service in curing the rupture. Ora is indeed the light of the household. Her father takes great pride and pleasure in her.

Mr. K. has some idea of giving up tanning and devoting himself to the raising of pigs, chickens and vegetables, and it would gratify me to have him do so, for I fear his health will fail totally by the severe labor of the yard. If he were to live wholly on the farm he would be constantly improving it in some way; would plant an orchard, make a duck pond and vineyard, build a large barn and finish and improve the house. We should have a fine flower garden and all sorts of conveniences.

A Tale Of
The Redwoods

———— ❧·❧ ————

W e had crossed and recrossed the river many times, now
wading its shallow depths, now springing from bowlder
to bowlder, and taking advantage of the tree-trunks that nearly
spanned it occasionally. It was high noon, and we were at length
glad to stop and rest in a jungle of undergrowth, shaded at this
point by some aromatic laurels. What a wealth of nature! Here
were hazel-bushes; huge ferns; the wide-spreading, elegant leaves
of the wild raspberry; young redwoods of freshest green, springing
so stately from the roots of their fallen elders; clumps of azaleas
in open spots; the polished leaf of the poison-oak, so noticeable for
its rich coloring and graceful outline—these, with hundreds of other
vines and shrubs, made a rare picture for the eye to wander over.

"What a romantic spot for 'love in a cottage!' " remarked the
youngest of our party, pointing from where he lay to a little knoll
that sloped backward from the river far enough to command a
glimpse of the purple mountain. "Come," he urged, "let's take
possession. I will carry all your tiger lilies and that sickly smelling
yerba buena. The air will be cooler up there."

We rose good-naturedly to second his wish, and pushed lazily
through the briar-crossed cattle-trail to the spot indicated. We were
not a little surprised, on reaching it, to find the remains of an old
shanty on our pre-emption; a low chimney, made of mud and
sticks and built outside the dwelling, and some blackened redwood
boards that had made part of the floor, being all that was left to

tell there had been a human habitation. Huge redwood stumps, interspersed between the young forest-trees, showed that the land had been formerly cleared to the river, and, strangely out of place in such a wilderness, two luxuriant rose-bushes stretched their unpruned branches hither and thither; a multiflora scrambled over and hid the remnant of a rough fence, and a La Marque clung for support to a mass of intertwined creepers frail as itself.

"This place," said L——, who now joined us with his empty trout-basket, "was the scene of a tragedy, of a kind only too common in our early history; but my wife can tell you the whole. I only came in just before the curtain dropped."

We begged to hear it, and simultaneously arranged ourselves in a seated circle to listen.

"It begins in the city, and the preface will, I fear, be too long," she objected. That, we insisted, was impossible, as we had two good hours to spare, and the scene would so admirably frame the story.

"It was shortly after our arrival in San Francisco," she began, "that I met the young girl, or young woman, whose life faded out so swiftly in the centre of this solitude. 'On this side,' as we say—that is, after crossing the isthmus—my sister Caroline was taken down with Panama fever, and I was nearly as ill from alarm and fatigue as she from disease. Still, I kept up, and watched and prayed, and we landed in San Francisco alive—not much more. L—— , who at this time was superintendent of the La Salud Mine, hurried down to meet us; but as the doctor declared it would be too serious a risk for Caroline to travel inland, he could only make arrangements for our remaining a month or two, and then hurry back to the situation he had so lately acquired. In order to lessen expenses somewhat (board at the American Hotel, on the Plaza, was $50 a week), it was decided we should go to a lodging-house, where, with such slender appetites, we were able to supply our wants from a restaurant at a much lower figure. You will judge, however, that our condition was anything but enviable, when I tell you that these lodging-rooms covered the entire second floor, the whole lower floor being used for gambling-hells and saloons, in which some sort of music was going on all day, and especially all night. A piano and a tolerable bass voice seemed to be fixtures of the establishment, and were only silent after three in the morning. Two boys with a harp had already reached the city, and did frequent duty below. The first barrel-organ on the coast also found patrons. Occasionally a stabbing affray or a suicide made a slight diversion, when, for a few hours, things would be quieted. Besides all these noises, which came undulled through the thin floors, and the racing of the rats on the cloth ceiling above (which sagged with their weight), the gamblers, whose dining and sleeping-rooms were on this floor, used our passage-way as a sort of parade-ground, and the steady tramp, tramp, tramp, so close to us, made me even more nervous than the music or murders. It was, as I said, a fearful time; among total strangers, dependent on a restaurant, no fire to heat gruel or a bottle of water, dreading the bold stare if you went out, dreading what might happen any moment within. The old doctor was kind, and did all he could; but Caroline showed slight promise of returning health, until after an event which would have killed any other invalid.

"The day had been extremely warm, and we had been obliged to have the door ajar as well as the window open. By some unaccountable oversight, I had forgotten to lock the former on retiring, and, at about one o'clock, I was startled by a loud knocking and a demand for entrance. Fearing that it meant fire (one-third of the city had been burned the week previous), I was out of bed in an instant, but in reply to my inquiries, the man, who now had his hand on the lock and turned it, declared that it was his room, and no one but himself should shut it; he would put a knife into Brown next morning for renting his room over his head. Good heavens! what could I do? I ordered him away peremptorily, but he was just enough under the influence of liquor to be insensible to appeals of any sort. I screamed for help through the crack that I had not strength to close. I shouted to the proprietor of the lodgings, who I knew must be in his chamber opposite. But no one came, and my forces decreased with each moment. Once, with superhuman effort, I closed the door, but before I could turn the key it was open again. Poor Caroline, in her skeleton condition, attempted to rise and come to my help. The more I screamed for assistance, the more exhausted my strength was. I stopped for an instant, when a bright thought flashed before me. I seized it as a drowning man might seize a straw. Gathering up my utmost force, I pushed furiously against the door, and then suddenly let go. Bang! came the villainous intruder, full length and flat on his very prominent nose. The pain must have been severe, for it sobered and restrained him instantly, and, picking himself up with difficulty, he beat an ignominious retreat, while I contemptuously tossed his hat after him. The real climax of the affair was his returning, after I had relocked the door, to say, in an affable tone:

" 'Beg pardon, ladies; I'm a little the worse for liquor, I believe. I'm not so bad a fellow as you imagine.'

"That, by the way, was a pretty fair sample of many apologies I have heard since then from men who, away from the sustaining and purifying influence of good women, in every-day life defied all laws of decency and amenity. 'You think me a rough, bad fellow, because I swear a little at times; but the fact is I have no concealed meanness like lots of other men you meet. I'm a pretty good fellow, now, let me tell you.'

"I gave poor Caroline a heavy dose of whisky, hoping thus to allay the effects of her fright and make sleep possible; then wrapping myself in a shawl, I kept watch the rest of the night. Well, the next morning the proprietor of the rooms came to congratulate me on my success in worsting my drunken visitor.

" 'But if you heard me call, and knew we were in danger, why did you not come and defend us?' I asked, indignantly. 'How could you be so unmanly as to leave two weak women to suffer such a dreadful outrage alone?'

" 'O, I knew you were an awful smart woman, and could just beat him, and another, too, if necessary. I was watching and listening, and I saw you could manage the business. I kept my six-shooter in my hand, ready to fire the moment he had got the better of you. Anyway, the moment I'd appeared he'd have pulled his knife on me, and I'd have been a dead man. It's dangerous interfering where a woman's concerned,' he concluded, shaking his head timidly, as he pictured to himself the fate he had so barely missed.

"My sister slept and slept. Her breathing was deep and regular, and the expression of her face more than usually serene. Now and then I fancied light footsteps paused at the door; but the noises of the busy day soon overpowered the fancy. At noon a gentle tap at the door aroused me from a waking dream, and Caroline opened her eyes with a smile. It was a young woman, in a yellow striped calico, bearing in her hand a small waiter covered with some delicately cooked food—broiled chicken and golden toast—on which Caroline at once cast a longing eye. The girl courtesied: 'Mr. Rush sends his compliments, Miss, and he hopes the other lady is none the worse for the trouble the drunken scoundrel gave you last night. All the gentlemen was mad at him, ma'am;' and she set down the tray close beside the sick one's pillow. Here was a quandary. I objected that we did not know Mr. Rush, that I had no acquaintance with—'such people,' I was going to say; but corrected myself in time, and said, 'those parties below.' The idea of being under an obligation to gamblers! and then, this pretty yellow-haired girl? I had seen her several times before in the same striking dress, now scrubbing the entry, now the dining-room (which I knew belonged to the gamblers), and again I had caught a glimpse of her in an emerald satin dress, presiding at the dinner-table. We had noticed her voice—sweet and strong, though uncultivated—so entirely in harmony with her eager, magnetic, but too girlish face. Caroline had only yesterday observed, 'How *can* she sing so like a bird in such a place as this, and with such a life as hers must be!' and now, here we were, mixed up with all this.

" 'O, please take it, Miss; it'll do you good, and they'll be so dashed if you don't. They're not your kind of gentlemen, ma'am, but they still have a kind feeling for women—ladies, that is.'

" 'Very well. I am extremely obliged to you for your trouble;

and will you give the gentleman' (how the word stuck in my throat!) 'my sister's thanks?'

" 'I will indeed, ma'am, and I'm glad the sick lady relishes it, and may I bring her a snack to-night myself? I have charge of everything the same as it was my own.'

"From this time there was no withstanding her womanly kindness. In the morning she came clothed in the yellow stripes, in the evening in the emerald satin, clasped with a gorgeous pearl brooch, always with some little nicety for Carry, who found in her her best physician. Her odd, vivacious chat at night made her believe she would be well in the morning, and mild meditation on the fresh oddities and crudities of her speech when she brought in the late breakfast took her mind off herself the rest of the day. How *could* there be anything dubious or wrong about such a hearty, unselfish creature? and yet we had avoided her as outside the pale. On her side she grew ever more kind and communicative, and in less than a month we possessed her entire history, together with her half-formed plans for the future.

"The daughter of a small tradesman at Melbourne, she had grown up on much work and little schooling. Always happy, always beloved, she had had many suitors, and at twenty married a man whom she loved passionately and trusted wholly. But her father, her watchful protector, dying shortly after the marriage, everything went wrong. Complaint took the place of praise, censure of thanks. Her English, her singing, her manners, her cheerfulness even, he found fault with, and set himself to subdue. She was wild with misery and disappointment. The baby brought rest and relief, but he was soon taken from her arms, and life was again full of despair. Then he brought her to this country, where in the mines he had fallen a victim in a mining-claim affray. Returning a stranger to San Francisco, she had sought work as a nurse, but that was too confining, and now she was cook, housekeeper, and chambermaid at this gambling establishment.

" 'O, *I* am in no danger, ma'am, from these gamblers. I could take care of myself when I was a mere child. *I* understand how to deal with them, and they understand me, you may be certain. No man ever frightened me but my husband, and where that love went to after we were married, was, and always will be, a mystery to me. O, if you could have seen the look in his eye when he said "it was my *duty* to love him." ' She shivered and her whole aspect changed as she remembered the old tyranny.

" 'But was it advisable for her to risk her good name in the way she was doing? Why not seek other employment?'

"She blushed, and explained that she had a friend. He was with the gamblers, but not of them. Next week he was to be paid for the billiard-tables he had invested his money in, and then they were to be married and go into the country. He was a lumberman and hated the city. She did not think people would concern themselves about the associations of hard-working people, etc.

"Three nights after this, she came, bringing a leather bag, in which was $500, and begged that it might remain with us, as she had a presentiment that it was not safe with Thane (her lover). Next morning, beneath the napkin that covered the breakfast-tray, she brought $500 more. On the following night, a disguised man entered Thane's room, stabbed him in several places, and, after rummaging his trunk, left him bleeding and speechless. Early the following morning, Jane, uneasy and fearing she knew not what, knocked at his door. Hearing only a faint moan, she opened it, and found him weltering in his blood. She at once informed the gamblers, who made a show of looking into the matter, but nothing came of it. Jane at once relinquished her situation as cook and housekeeper, and devoted herself to nursing her lover. He was just pronounced out of danger when L—— came again to the city and brought us down to the ranch, where we have been ever since. A year passed before L—— brought me for the first time to look at these big trees. The horseback ride—the only mode of traveling in those days—had been delightfully exhilarating. We rode round this way, as husband had some business with the mill over there, and I pulled up at this shanty to get a drink and rest awhile before returning. Some marigolds and great double sun-flowers proclaimed the presence of a woman, and a cheery voice was singing within. The door opened, and, to our astonishment, who should appear but Jane Harkness, in the identical yellow striped dress. She stood on no ceremony, but, throwing her arms around me, laughed and cried by turns, exclaiming:

" 'You dear soul! But is it you or a ghost? You have come straight from heaven to see how happy I am.' Then, ensconcing me in the one rocking-chair of the establishment, she went back to where I had left them, and explained how Thane, when sufficiently recovered, had been engaged as top-sawyer by Old G—— of the mill, that they were prospering, and he had already invested what he had in a venture of lumber for Los Angeles. He hoped in a few years to make his pile, and then they would live a little nearer town. Her face, toned down and more sweetly womanly, bore testimony to the value of the life they had led together. After this, we saw each other pretty frequently, considering the distance that divided us. Thane was held to be a thriving, honest business man. He was glad to serve us whenever he could, and the more we saw of him the more we liked him. Sitting by the dam with him once, he told me of his flattering prospects. 'This is the happiest year of my life,' he said, with a wistful backward glance at the shanty; 'God grant that it may continue.'

" 'You are so good to Jane that I am certain it will,' I replied.

"The first rains had laid the dust and made the roads once more pleasant for traveling. The hills were gay in new spring dresses. Every one was hopeful about the market for the abundant crops, only fairly harvested when the rain had appeared. L—— was particularly buoyant because our new house was contained in the schooner-load of potatoes he had just shipped to San Francisco, when, instead of the rainy nights and bright, sunshiny days of the previous winter and the beginning of this, 1852–3 concluded to favor us with an illustration of what in childhood we had pictured to ourselves as a rainy season in the tropics. For three weeks it poured down, with slight variation in degree, day and night. The brooks were swollen to rivers, and the rivers—black, roaring, sullen—spread over wide areas of valley and forest land, carrying off first the scantling and *débris* of the mills, and later logs, lumber, and huge trees, which the flood had torn up by the roots, and at last often the mills themselves. There were no bridges or fences, such as we lost this last winter, to be washed away, and, as the roads were with slight exception merely trails, if one disappeared here or there, you had but to initiate another on either side, as the whole country was before you. I will explain here, that at this period the danger of the southerly winds that bring our rain was not sufficiently appreciated, and within a few weeks, nine schooners went ashore between this point and the city, the one containing our new house among the others. Fortunately no lives were lost, for the little craft were driven so firmly and steadily landward that the small crews and few passengers waded or swam safely to shore. But what I was coming at is, that one of these schooners on her down trip had landed, on the booming surf, as usual, one lady passenger, and very soon a rumor spread through the town that Thane's wife had arrived from the East. His wife! What wife? Had he any other wife than the one who, for love of him, had been willing to turn her back on the high salaries and gayer aspects of a city life, and bury herself in the forests of the Syante? I begged L—— to go at once and learn the truth or falsity of the report, for if it were true, no matter what the condition of the roads or the skies, he must at once go up and fetch Jane to our house. The rumor he found, alas! had truth for a basis; and the legitimate Mrs. Thane, who had come, piloted by the regular installments of money sent by her husband, was at that moment at the tavern, occupied in making close and rigid inquiry respecting her husband. She was, as we afterward knew her, a tall, dark, formal, but by no means unattractive woman, and noticeable principally for the uncompromising willfulness of her mental vision, by which she saw every fact, every character, in a false light, and made all her deductions, interpretations, and plans, from crooked or false premises, and she clung to them with such smiling tenacity, such self-

satisfied positiveness, that to sympathize with her it was first necessary to cast aside all your own past experience and start anew with
herself for guide. For peace, one must yield or fly. But, to return.
Before L—— could give a few orders and saddle his horse, I saw
Thane turn up the lane, his haggard face and bent form giving
him the air of a much older man than he was. He read in my eyes
that I knew all, and followed me without a word into the sitting-
room, where, after closing the door, he sunk into a chair, and,
passing his hand with weary, perplexed air across his brow, he said:

" 'You have heard the news; it's all up with me. I saw her name
in the steamer passenger-list the day before the schooner got in.
Good God! what am I to do? I tell you, Mrs. L——, I never knew
a happy day till I met Jane. But don't think I am here to apologize;
I took the risk and am overtaken by the consequences.'

" 'Was not your wife a good woman?' I asked, anxious to account
for such conduct in a man apparently so honest and unselfish.

" 'She's a thorough good woman, and a great deal smarter than
I am. She had more schooling and knows more about books than
I ever did, or shall. She's very pretty, too, and I fell in love, as
they call it, with that, before I knew how different we were. She
sees everything opposite to the way I do, and I know *now* that
she never loved me, though I am certain also that she loves no
one else. I never had an hour's happiness till I met Jane,' he reiterated.

" 'Then, why don't you offer her some liberal terms, and endeavor to procure a divorce?' I asked; remembering, curiously
enough, Southey's remark in reference to Shelley's affairs, that he
did not see why a man could not love, and be happy with *'any
good woman.'*

" 'I've done that already,' he replied, drearily. 'We'd give her
all, gladly; but she's indignant, and talks in a business way of
setting everything straight again, and forgiving me. You see she
doesn't suffer herself. She's not affectionate like other women.'

" 'I'm forced to tell you, that in my opinion, you've behaved
very dishonorably with both your wife and Jane,' I said.

" 'Naturally, you would feel so'—with the same perplexed motion of the hand. 'I'm only too thankful to have you talk with me at all. I know you'll pity Jane. Poor Jane! *I* shall go to the d——l straight. My principal object in coming to you, though, is to beg you to come up and see Jane. She takes the thing too quiet-like, and I'm afraid. After I had told her all, she shuddered a little, and then fixed her eyes on the stove, and I couldn't get her to answer a word. In fact, she looked as if she didn't understand quite. She loves you so, ma'am, I thought if you'd come up, you could get her to talk. I think the clouds won't gather again till night, and I've got a horse there with a side-saddle.'

"Yes, I would like to go. I would advise with Mr. L——, and go without delay, but I should prefer my own Rosea to another horse. Mr. L—— agreed, and, full of anxious solicitude himself, saw that Rosea was carefully 'sinched' for the slippery hills and swollen creeks.

" 'Bring her back with you, if you can,' he whispered, after lifting me to the saddle. 'Bring her back to live with us, and let the world howl if it will. She's a woman, a good woman, and that's all we need to know.'

"Rosea seemed to appreciate the urgency of the occasion, for he started off at once in a generous lope, which he only left when forced to slide down the deep and slippery gullies. Such fearful climbing and jumping over washed-out places! There was little to be said, so we rode on in silence. Before we were half-way here, the horizon closed in on us, only a little less gloomy than the fast-approaching night. Rosea, however, had a wonderful instinct—only 'give him his head,' as L—— used to say, and he would select on the blackest night the right one out of three divergent trails. So far, we were safe; but before we neared the bowlder hill, the heavy splashing drops converged into continuous streams. Still, Rosea loped and snorted as if the day were before him.

"It was ominous of trouble that, as we approached the shanty, no friendly light glimmered from the window, and no welcome met us at the door. Such alarm did this waken in Thane, that, leaving me to dismount and fasten Rosea myself, in the darkness, he opened the door and called, in tender, anxious tones, as he entered:

" 'Jane, dear! Where are you, darling? Here is dear Mrs. L—— with me.'

"But there was no reply—nothing but an increase of forebodings. I flung the saddle on the sitting-room floor, and went with him to the back door, calling with him:

" 'Jane, dear! Come to us, come.' Just then something flashed past us in the direction of the river; and yet how can I talk of flashing, where there was no light seen! The darkness and the driving rain effectually forbade seeing. It could not be that she was wandering about alone on such a stormy night. It was awe-inspiring just to listen to the surging of the wind through the forest, and the turbulent roar of the floods, which swallowed up in one continuous hoarse booming all lesser sounds. Thane searched for some matches, and with trembling fingers lit a candle. No, it was plain she was in neither of the three little rooms, and the dress she had worn in the morning was hanging over a chair. We gazed at each other in dismay and utter helplessness. Why had we not stopped at Bill Smith's to inquire? Why had we not anticipated some desperate step under such desperate circumstances? The mill was the nearest habitation, but there was no one living there now. It had not been running for a month. Only two days previous the dam gave way, and the banks of the river had altered, as she knew. It would be useless to seek her there. Still, Thane took a lantern, and screening it under his heavy coat, went as near as he could to the mill, still calling, and still hurrying back, hoping to find her here. I had taken a heavy blanket from the bed, and, divesting myself of my wet riding-habit, had wrapped it about me as the best I could do; and at last, overcome by wretchedness and fatigue, I sunk into a heavy slumber, sitting with my head resting on the bed. It must have been nearly one o'clock, when a wild gust blew open the door, and I was intensely awake instantly, shivering as I realized a chill, indefinable horror that filled the room like a living presence. I stood up and shook myself, in the hope of freeing my mind from the death-like sensation. I knew I was alone, yet I had no voice with which to call on Thane, who might, indeed, be miles away. My stiffened limbs refused to sustain me, and the door I would not close if I could remained open. I knew not how long this state of things lasted. It seemed to me an hour at least, when I became aware of Thane's approach. He hesitated on the threshold, a painful apprehension holding him back; then, forcing himself to meet the worst, he stepped toward me with a terrible inquiry in his eyes.

" 'Do you feel it? What is it?' I found tongue to say, and the sound of my voice broke the spell. The horror had vanished, and simultaneously I could hear the rain beating monotonously on the roof, and pouring in gurgling streams from the eaves.

" 'It was *there!*' he said, pointing out into the blackness. The gesture, for some reason, brought vividly before me the dreams I had just left behind me, and whose shadows hung yet around me. I thought we were gliding through the forest in search of our poor friend, guided by the feeble light of a lamp. The waters howled savagely, and drove monstrous trees with a thud against the bank near which we passed. She seemed ever near—nearer; and above the deafening tempest, her voice, clear and bell-like, called to us, 'Come, come. I love you! Dearest, come! I love, love!' Then, when we had arrived at the spot whence the sound had proceeded, it had floated far, far away, and still the liquid, wailing voice entreated, implored: 'I love you! Come, dearest, come!' Then the scene changed. Jane was on the deck of an outward-bound vessel, smiling me a kind farewell. The fastenings were parted, and the ship swept onward with full sun-lit sails, when Jane took from her bosom the pearl pin, Thane's first present to her, and flung it across the waters to me. The distance was too great, and it fell, lost in the waves. When I looked again, no ship was anywhere to be seen, only some gulls screamed beneath the lowering storm.

"Morning broke slowly and gloomily. At my request, Thane gave Rosea some oats, and I made preparation to return home.

My husband would be anxious, I knew, for several reasons, and my remaining longer was of no avail so far as Jane was concerned. Thane made no objection. Had I eaten? Yes, I had found bread in the closet. Listlessly and mechanically he lifted me into the saddle, gave me one glance full of gratitude and despair, and I was on my way, feeling that with each spring of my horse I left farther behind me a weird and awful mystery. I longed to get out of the valley and upon some height, where I could breathe freely and look abroad on the world with healthy eyes. What, then, was my joy as I made the top of Lone Point, to descry L—— ascending the long slope below me. Never did his Mexican *serape* suggest such a rainbow of promise, or his little willful roan, with the cropped ears, seem so human in his relation to me. He also had had his misgivings, and reproached himself for consenting to my leaving home when the storm offered such indefinite prospect of return. But he had another tale than this in his eyes—a gravity which gave unusual gentleness to his manner, and something of purpose, too, for he did not turn his horse's head homeward.

" 'What news, dear? Tell me at once. Are the children well?' I inquired, full of apprehension. Yes, all was right at home; but Jane was dead—drowned—lying that moment beside a mountain of *débris* that blocked the bight of Bill Smith's. He was going to Thane, and I accompanied him. It seemed that Smith, having been disturbed in the night by a visit from Thane, and having casually learned the news of the day before, rose early to reconnoitre, and with a sailor's instinct directed his steps to that point where the bed of the river was narrowed by advancing, precipitous, rocky banks, and where, as it happened, large quantities of floating logs were continually being piled up, and as regularly flooded off when a slight increase of current dislodged the clumsy dam. At first, struck with wonder at sight of the massive confusion, made up of logs, planks, fence-rails, and trees, that were jammed into the narrow pass, he overlooked the object of his search. Presently, however, while observing on the top the green straggling branches of a madroña, with its bright red bark, he detected a bit of floating drapery, and without stopping to calculate closely the possible danger, climbed cautiously and swiftly to the top of the treacherous pile. There, hidden, sheltered apparently, beneath the cheerful evergreen foliage, but in reality dress and hair entangled in the *débris,* and one poor hand pitilessly crushed—there lay kind-hearted Jane; the emerald satin dress still contrasting happily with the fair, deathly fair complexion and yellow hair, and the pearl pin— emblem of purity—gleaming at her throat. There was no time for reflection. Immediate action was called for, since at any moment the mass might break up. A rope to secure her was the first thought, as it was evident that to extricate her would be no easy task. The clothing was pinched tight in the gripe of two solid logs, and the hair was interwoven in the rough fibre of the loose bark. It was while returning with the rope he had so opportunely discovered L——, and together they consulted while making the best of their way to the stream. It was not safe for both to leave the bank, so L—— took the rope and clambered up, and having secured it to the body, tossed the other end to Bill. Then he quickly cut the clothing loose with his knife, and partly cut and partly freed the hair, when the two lifted her down reverently from the funeral pile to the bank, and then as far as might be concealed the damage and defacement of person and clothing.

" 'Poor creeter!' said Bill, when they had thus disposed of their burden. 'Poor creeeter! She never knowed such a trouble as this was afore her. I've heerd them mill-men tell a sight about her, how spry she was, and how one while, as she boarded the hands, she cooked their vittles as purtickelar as if they were rich folks. They allus said there warn't no woman in these parts as good as Mrs. Thane, and now it seems as she aint no Mrs. Thane at all. It beats all natur' what a world this is!'

"When Thane sat down on the wet ground beside the body of the woman he had loved well but not wisely, and took up some of the damp hair and laid it against his cheek, his appearance was nearly as death-like as hers. They had covered the crushed hand with the dress, but he drew it out, and the sickening, pitiful spectacle filled him with anguish he did not attempt to conceal. I was glad to see the tears flow, and to hear him sob and groan aloud in all the *abandon* of grief. Then a rough litter was constructed, and they carried her to the dwelling from which, with wild despair, she had fled but a few hours before. A funeral was arranged for immediately, and as no minister could be procured (the river being unsafe for fording, and the only boat carried out to sea) L——offered to read the Odd Fellows' funeral service, which was gladly acceded to. I would remain. (How fortunate it was that our ranch was this side of the river, and there was an effectual separation for the time between Thane and his wife.) A plain coffin was procured, and on the following morning, amid torrents of rain and in the presence of half-a-dozen men and one woman (myself), the earthly garment that had been so violently rent was laid away on the hillside yonder. Sincere sorrow was felt by the few who remembered how she had lightened their rough labor by her cheerful presence, and how no one had ever sought her sympathy or assistance in vain. The last shovelful of earth filled in, Thane returned to the cabin, and proceeded to lock up in an old carpenter's-chest what remained of her wardrobe, which he begged I would take charge of for awhile at least. I wanted that the much-treasured pearl pin should be buried with her, but Thane insisted that I must keep it in memory of one who so loved me; and here it is now," she continued, taking the elegant brooch from her dress to pass around for our inspection.

"Thane never returned to the cabin. He sold out his interest in the lumberyard, and, as soon as the storm abated and vessels were running, he left with his wife for San Francisco, and thence to Los Angeles. However, he did not live long. Two years afterward he died of consumption, brought on, I've no doubt, by the exposure of that fearful night, and encouraged by his inevitable remorse.

"His wife, who managed the little property with decision and skill, afterward married Haleton, the lawyer who won the big cinnabar case, and she was greatly instrumental, I heard, in securing her husband's election to the State Senate. She made quite a prominent figure at the capital in '57.

"I was talking the other day with one of the old mill-hands, now a wealthy stock-raiser, about those early times; especially of poor Jane, and the remarkable discrepancy between Mrs. Thane and her quiet, unambitious husband.

" 'Well, I've always held it a mystery,' he concluded, 'what that stylish, high-talking woman wanted with our top-sawyer.' "

The shadows were lengthening as Mrs. L—— closed her sad tale, and the heat had given place to an agreeable coolness. The smoky blue atmosphere of the forest had deepened to a dusky purple, when, single file, at a funeral pace, we moved off, turning our backs on the monumental rose-bushes, and sought our original camping-ground, where the happy faces of the children, shouting still at each new delight, gave us to ourselves again.

*Ina Coolbrith (1841–1928), photograph circa
1863. Courtesy of the Oakland Public Library,
Oakland History Room.*

Ina Coolbrith (1841–1928)

Somewhat mysterious in her lifetime, often said to be romantically aligned with male writers of the time—Mark Twain, Bret Harte, Charles Warren Stoddard, Joaquin Miller—Ina Coolbrith was an alluring and private woman. As was discovered upon her death in 1928, she had reason to be protective of her past, knowing that the respect she enjoyed in the Bay Area could be swept away by the misinterpretation of local gossips.

She was born Josephine Smith, the last of three daughters of Agnes Coolbrith Smith and Don Carlos Smith, brother of the Mormon leader Joseph Smith. Born four months before her father's death and five months before the death of her sister, Josephine Smith was still an infant when her mother, fleeing the Mormon Church and polygamy, married William Pickett, a St. Louis printer. The Picketts added twin sons to their family, and in 1851 they migrated over the Rockies to California.

Once settled in Los Angeles, Josephine Smith began to write poetry, inspired by Shakespeare and Lord Byron, whose works came across the prairie with the Picketts. Soon her poems were being published in local newspapers.

Exceptionally pretty, vivacious and popular, and driven by youthful passion, Josephine Smith married Robert Carsely in April 1858. Carsely was an established iron worker and part-time actor. But just two years later, amid rumors that Carsely was abusive, the marriage failed—though not quietly. In the end there was an altercation between Josephine's stepfather and Carsely. The irate young husband suffered a mutilating bullet wound to the hand, which was later amputated. A sensational divorce trial ensued, ending in dissolution of the marriage in December 1861. Young Josephine went into a deep depression, withdrawing for a year, and then moved to San Francisco. Later, she published "A Mother's Grief," but it was only at her death, when her personal papers were catalogued, that it was ascertained that the poem was a eulogy to an infant son who had died during the disastrous time in Los Angeles.

San Francisco was good to Josephine Smith Carsely, who upon arrival immediately changed her name to Ina Coolbrith. By the mid-sixties, now a slender, graceful woman with a serious mien, she was well known as one of the Golden Gate Trinity. This trio's exclusive membership consisted of the most highly visible and sought-after California writers of the period—Bret Harte, Charles Warren Stoddard, and Coolbrith.

Coolbrith's poems were printed in the *Overland Monthly,* the *Golden Era,* the *Californian*—literally all over the Bay Area—and reprinted in Eastern magazines as well. She drew praise from James Greenleaf Whittier, William Dean Howells and others for her refined classic verse. She was as beautiful as she was talented, with large dark eyes, a smooth olive complexion, and long bouncy dark curls, and was linked romantically with literary figures and businessmen alike. Perhaps because she was afraid to repeat the past, she abstained from any relationship that might become permanent.

When the frontier literary period in California began to wane after 1869, Mark Twain, Bret Harte, Joaquin Miller, Charles Warren Stoddard and others left for New York and Europe. Ina Coolbrith did not go, though she had offers from Eastern and San Francisco publishers for travel poetry from Europe. Ina believed she was obligated to stay in the Bay Area and support a rather large family: her mother, a niece and nephew left orphaned by the death of her sister, and a young half-Indian girl named Calle Shasta—Joaquin Miller's daughter, left on Ina's doorstep one night as Miller left town. Coolbrith regretted she could not move toward the expansive literary career offered her outside California, but she had always possessed strong convictions and a solid sense of right and wrong, and felt she could not leave those who depended on her.

In September of 1873 Coolbrith was named librarian for the Oakland Free Library, with a respectable monthly salary of $80. The new position left her little time to write, but she was content to be around books and book lovers, and as librarian for two decades she inspired many talented Californians, such as Jack London and Isadora Duncan. But, in 1892 the library board discharged Coolbrith with only three days' notice and without any pension or compensation, after nearly twenty years of service, reportedly for admitting to the press that the library building was in need of repair, which it was. The discharge was a blow, personally and financially, and Coolbrith struggled the rest of her life to meet her financial needs. On at least two occasions she was helped by the Bohemian Club, which voted her an honorary member—the only woman in their group—and set up a small stipend that helped ease her financial worries.

In "retirement" Ina Coolbrith wrote poetry and organized local literary groups—the California Literature Society and the Women's Press Association among them. For the Pan Pacific Exposition held in San Francisco in 1915, she was president of the Congress of Authors, and was also honored as California's first Poet Laureate, the first named in the nation. She shared the stage with her longtime friend and fellow writer, Josephine Clifford McCrackin, and together they reminisced about the 1860s and the *Overland Monthly* office.

The poems included here represent her early work, written in San Francisco. "The Mother's Grief" appeared first in the *Californian* in 1865; "Mariposa Lily" in *A Christmas Greeting* in 1885; and "A Memory" in *Scribners* in 1895. She was strongly influenced by her early experiences in life, and an intense, lifelong connection with nature, which it seems was a healing force for her. Her poetic themes—nature, a rather existential philosophy, and personal autonomy—resound with these influences. Her form is traditional and unerring, her metaphor clear, her tone controlled. Her later poetry is more ironic and pessimistic, but generally also more revealing of its author.

Ina Coolbrith died February 29, 1928 at her home in Berkeley, California. As evidence of her years and her artistic talent, she left eight volumes of poetry, including *Songs from the Golden Gate, The Singer of the Sea,* and a posthumous collection called *Wings of Sunset.*

THE MOTHER'S GRIEF

— ❧·❧ —

So fair the sun rose yester-morn,
  The mountain cliffs adorning;
The golden tassels of the corn
  Danced in the breath of morning;
The cool, clear stream that runs before,
  Such happy words was saying,
And in the open cottage door
  My pretty babe was playing.
Aslant the sill a sunbeam lay:
  I laughed in careless pleasure,
To see his little hand essay
  To grasp the shining treasure.

To-day no shafts of golden flame
  Across the sill are lying;
To-day I call my baby's name,
  And hear no lisped replying;
To-day—ah, baby mine, to-day—
  God holds thee in His keeping!
And yet I weep, as one pale ray
  Breaks in upon thy sleeping—
I weep to see its shining bands
  Reach, with a fond endeavor,
To where the little restless hands
  Are crossed in rest forever!

THE MARIPOSA LILY

— ❧·❦ —

Insect or blossom? Fragile, fairy thing,
Poised upon slender tip, and quivering
  To flight! a flower of the fields of air;
  A jeweled moth; a butterfly, with rare
And tender tints upon his downy wing
  A moment resting in our happy sight;
  A flower held captive by a thread so slight
Its petal-wings of broidered gossamer
Are, light as the wind, with every wind astir,—
  Wafting sweet odor, faint and exquisite.
O dainty nursling of the field and sky,
  What fairer thing looks up to heaven's blue
  And drinks the noontide sun, the dawning's dew?
Thou winged bloom! thou blossom-butterfly!

A Memory

— ❧·❦ —

Through rifts of cloud the moon's soft silver slips;
  A little rain has fallen with the night,
Which from the emerald under-sky still drips
  Where the magnolias open, broad and white.

So near my window I might reach my hand
  And touch these milky stars, that to and fro
Wave, odorous. . . . Yet 't was in another land—
  How long ago, my love, how long ago!

Mary Hallock Foote (1847–1938)

From the moment Mary Hallock Foote arrived in California in 1876, she was captivated by the landscape—both physical and social—and she made it her goal to articulate the "real West" as only a resident could. A talented illustrator and a prolific writer, she expressed the energy, beauty and drama of the new western states in both media.

Foote was born in 1847 in Milton, New York. She was the daughter of Quakers who were intent upon educating her in the ideals of the Society of Friends. Her father read congressional debates and newspaper editorials to his children regularly, while offering them free access to his impressive personal library. Foote counted Free Soil Republicans and abolitionists like Susan B. Anthony and Ernestine L. Rose among the regular visitors to her childhood home.

As a young woman, Mary Hallock Foote attended the Poughkeepsie Female Collegiate Seminary. Later she attended the Cooper Union Institute School of Design in New York City, where she developed her skills as an illustrator, securing commissions to illustrate some of Longfellow's poems and some editions of *Harper's Weekly*. It was also at Cooper Union that she discovered her fondness for language and literature, mainly through the influence of friends Helena De Kay and Emma Beach.

When Mary met Emma's first cousin, Arthur De Wint Foote, he was a young civil engineer at Tehachapi Pass in California. A contrast to the literati with whom Mary was associating, Arthur, although a Bostonian, was an outdoorsman, more noble than refined, and hopelessly in love with the new West.

Shortly after their meeting Arthur returned to the West, carrying on a courtship by mail. They married in 1876, in Mary's home town of Milton. Late that summer she was on a train to California, noting that "no girl ever wanted less to 'go West' with any man, or paid a man a greater compliment by doing so." But once she arrived in California, she was moved by the countryside and its people and quickly realized the literary and illustrative possibilities. In 1878 she had two articles published in *Scribner's Monthly,* only months after the birth of her first child, Arthur Burling Foote. Arthur Jr. was later joined by two sisters, Agnes and Betty.

Mary Hallock Foote (1847–1938), photograph taken May 29, 1921.
Courtesy of the California Historical Society, San Francisco. FN-16661.

During the years when the children were born, and for several years that followed, the family moved many times: to Leadville, Colorado; to the Michoacán province of Mexico; to Boise, Idaho; and twice back to Milton. These were years of heartbreak, failure and discouragement, and finally they moved back to California and settled in Grass Valley in 1895. All the while, Mary was writing novels, short stories and articles, and drawing the landscapes as she adopted them one by one. In Leadville she met Helen Hunt Jackson and Clarence King, and their enthusiasm for literature buoyed her own. In all, before 1920 she completed twelve novels, four collections of short stories, and a collection of splendid illustrations which detail the unique panorama of the early American West.

Throughout her early adult years, Mary Foote kept life notes that she called her "Reminiscences," but these notes stopped abruptly in 1904 with the death of her daughter Agnes. Ten years later Arthur retired and their son took his place as manager of the North Star Mine. Their daughter Betty lived with them during their last years. Arthur died in 1934 at 84 and Mary Hallock Foote died in 1938 at 91.

In much of her work, Foote contrasted East with West in a narrative voice that elucidated her own female point of view. She saw the West as a "genesis, a formless record of beginnings, tragic, grotesque, sorrowful, unrelated, except as illustrations of a tendency towards confusion and failure, with contrasting lights of character, and high personal achievement." Her two final novels, *Edith Bonham* and *The Ground-Swell* are hailed as her best, but some of her earlier novels and stories more clearly articulate images of pioneer California—especially as experienced by women. As time went on, Foote lamented the decline of women's western literature as a viable genre, saying "so completely has my vogue passed away."

The piece included in this collection, "In Exile," first appeared in *The Last Assembly Ball and the Fate of a Voice,* published by Houghton Mifflin in 1889.

IN EXILE

I.

Nicky Dyer and the schoolmistress sat upon the slope of a hill, one of a low range overlooking an arid Californian valley. These sunburnt slopes were traversed by many narrow footpaths, descending, ascending, winding among the tangle of poison-oak and wild-rose bushes, leading from the miners' cabins to the shaft-houses and tunnels of the mine which gave to the hills their only importance. Nicky was a stout Cornish lad of thirteen, with large light eyes that seemed mildly to protest against the sportive relation which a broad, freckled, turned-up nose bore to the rest of his countenance; he was doing nothing in particular, and did it as if he were used to it. The schoolmistress sat with her skirts tucked round her ankles, the heels of her stout little boots driven well into the dry, gritty soil. There was in her attitude the tension of some slight habitual strain—perhaps of endurance—as she leaned forward, her arms stretched straight before her, with her delicate fingers interlocked. Whatever may be the type of Californian young womanhood, it was not her type; you felt, looking at her cool, clear tints and slight, straight outlines, that she had winter in her blood.

She was gazing down into the valley, as one looks at a landscape who has not yet mastered all its changes of expression; its details were blurred in the hot, dusty glare; the mountains opposite had faded to a flat outline against the indomitable sky. A light wind blew up the slope, flickering the pale leaves of a manzanita, whose burnished, cinnamon-colored stems glowed in the sun. As the breeze strengthened, the young girl stood up, lifting her arms, to welcome its coolness on her bare wrists.

"Nicky, why do the trees in that hollow between the hills look so green?"

"There'll be water over there, miss; that's the Chilano's spring. I'm thinkin' the old cow might 'a' strayed over that way somewheres; they mostly goes for the water, wherever it is."

"Is it running water, Nicky—not water in a tank?"

"Why, no, miss; it cooms right out o' the rock as pretty as iver you saw! I often goes there myself for a drink, cos it tastes sort o' different, coomin' out o' the ground like. We wos used to that kind o' water at 'ome."

"Let us go, Nicky," said the girl. "I should like to taste that water, too. Do we cross the hill first, or is there a shorter way?"

"Over the 'ill's the shortest, miss. It's a bit of a ways, but you've been longer ways nor they for less at th' end on 't."

They "tacked" down the steepest part of the hill, and waded through a shady hollow, where ferns grew rank and tall,—crisp, faded ferns, with an aromatic odor which escaped by the friction of their garments, like the perfume of warmed amber. They reached at length the green trees, a clump of young cottonwoods at the entrance to a narrow cañon, and followed the dry bed of a stream for some distance, until water began to show among the stones. The principal outlet of the spring was on a small plantation at the head of the cañon, rented of the "company" by a Chilian, or "the Chilano," as he was called; he was not at all a pastoral-looking personage, but, with the aid of his good water, he earned a moderately respectable living by supplying the neighboring cabins and the miners' boarding-house with green vegetables. After a temporary disappearance, as if to purge its memory of the Chilano's water-buckets, the spring again revealed itself in a thin, clear trickle down the hollowed surface of a rock which closed the narrow passage of the cañon. Young sycamores and cottonwoods shut out the sun above; their tangled roots, interlaced with vines still green and growing, trailed over the edge of the rock, where a mass of earth had fallen; green moss lined the hollows of the rock, and water-plants grew in the dark pools below.

The strollers had left behind them the heat and glare; only the breeze followed them into this green stillness, stirring the boughs overhead and scattering spots of sunlight over the wet stones. Nicky, after enjoying for a few moments the schoolmistress' surprised delight, proposed that she should wait for him at the spring, while he went "down along" in search of his cow. Nicky was not without a certain awe of the schoolmistress, as a part of creation he had not fathomed in all its bearings; but when they rambled on the hills together, he found himself less uneasily conscious of her personality, and more comfortably aware of the fact that, after all, she was "nothin' but a woman." He was a trifle disappointed that she showed no uneasiness at being left alone, but consoled himself by the reflection that she was "a good un to 'old 'er tongue," and probably felt more than she expressed.

The schoolmistress did not look in the least disconsolate after Nicky's departure. She gazed about her very contentedly for a while, and then prepared to help herself to a drink of water. She hollowed her two hands into a cup, and waited for it to fill, stooping below the rock, her lifted skirt held against her side by one elbow, while she watched with a childish eagerness the water trickle into her pink palms. Miss Frances Newell had never looked prettier in her life. A pretty girl is always prettier in the open air, with her head uncovered. Her cheeks were red; the sun just touched the roughened braids of dark brown hair, and intensified the glow of a little ear which showed beneath. She stooped to drink; but Miss Frances was destined never to taste that virgin cup of water. There was a trampling among the bushes, overhead; a little shower of dust and pebbles pattered down upon her bent head, soiling the water. She let her hands fall as she looked up, with a startled "Oh!"

A pair of large boots were rapidly making their way down the bank, and the cause of all this disturbance stood before her—a young man in a canvas jacket, with a leathern case slung across his shoulder, and a small tin lamp fastened in front of the hat which he took off while he apologized to the girl for his intrusion.

"Miss Newell! Forgive me for dropping down on you like a thousand of brick! You've found the spring, I see."

Miss Frances stood with her elbows still pressed to her sides, though her skirt had slipped down into the water, her wet palms helplessly extended. "I was getting a drink," she said, searching with the tips of her fingers among the folds of her dress for a handkerchief. "You came just in time to remind me of the slip between the cup and the lip."

"I'm very sorry, but there is plenty of water left. I came for some myself. Let me help you." He took from one of the many pockets stitched into the breast and sides of his jacket a covered flask, detached the cup, and, after carefully rinsing, filled and handed it to the girl. "I hope it doesn't taste of 'store claret;' the water underground is just a shade worse that that exalted vintage."

"It is delicious, thank you, and it doesn't taste in the least of claret. Have you just come out of the mine?"

"Yes. It is measuring-up day. I've been toddling through the drifts and sliding down chiflons"—he looked ruefully at the backs of his trousers legs—"ever since seven o'clock this morning. Haven't had time to eat any luncheon yet, you see." He took from another pocket a small package folded in a coarse napkin. "I came here to satisfy the pangs of hunger and enjoy the beauties of nature at the same time—such nature as we have here. Will you excuse me, Miss Newell? I'll promise to eat very fast."

"I'll excuse you if you will not ask me to eat with you."

"Oh, I've entirely too much consideration for myself to think of such a thing; there isn't enough for two."

He seated himself, with a little sigh, and opened the napkin on the ground before him. Miss Newell stood leaning against a rock on the opposite side of the brook, regarding the young man with a shy and smiling curiosity. "Meals," he continued, "are a reckless tribute to the weakness of the flesh we all engage in three times a day at the boarding-house; a man must eat, you know, if he expects to live. Have you ever tried any of Mrs. Bondy's fare, Miss Newell?"

"I'm sure Mrs. Bondy tries to have everything very nice," the young girl replied, with some embarrassment.

"Of course she does; she is a very good old girl. I think a great deal of Mrs. Bondy; but when she asks me if I have enjoyed my dinner, I always make a point of telling her the truth; she respects me for it. This is her idea of sponge cake, you see." He held up admiringly a damp slab of some compact pale-yellow substance, with crumbs of bread adhering to one side. "It is a little mashed, but otherwise a fair specimen."

Miss Frances laughed. "Mr. Arnold, I think you are too bad. How can she help it, with those dreadful Chinamen? But I would really advise you not to eat that cake; it doesn't look wholesome."

"Oh, as to that, I've never observed any difference; one thing is about as wholesome as another. Did you ever eat bacon fried by China Sam? The sandwiches were made of that. You see I still live." The sponge cake was rapidly disappearing. "Miss Newell, you look at me as if I were making away with myself, instead of the cake—will you appear at the inquest?"

"No, I will not testify to anything so unromantic; besides, it might be inconvenient for Mrs. Bondy's cook." She put on her hat, and stepped along the stones towards the entrance to the glen.

"You are not going to refuse me the last offices?"

"I am going to look for Nicky Dyer. He came with me to show me the spring, and now he has gone to hunt for his cow."

"And you are going to hunt for him? I hope you won't try it, Miss Frances: a boy on the track of a cow is a very uncertain object in life. Let me call him, if you really must have him."

"Oh, don't trouble yourself. I suppose he will come after a while. I said I would wait for him here."

"Then permit me to say that I think you had better do as you promised."

Miss Frances recrossed the stones, and seated herself, with a faint deprecatory smile.

"I hope you don't mind if I stay," Arnold said, moving some loose stones to make her seat more comfortable. "You have the prior right to-day, but this is an old haunt of mine. I feel as if I were doing the honors; and to tell you the truth, I am rather used up. The new workings are very hot and the drifts are low. It's a combination of steam-bath and hoeing corn."

The girl's face cleared, as she looked at him. His thin cheek was pale under the tan, and where his hat was pushed back the hair clung in damp points to his forehead and temples.

"I should be very sorry to drive you away," she said. "I thought you looked tired. If you want to go to sleep, or anything, I will promise to be very quiet."

Arnold laughed. "Oh, I'm not such an utter wreck; but I'm glad you can be very quiet. I was afraid you might be a little uproarious at times, you know."

The girl gave a sudden shy laugh. It was really a giggle, but a very sweet, girlish giggle. It called up a look of keen pleasure to Arnold's face.

"Now I call this decidedly gay," he remarked, stretching out his long legs slowly, and leaning against a slanting rock, with one arm behind his head. "Miss Frances, will you be good enough to tell me that my face isn't dirty?"

"Truth compels me to admit that you have one little daub over your left eyebrow."

"Thank you," said Arnold, rubbing it languidly with his handkerchief. His hat had dropped off, and he did not replace it; he did not look at the girl, but let his eyes rest on the thread of falling water that gleamed from the spring. Miss Frances, regarding him with some timidity, thought: How much younger he looks without his hat! He had that sensitive fairness which in itself gives a look of youth and purity; the sternness of his face lay in the curves which showed under his mustache, and in the silent, dominant eye.

"You've no idea how good it sounds to a lonely fellow like me," he said, "to hear a girl's laugh."

"But there are a great many women here," Miss Frances observed.

"Oh yes, there are women everywhere, such as they are; but it takes a nice girl, a lady, to laugh!"

"I don't agree with you at all," replied Miss Frances coldly. "Some of those Mexican women have the sweetest voices, speaking or laughing, that I have ever heard; and the Cornish women, too, have very fresh, pure voices. I often listen to them in the evening when I sit alone in my room. Their voices sound so happy"—

"Well, then it is the home accent—or I'm prejudiced. Don't laugh again, please, Miss Frances; it breaks me all up." He moved his head a little, and looked across at the girl to assure himself that her silence did not mean disapproval. "I admit," he went on, "that I like our Eastern girls. I know you are from the East, Miss Newell."

"I am from what I used to think East," she said smiling. "But everything is East here; people from Indiana and Wisconsin say they are from the East."

"Ah, but you are from our old Atlantic coast. I was sure of it when I first saw you. If you will pardon me, I knew it by your way of dressing."

The young girl flushed with pleasure; then, with a reflective air: "I confess myself, since you speak of clothes, to a feeling of relief when I saw your hat the first Sunday after I came. Western men wear such dreadful hats."

"Good!" he cried gayly. "You mean my hat that I *call* a hat." He reached for the one behind his head, and spun it lightly upward, where it settled on a projecting branch. "I respect that hat myself,— my *other* hat, I mean; I'm trying to live up to it. Now, let me guess your State, Miss Newell: is it Massachusetts?"

"No—Connecticut; but at this distance it seems like the same thing."

"Oh, pardon me, there are very decided differences. I'm from Massachusetts myself. Perhaps the points of difference show more in the women—the ones who stay at home, I mean, and become more local and idiomatic than the men. You are not one of the daughters of the soil, Miss Newell."

She looked pained as she said, "I wish I were; but there is not room for us all, where there is so little soil."

Arnold moved uneasily, extracted a stone from under the small of his back and tossed it out of sight with some vehemence. "You think it goes rather hard with women who are uprooted, then," he said. "I suppose it is something a roving man can hardly conceive of—a woman's attachment to places, and objects, and associations; they are like cats."

Miss Newell was silent.

Arnold moved restlessly; then began again, with his eyes still on the trickle of water: "Miss Newell, do you remember a poem—I think it is Bryant's—called 'The Hunter of the Prairies'? It's no disgrace not to remember it, and it may not be Bryant's."

"I remember seeing it, but I never read it. I always skipped those Western things."

Arnold gave a short laugh, and said, "Well, you are punished, you see, by going West yourself to hear me repeat it to you. I think I can give you the idea in the Hunter's own words:

" 'Here, with my rifle and my steed,
    And her who left the world for me—' "

The sound of his own voice in the stillness of the little glen, and a look of surprise in the young girl's quiet eyes, brought a sudden access of color to Arnold's face. "Hm-m-m," he murmured to himself, "it's queer how rhymes slip away. Well, the last line ends in *free*. You see, it is a man's idea of happiness—a young man's. Now, how do you suppose *she* liked it—the girl, you know, who left the world, and all that? Did you ever happen to see a poem or a story, written by a woman, celebrating the joys of a solitary existence with the man of her heart?"

"I suppose that many a woman has tried it," Miss Newell said evasively, "but I'm sure she"—

"Never lived to tell the tale?" cried Arnold.

"She probably had something else to do, while the hunter was riding around with his gun," Miss Frances continued.

"Well, give her the odds of the rifle and the steed; give the man some commonplace employment to take the swagger out of him; let him come home reasonably tired and cross at night,—do you suppose he would find the 'kind' eyes and the 'smile'? I forgot to tell you that the Hunter of the Prairies is always welcomed by a smile at night."

"He must have been an uncommonly fortunate man," she said.

"Of course, he was; but the question is: Could any living man be so fortunate? Come, Miss Frances, don't prevaricate!"

"Well, am I speaking for the average woman?"

"Oh, not at all—you are speaking for the very nicest of women; any other kind would be intolerable on a prairie."

"I should think, if she were very healthy," said Miss Newell, hesitating between mischief and shyness, "and not too imaginative, and of a cheerful disposition; and if he, the hunter, were above the average—supposing that she cared for him in the beginning—I should think the smile might last a year or two."

"Heavens, what a cynic you are! I feel like a mere daub of sentiment beside you. There have been moments, do you know, even in this benighted mining camp, when I have believed in that hunter and his smile!"

He got up suddenly, and stood against the rock, facing her. Although he kept his cool, bantering tone, his breathing had quickened, and his eyes looked darker. "You may consider me a representative man, if you please: I speak for hundreds of us scattered about in mining camps and on cattle ranches, in lighthouses and frontier farms and military posts, and all the God-forsaken holes you can conceive of, where men are trying to earn a living, or lose one—we are all going to the dogs for the want of that smile! What is to become of us if the women whose smiles we care for cannot support life in the places where we have to live? Come, Miss Frances, can't you make that smile last at least two years?" He gathered a handful of dry leaves from a broken branch above his head and crushed them in his long hands, sifting the yellow dust upon the water below.

"The places you speak of are very different," the girl answered, with a shade of uneasiness in her manner. "A mining camp is anything but a solitude, and a military post may be very gay."

"Oh, the principle is the same. It is the absolute giving up of everything. You know most women require a background of family and friends and congenial surroundings; the question is whether *any* woman can do without them."

The young girl moved in a constrained way, and flushed as she said, "It must always be an experiment, I suppose, and its success would depend, as I said before, on the woman and on the man."

"An 'experiment' is good!" said Arnold, rather savagely. "I see you won't say anything you can't swear to."

"I really do not see that I am called upon to say anything on the subject at all!" said the girl, rising and looking at him across the brook with indignant eyes and a hot glow on her cheek.

He did not appear to notice her annoyance.

"You are, because you know something about it, and most women don't: your testimony is worth something. How long have you been here—a year? I wonder how it seems to a woman to live in a place like this a year! I hate it all, you know—I've seen so much of it. But is there really any beauty here? I suppose beauty, and all that sort of thing, is partly within us, isn't it—at least, that's what the goody little poems tell us."

"I think it is very beautiful here," said Miss Frances, softening, as he laid aside his strained manner, and spoke more quietly. "It is the kind of place a happy woman might be very happy in; but if she were sad—or—disappointed"—

"Well?" said Arnold, pulling at his mustache, and fixing a rather gloomy gaze upon her.

"She would die of it! I really do not think there would be any hope for her in a place like this."

"But if she were happy, as you say," persisted the young man, "don't you think her woman's adaptability and quick imagination would help her immensely? She wouldn't see what I, for instance, know to be ugly and coarse; her very ignorance of the world would help her."

There was a vague, pleading look in his eyes. "Arrange it to suit yourself," she said. "Only, I can assure you, if anything should happen to her, it will be the—the hunter's fault."

"All right," said he, rousing himself. "That hunter, if I know him, is a man who is used to taking risks! Where are you going?"

"I thought I heard Nicky."

They were both silent, and as they listened, footsteps, with a tinkling accompaniment, crackled among the bushes below the cañon. Miss Newell turned towards the spring again. "I want one more drink before I go," she said.

Arnold followed her. "Let us drink to our return. Let this be our fountain of Trevi."

"Oh, no," said Miss Frances. "Don't you remember what your favorite Bryant says about bringing the 'faded fancies of an elder world' into these 'virgin solitudes?' "

"Faded fancies!" cried Arnold. "Do you call that a faded fancy? It is as fresh and graceful as youth itself, and as natural. I should have thought of it myself, if there had been no fountain of Trevi."

"Do you think so?" smiled the girl. "Then imagination, it would seem, is not entirely confined to homesick women."

"Come, fill the cup, Miss Frances! Nicky is almost here."

The girl held her hands beneath the trickle again, until they were brimming with the clear sweet water.

"Drink first," said Arnold.

"I'm not sure that I want to return," she replied, smiling, with her eyes on the space of sky between the treetops.

"Nonsense—you must be morbid. Drink, drink!"

"Drink yourself; the water is all running away!"

He bent his head, and took a vigorous sip of the water, holding his hands beneath hers, inclosing the small cup in the larger one. The small cup trembled a little. He was laughing and wiping his mustache, when Nicky appeared; and Miss Frances, suddenly brightening and recovering her freedom of movement, exclaimed, "Why, Nicky! You have been *forever!* We must go at once, Mr. Anold; so good-by! I hope"—

She did not say what she hoped, and Arnold, after looking at her with an interrogative smile a moment, caught his hat from the branch overhead, and made her a great flourishing bow with it in his hand.

He did not follow her, pushing her way through the swaying, rustling ferns, but he watched her light figure out of sight. "What an extraordinary ass I've been making of myself!" He confided this remark to the stillness of the little cañon, and then, with long strides, took his way over the hills in an opposite direction.

It was the middle of July when this little episode of the spring occurred. The summer had reached its climax. The dust did not grow perceptibly deeper, nor the fields browner, during the long brazen weeks that followed; one only wearied of it all, more and more.

So thought Miss Newell, at least. It was her second summer in California, and the phenomenon of the dry season was not so impressive on its repetition. She had been surprised to observe how very brief had been the charm of strangeness, in her experience of life in a new country. She began to wonder if a girl, born and brought up among the hills of Connecticut, could have the seeds of *ennui* subtly distributed through her frame, to reach a sudden development in the heat of a Californian summer. She longed for the rains to begin, that in their violence and the sound of the wind she might gain a sense of life in action by which to eke out her dull and expressionless days. She was, as Nicky Dyer had said, "a good un to 'old 'er tongue," and therein lay her greatest strength as well as her greatest danger.

Miss Newell boarded at Captain Dyer's. The prosperous ex-mining captain was a good deal nearer to the primitive type than any man Miss Newell had ever sat at table with in her life before, but she had a thorough respect for him, and she felt that the time might come when she could enjoy him—as a reminiscence. Mrs.

Dyer was kindly, and not more of a gossip than her neighbors; and there were no children—only one grandchild, the inoffensive Nicky. The ways of the house were somewhat uncouth, but everything was clean and in a certain sense homelike. To Miss Newell's homesick sensitiveness it seemed better than being stared at across the boarding-house table by Boker and Pratt, and pitied by the engineer. She had a little room at the Dyers', which was a reflection of herself so far as a year's occupancy and very moderate resources could make it; perhaps for that very reason she often found her little room an intolerable prison. One night her homesickness had taken its worst form, a restlessness, which began in a nervous inward throbbing and extended to her cold and tremulous fingertips. She went softly downstairs and out on the piazza, where the moonlight lay in a brilliant square on the unpainted boards. The moonlight increased her restlessness, but she could not keep away from it. She dared not walk up and down the piazza, because the people in the street below would see her; she stood there perfectly still, holding her elbows with her hands, crouched into a little dark heap against the side of the house.

Lights were twinkling, far and near, over the hills, singly, and in clusters. Black figures moved across the moonlit spaces in the street. There were sounds of talking, laughing, and singing; dogs barking; occasionally a stir and tinkle in the scrub, as a cow wandered past. The engines throbbed from the distant shaft-houses. A miner's wife was hushing her baby in the next house, and across the street a group of Mexicans were talking all at once in a loud, monotonous cadence.

In her early days at the mines there had been a certain piquancy in her sense of the contrast between herself and her circumstances, but that had long passed into a dreary recognition of the fact that she had no real part in the life of the place.

She recalled one afternoon when Arnold had passed the schoolhouse, and found her sitting alone on the doorstep. He had stopped to ask if that "mongrel pack on the hill were worrying the life out of her," and had added with a laugh, in answer to her look of silent disapproval, "Oh, I mean the dear lambs of your flock. I saw two of them just now on the trail, fighting over a lame donkey. The clans were gathering on both sides; there will be a pitched battle in a few minutes. The donkey was enjoying it. I think he was asleep!" The day had been an unusually hard one, and the patient little schoolmistress was just then struggling with a distracted sense of unavailing effort. Arnold's grim banter had brought the tears, as blood follows a blow. He got down from his horse, looking wretched at what he had done. "I am a brute, I believe—worse than any of the pack. You have so much patience with them—please have a little with me. Trust me, I am not utterly blind to your sufferings. Indeed, Miss Newell, I see them, and they make me savage!" With the gentlest touch he had lifted her hand, held it in his a moment, and then had mounted his horse and ridden away.

Yes, he *did* understand—she felt sure of that. What an unutterable rest it would be if she could go to some one with the small worries of her life! But she could not yield to such impulses. It was different with men. She had often thought of Arnold's words that day at the spring, all the more that he had never, before or since, revealed so much of himself to her. Under an apparently careless frankness and extravagance of speech he was a reticent man; but lightly spoken as the words had been, were they not the sparks and ashes blown from a deep and smothered core of fire? She seemed to feel its glow on her cheek as she recalled his singular persistence and the darkening of his imperious eyes. No, she would not permit herself to think of that day at the spring.

There was a bright light in the engineer's office across the street. She could see Arnold through the windows (for, like a man, he did not pull his shades down) at one of the long drawing-tables. He worked late, it seemed. He was writing; he wrote rapidly page after page, tearing each sheet from what appeared to be a paper block, and tossing it on the table beside him; he covered only one side of the paper, she noticed, thinking with a smile of her own small economies. Presently he got up, swept the papers together in his hands, and stooped over them. He is numbering and folding them, she thought, and now he is directing the envelope—to whom, I wonder! He turned, and as he walked towards the window she saw him put something into the pocket of his coat. He lighted a cigar, and began walking, with long strides, up and down the room, one hand in his pocket; the other he occasionally rubbed over his eyes and head, as if they hurt him. She remembered that the engineer had headaches, and wished that somebody would ask him to try valerian. Is he ever really lonely? she thought. What can he, what can any man, know of loneliness? He may go out and walk about on the hills; he may go away altogether, and take the risks of life somewhere else. A woman must take no risks. There is not a house in the camp where he might not enter to-night, if he chose; he might come over here and talk to me. The East, with all its cherished memories and prejudices and associations, seemed so hopelessly far away; they two alone, in that strange, uncongenial new world which had crowded out the old, seemed to speak a common language: and yet how little she really knew of him!

Suddenly the lights disappeared from the windows of the office. She heard a door unlock, and presently the young man's figure crossed the street and turned up the trail past the house.

Two other figures going up halted, and the taller one said, "Will you go up on the hill, to-night, Arnold?"

"What for?" said Arnold, slackening his pace without stopping.

"Oh, nothing in particular—to see the señoritas."

"Oh, thank you, Boker, I've seen the señoritas."

He walked quickly past the men, and the shorter one, who had not spoken, called after him rather huskily—

"W-what do you think of the little school-ma'am?"

Arnold turned back and confronted the speaker in silence.

"I say! Is she thin 'nough to suit you?" the heavy-playful one persisted.

"Shut up, Jack!" said his comrade. "You're a little high now, you know."

He dragged him on, up the trail; the voices of the two men

blended with the night chorus of the camp as they passed out of sight.

Miss Newell sat perfectly still for a while; then she went to her room, and threw herself down on the bed, listening to an endless mental repetition of those words that the faithless night had brought to her ear. The moonlight had left the piazza, and crept round to the side of the house; it shone in at the window, touching the girl's cold fingers pressed to her burning cheeks and temples. She got up, drew the curtain, and groped her way back to the bed, where she lay for hours, trying to convince herself that her misery was out of all proportion to the cause, and that those coarse words could make no real difference in her life.

They did make a little difference: they loosened the slight, indefinite threads of intercourse which a year had woven between these two exiles. Miss Newell was prepared to withdraw from any further overtures of friendship from the engineer; but he made it unnecessary for her to do so—he made no overtures. On the night of Pratt's tipsy salutation he had abruptly decided that a mining camp was no place for a nice girl, with no acknowledged masculine protector. In Miss Newell's circumstances a girl must be left entirely alone, or exposed to the gossip of the camp. He knew very well which she would choose, and so he kept away—though at considerable loss to himself, he felt. It made him cross to watch her pretty figure going up the trail every morning and to reflect that so much sweetness and refinement should not be having its ameliorating influence on his own barren and somewhat defiant existence.

II.

The autumn rains set in early, and the winter was unusually severe. Arnold had a purpose which kept him hard at work and very happy in those days.

During the long December nights he was shut up in his office, plodding over his maps and papers, or smoking in dreamy comfort by the fire. He was seldom interrupted, for he had earned the character of a social ingrate and hardened recluse in the camp. He had earned it quite unconsciously, and was as little troubled by the fact as by its consequences. On the evening of New Year's Day he crossed the street to the Dyers' and asked for Miss Newell. She presently greeted him in the parlor, where she looked, Arnold thought, more than ever out of place, among the bead baskets, and splint frames inclosing photographs of deceased members of the Dyer family, and the pallid walls, weak-legged chairs, and crude imaginings in worsted work. Her apparent unconsciousness of these abominations was another source of irritation. It is always irritating to a man to see a charming woman in an unhappy and false position, where he is powerless to help her. Arnold had not expected that it would be a very exhilarating occasion—he remembered the Dyer parlor—but it was even less pleasant than he had expected. He sat down, carefully, in a glued chair whose joints had opened with the dry season and refused to close again; he did not know where the transfer of his person might end. Captain Dyer was present, and told a great many stories in a loud, tiring voice. Miss Frances sat by with some soft white knitting in her hands, and her attitude of patient attention made Arnold long to attack her with some savage pleasantries on the subject of Christmas in a mining camp; it seemed to him that patience was a virtue that could be carried too far, even in woman. Then Mrs. Dyer came in, and manoeuvred her husband out into the passage; after some loudly suggestive whispering there, she succeeded in getting him into the kitchen, and shut the door. Arnold got up soon after that, and said good-evening.

Miss Newell remained in the parlor for some time, after he had gone, moving softly about. She had gathered her knitting closely into her clasped hands; the ball trailed after her, among the legs of the chairs, and when in her silent promenade she had spun a grievous tangle of wool she sat down, and dropped the work out of her hands with a helpless gesture. Her head drooped, and tears trickled slowly between the slender white fingers which covered her face. Presently the fingers descended to her throat and clasped it close, as if to still an intolerable throbbing ache which her half-suppressed tears had left.

At length she rose, picked up her work, and patiently followed the tangled clue until she had recovered her ball; then she wound it all up neatly, wrapped the knitting in a thin white handkerchief, and went to her room.

With the fine March weather—fine in spite of the light rains—the engineer was laying out a road to the new shaft; it wound along the hillside where Miss Newell had first seen the green trees, by the spring. The engineer's orders included the building of a flume, carrying the water down from the Chilano's plantation into a tank, built on the ruins of the rock which had guarded the sylvan spring. The discordant voices of a gang of Chinamen profaned the stillness which had framed Miss Frances' girlish laughter; the blasting of the rock had loosened, to their fall, the clustering trees above, and the brook below was a mass of trampled mud.

The engineer's visits to the spring gave him no pleasure, in those days. He felt that he was the inevitable instrument of its desecration; but over the hill, just in sight from the spring, carpenters were putting a new piazza round a cottage that stood remote from the camp, where a spur of the hills descended steeply towards the valley. Arnold took a great interest in this cottage. He was frequently to be seen there in the evening, tramping up and down the new piazza, and offering to the moon, that looked in through the boughs of a live-oak at the end of the gallery, the incense of his lonely cigar. Sometimes he would take the key of the front door from his pocket, enter the silent house, and wander from one room to another, like a restless but not unhappy ghost; the moonlight, touching his face, showed it strangely stirred and softened. His was no melancholy madness.

Arnold was leaning on the gate of this cottage, one afternoon, when the schoolmistress came down the trail from the camp. She did not appear to see him, but turned off the trail at a little distance from the cottage, and took her way across the hill behind it. Arnold watched her a few minutes, and then followed, overtaking her on the hills above the new road, where she had sat with Nicky Dyer nearly a year ago.

"I don't like to see you wandering about here, alone," he said. "The men on the road are a scratch gang, picked up anyhow, not like the regular miners. I hope you are not going to the spring!"

"Why?" said she. "Did you not drink to our return?"

"But you would not drink with me, so the spell did not work; and now the spring is gone—all its beauty, I mean. The water is there, in a tank, where the Chinamen fill their buckets night and morning, and the teamsters water their horses. We'll go over there, if you would like to see the march of modern improvements."

"No," she said; "I had rather remember it as it was; still, I don't believe in being sentimental about such things. Let us sit down a while."

A vague depression, which Arnold had been aware of in her manner when they met, became suddenly manifest in her paleness and in a look of dull pain in her eyes.

"But you are hurt about it," he said. "I wish I hadn't told you in that brutal way. I'm afraid I'm not many degrees removed from the primeval savage, after all."

"Oh, you needn't mind," she said, after a moment. "That was the only place I cared for, here, so now there will be nothing to regret when I go away."

"Are you going away, then? I'm very sorry to hear it; but of course I'm not surprised. You couldn't be expected to stand it another year; those children must have been something fearful."

"Oh, it wasn't the children."

"Well, I'm sorry. I had hoped"—

"Yes," said she, with a modest interrogation, as he hesitated, "what is it you had hoped?"

"That I might indirectly be the means of making your life less lonely here. You remember that 'experiment' we talked about at the spring?"

"That *you* talked about, you mean."

"I am going to try it myself. Not because you were so encouraging—but—it's a risk anyway, you know, and I'm not sure the circumstances make so much difference. I've known people to be wretched with all the modern conveniences. I am going East for her in about two weeks. How sorry she will be to find you gone! I wrote to her about you. You might have helped each other; couldn't you stand it, Miss Newell, don't you think, if you had another girl?"

"I'm afraid not," she said very gently. "I *must* go home. You may be sure she will not need me; you must see to it that she doesn't need—any one."

They were walking back and forth on the hill.

"I was just looking for the cottonwood-trees; are they gone too?" she asked.

"Oh yes; there isn't a tree left in the cañon. Don't you envy me my work?"

"I suppose everything we do seems like desecration to somebody. Here am I making history very rapidly for this colony of ants." She looked down with a rueful smile as she spoke.

"I wish you had the history of the entire species under your foot, and could finish it at once."

"I'm not sure that I would; I'm not so fond of extermination as you pretend to be."

"Well, keep the ants if you like them, but I am firm on the subject of the camp children. There *are* blessings that brighten as they take their flight. I pay my monthly assessment for the doctor with the greatest cheerfulness; if it wasn't for him, in this climate, they would crowd us off the hill."

"Please don't!" she said wearily. "Even *I* don't like to hear you talk like that; I am sure *she* will not."

He laughed softly. "You have often reminded me of her in little ways: that was what upset me at the spring. I was very near telling you all about her that day."

"I wish that you had!" she said. They were walking towards home now. "I suppose you know it is talked of in the camp," she said, after a pause. "Mr. Dyer told me, and showed me the house, a week ago. And now I must tell you about my violets. I had them in a box in my room all winter. I should like to leave them as a little welcome to her. Last night Nicky Dyer and I planted them on the bank by the piazza under the climbing-rose; it was a secret between Nicky and me, and Nicky promised to water them until she came; but of course I meant to tell you. Will you look at them to-night, please, and see if Nicky has been faithful?"

"I will, indeed," said Arnold. "That is just the kind of thing she will delight in. If you are going East, Miss Newell, shall we not be fellow-travelers? I should be so glad to be of any service."

"No, thank you. I am to spend a month in Santa Barbara, and escort an invalid friend home. I shall have to say good-by, now. Don't go any farther with me, please."

That night Arnold mused late, leaning over the railing of the new piazza in the moonlight. He fancied that a faint perfume of violets came from the damp earth below; but it could have been only fancy, for when he searched the bank for them they were not there. The new sod was trampled, and a few leaves and slight, uptorn roots lay scattered about, with some broken twigs from the climbing-rose. He had found the gate open when he came, and the Dyer cow had passed him, meandering peacefully up the trail.

The crescent moon had waxed and waned since the night when it lighted the engineer's musings through the wind-parted live-oak boughs, and another slender bow gleamed in the pale, tinted haze of twilight. The month had gone, like a feverish dream, to the young schoolmistress, as she lay in her small, upper chamber, unconscious of all save alternate light and darkness, and rest following pain. When, at last, she crept down the short staircase to breathe the evening coolness, clinging to the stair-rail and holding her soft white draperies close around her, she saw the pink light lingering on the mountains, and heard the chorus to the "Sweet By and By" from the miners' chapel on the hill. It was Sunday evening, and the house was piously "emptied of its folk." She took her old seat by the parlor window, and looked across to the engineer's office; its windows and doors were shut, and the dogs of the camp were chasing each other over the loose boards of the piazza floor. She laughed a weak, convulsive laugh, thinking of the engineer's sallies of old upon that band of Ishmaelites, and of the scrambling, yelping rush that followed. He must have gone East, else the dogs had not been so bold. She looked down the valley where the mountains parted seaward, the only break in the continuous barrier of land that cut off her retreat and closed in about the atom of her own identity. The thought of that immensity of distance made her faint.

There were steps on the porch—not Captain Dyer's, for he and his good wife were lending their voices to swell the stentorian chorus that was shaking the church on the hill; the footsteps paused at the door, and Arnold himself opened it. He had not, evidently, expected to see her.

"I was looking for some one to ask about you," he said. "Are you sure you are able to be down?"

"Oh yes. I've been sitting up for several days. I wanted to see the mountains again."

He was looking at her intently, while she flushed with weakness, and drew the fringes of her shawl over her tremulous hands.

"How ill you have been! I have wished myself a woman, that I might do something for you! I suppose Mrs. Dyer nursed you like a horse."

"Oh, no; she was very good; but I don't remember much about the worst of it. I thought you had gone home."

"Home! Where do you mean? I didn't know that I had ever boasted of any reserved rights of that kind. I have no mortgage, in fact or sentiment, on any part of the earth's surface, that I'm acquainted with!"

He spoke with a hard carelessness in his manner which made her shrink.

"I mean the East. I am homeless, too, but all the East seems like home to me."

"You had better get rid of those sentimental, backward fancies as soon as possible. The East concerns itself very little about us, I can tell you! It can spare us."

She thrilled with pain at his words. "I should think you would be the last one to say so—you, who have so much treasure there."

"Will you please to understand," he said, turning upon her a face of bitter calmness, "that I claim no treasure anywhere—not even in heaven!"

She sat perfectly still, conscious that by some fatality of helpless incomprehension every word that she said goaded him, and she feared to speak again.

"Now I have hurt you," he said in his gentlest voice. "I am always hurting you. I oughtn't to come near you with my rough edges! I'll go away now, if you will tell me that you forgive me!"

She smiled at him without speaking, while her fair throat trembled with a pulse of pain.

"Will you let me take your hand a moment? It is so long since I have touched a woman's hand! God! how lonely I am! Don't look at me in that way; don't pity me, or I shall lose what little manhood I have left!"

"What is it?" she said, leaning towards him. "There is something strange in your face. If you are in trouble, tell me; it will help me to hear it. I am not so very happy myself."

"Why should I add my load to yours? I seem always to impose myself upon you, first my hopes, and now my—no, it isn't despair; it is only a kind of brutal numbness. You must have the fatal gift of sympathy, or you would never have seen my little hurt."

Miss Frances was not strong enough to bear the look in his eyes as he turned them upon her, with a dreary smile. She covered her face with one hand, while she whispered—

"Is it—you have not lost her?"

"Yes! Or, rather, I never had her. I've been dreaming like a boy all these years—'In sleep a king, but waking, no such matter.' "

"It is not death, then?"

"No, she is not dead. She is not even false; that is, not very false. How can I tell you how little it is, and yet how much! She is only a trifle selfish. Why shouldn't she be? Why should we men claim the exclusive right to choose the best for ourselves? It was selfish of me to ask her to share such a life as mine; and she has gently and reasonably reminded me that I'm not worth the sacrifice. It's quite true. I always knew I wasn't. She put it very delicately and sweetly—she's the sweetest girl you ever saw. She'd marry me to-morrow if I could add myself, such as I am—she doesn't overrate me—to what she has already; but an exchange she wasn't prepared for. In all my life I never was so clearly estimated, body and soul. I don't blame her, you understand. When I left her, three years ago, I saw my way easily enough to a reputation, and an income, and a home in the East; she never thought of anything else; I never taught her to look for anything else. I dare say she rather enjoyed having a lover working for her in the unknown West; she enjoyed the pretty letters she wrote me; but when it came to the bare bones of existence in a mining camp, with a husband not very rich or very distinguished, she had nothing to clothe them with. You said once that to be happy here a woman must not have too much imagination; she hadn't quite enough. I had to be dead honest with her when I asked her to come. I told her there was nothing here but the mountains and the sunsets, and a few items of picturesqueness which count with some people. Of course I had to tell her I was but little better off than when I left. A man's experience is something he cannot set forth at its value to himself; she passed it over as a word of no practical meaning. There her imagination failed her again. She took me frankly at my own estimate; and in justice to her I must say I put myself at the lowest figures. I made a very poor show on paper."

"You wrote to her!" exclaimed Miss Frances. "You did not go on? Oh, you have made a great mistake! Do go: it cannot be too late. Letters are the most untrusty things!"

"Wait," he said. "There is something else. She has a head for business; she proposed that I come East, and accept a superintendentship from a cousin of hers, the owner of a gun-factory in one of those shady New England towns women are so fond of. She intimated that he was in politics, this cousin, and of course would expect his employees to become part of his constituency. It's a very pretty little bribe, you see; when you add the—the girl, it's enough to shake a man—who wants that girl. I'm not worth much to myself, or to anybody else, apparently, but by Heaven I'll not sell out as cheap as that!

"It all amounts to nothing except one more illusion gone. If there is a woman on this earth that can love a man without knowing for what, and take the chances of life with him without counting the cost, I have never known her. I asked you once if a woman could do that. You hadn't the courage to tell me the truth. I wouldn't have been satisfied if you had; but I'm satisfied now."

"I believed she would be happy; I believe she would be, now, if only you would go to her and persuade her to try."

"I persuade her! I would never try to persuade a woman to be my wife were I dying for love of her! I don't think myself invented by nature to promote the happiness of woman, in the aggregate or singly. I know there are men who do: let them urge their claims. I thought that she loved me; that was another illusion. She will probably marry the cousin, and become the most loyal of his constituents. He is welcome to her; but there's a ghostly blank somewhere. How I have tired you! You'll be in bed another week for this selfishness of mine." He stopped, while a sudden thought brought a change to his face. "But when are you going home?"

"I cannot go," she said. Her weakness came over her like a cloud, darkening the room and pressing upon her heavily. "Will you give me your arm?"

At the stairs she stopped, and leaning against the wall looked at him with wide, hopeless eyes.

"We are cut off from everything. My friend does not need me now; she has gone home—alone. She is dead!"

Arnold took a long walk upon the hills that night, and smoked a great many cigars in gloomy meditation. He was thinking of two girls, as young men who smoke a great many cigars without counting them often are; he was also thinking of Arizona. He had fully made up his mind to resign, and depart for that problematic region as soon as his place was filled; but an alternative had presented itself to him with a pensive attractiveness—an alternative unmistakably associated with the fact that the schoolmistress was to remain in her present isolated circumstances. It even had occurred to him that there might be some question of duty involved in his "standing by her," as he phrased it to himself, "till she got her color back." There was an unconscious appeal in the last words he had heard her speak which constrained him to do so. He was not in the habit of pitying himself, but had there been another soul to follow this mental readjustment of himself to his mutilated life, it would surely have pitied the eagerness with which he clung to this one shadow of a duty to a fellow-creature. It was the measure of his loneliness.

It was late in November. The rains had begun again with sound and fury; with ranks of clouds forming along the mountain sides, and driven before the sea-winds upward through the gulches; with days of breeze and sunshine, when the fog veil was lightly lifted and blown apart, showing the valley always greener; with days of lowering stillness, when the veil descended and left the mountains alone, like islands of shadow rising from a sea of misty whiteness.

On such a lowering day, Miss Frances stood at the junction of three trails, in front of the door of the blacksmith's shop. She was wrapped in a dark blue cloak, with the hood drawn over her head; the cool dampness had given to her cheeks a clear, pure glow, and her brown eyes looked out with a cheerful light. She was watching the parting of the mist in the valley below; for a wind had sprung up, and now the rift widened, as the windows of heaven might have opened, giving a glimpse of the world to the "Blessed Damozel." All was dark above and around her; only a single shaft of sunlight pierced the fog, and started into life a hundred tints of brightness in the valley. She caught the sparkle on the roofs and windows of the town ten miles away; the fields of sunburnt stubble glowed a deep Indian red; the young crops were tenderest emerald; and the line of the distant bay, a steel-blue thread against the horizon.

Arnold was plodding up the lower trail on his gray mare, fetlock deep in mud. He dismounted at the door of the shop, and called to him a small Mexican lad with a cheek of the tint of ripe corn.

"Here, Pedro Segundo! Take this mare up to the camp! Can you catch?" He tossed him a coin. "Bueno!"

"Mucho bueno!" said Pedro the First, looking on approvingly from the door of his shop.

Arnold turned to the schoolmistress, who was smiling from her perch on a pile of wet logs.

"I'm perfectly happy!" she said. "This east wind takes me home. I hear the bluebirds, and smell the salt-marshes and the wood-mosses. I'm not sure but that when the fog lifts we shall see white caps in the valley."

"I dare say there are some very good people down there," said Arnold, with deliberation, "but all the same I should welcome an inundation. Think what a climate this would be, if we could have the sea below us, knocking against the rocks on still nights, and thundering at us in a storm!"

"Don't speak of it! It makes me long for a miracle, or a judgment, or something that's not likely to happen."

"Meantime, I want you to come down the trail, and pass judgment on my bachelor quarters. I can't stand the boarding-house any longer! By Jove, I'm like the British footman in 'Punch'—'what with them legs o' mutton and legs o' pork, I'm a'most wore out! I want a new hanimal inwented!' I've found an old girl down in the valley who consents to look after me and vary the monotony of my dinners at the highest market price. She isn't here yet, but the cabin is about ready. I want you to come down and look it over. I'm a perfect barbarian about color! You can't put it on too thick and strong to suit me. I dare say I need toning down."

They were slipping and sliding down the muddy trail, brushing the raindrops from the live-oak scrub as they passed. A subtle underlying content had lulled them both, of late, into an easier companionship than they had ever found possible before, and they were gay with that enjoyment of wet weather which is like an intoxication after seven months of drought.

"Now I suppose you like soft, harmonious tints and neutral effects. You 're a bit of a conservative in everything, I fear."

"I think I should like plenty of color here, or else positive white; the monotony of the landscape and its own deep, low tones demand it. A neutral house would fade into an ash heap under this sun."

"Good! Then you'll like my dark little den, with its barbaric reds and blues."

They were at the gate of the little cottage, overlooking the valley. The gleam of sunlight had faded and the fog curtain rolled back. The house did indeed seem very dark as they entered. It was only a little after four o'clock, but the cloudy twilight of a short November day was suddenly descending upon them. The school-mistress looked shyly around, while Arnold tramped about the rooms and sprung the shades up as high as they would go.

They were in a small, irregular parlor, wainscoted and floored in redwood, and lightly furnished with bamboo. This room communicated by a low arch with the dining-room beyond.

"I have some flags and spurs and old trophies to hang up there," he said, pointing to the arch; "and perhaps I can get you to sew the rings on the curtain that's to hang underneath. I don't want too much of the society of my angel from the valley, you know; besides, I want to shield her from the vulgar gaze, as they do the picture of the Madonna."

"It will serve you right if she never comes at all!"

"Oh, she's pining to come. She's dying to sacrifice herself for twenty-five dollars a month. Did I tell you, by the way, that I've had a rise in my salary? There is a rise in the work, too, which rather overbalances the increase of pay, but that's understood; for a good many years it will be more work than wage, but at the other end I hope it will be more wage than work. You don't seem to be very much interested in my affairs; if you knew how seldom

I speak of them to any one but yourself, you might perhaps deign to listen."

"I am listening; but I'm thinking, too, that it's getting very late."

"See, here is my curtain!" he said, dragging out a breadth of heavy stuff. He took it to the window, and threw it over a Chinese lounge that stood beneath. "It's an old serape I picked up at Guadalajara five years ago: the beauty of having a house is that all the old rubbish you have bored yourself with for years immediately becomes respectable and useful. I expect to become so myself. You don't say that you like my curtain!"

"I think it is very pagan looking, and rather—dirty."

"Well, I shan't make a point of the dirt. I dare say the thing would look just as well if it was clean. Won't you try my lounge?" he said, as she looked restlessly towards the door. "It was invented by a race that can loaf more naturally than we do: it takes an American back some time to relax enough to appreciate it."

Miss Frances half reluctantly drew her cloak about her, and yielded her Northern slenderness to the long Oriental undulations of the couch. Her head was thrown back, showing her fair throat and the sweet upward curves of her lips and brows.

Arnold gazed at her with too evident delight.

"Why won't you sit still? You cannot deny that you have never been so comfortable in your life before."

"It's a very good place to 'loaf and invite one's soul,' " she said, rising to a sitting position; but that isn't my occupation at present. I must go home. It is almost dark."

"There is no hurry. I'm going with you. I want you to see how the little room lights up. I've never seen it by firelight, and I'll have my house-warming to-night!"

"Oh no, indeed! I must go back. There's the five o'clock whistle, now!"

"Well, we've an hour yet. You must get warm before you go."

He went out, and quickly returned with an armful of wood and shavings, which he crammed into the cold fireplace.

"What a litter you have made! Do you think your mature angel from the valley will stand that sort of thing?"

As she spoke, the rain descended in violence, sweeping across the piazza, and obliterating the fast-fading landscape. They could scarcely see each other in the darkness, and the trampling on the roof overhead made speech a useless effort. Almost as suddenly as it had opened upon them the tumult ceased, and in the silence that followed they listened to the heavy raindrops spattering from the eaves.

Arnold crossed to the window, where Miss Frances stood shivering and silent, with her hands clasped before her.

"I want you to light my fire," he said, with a certain concentration in his voice.

"Why do you not light it yourself?" She drew away from his outstretched hand. "It seems to me you are a bit of a tyrant in your own house."

He drew a match across his knee and held it towards her: by its gleam she saw his pale, unsmiling face, and again that darkening of the eyes which she remembered.

"Do you refuse me such a little thing—my first guest? I ask it as a most especial grace!"

She took the match, and knelt with it in her hands; but it only flickered a moment, and went out. "It will not go for me. You must light it yourself."

He knelt beside her and struck another match. "We will try together," he said, placing it in her fingers and closing his hand about them. He held the trembling fingers and the little spark they guarded steadily against the shaving. It kindled; the flame breathed and brightened and curled upward among the crooked manzanita stumps, illuminating the two entranced young faces bending before it. Miss Frances rose to her feet, and Arnold, rising too, looked at her with a growing dread and longing in his eyes.

"You said to-day that you were happy, because in fancy you were at home. Is that the only happiness possible to you here?"

"I am quite contented here," she said. "I am getting acclimated."

"Oh, don't be content: I am not; I am horribly otherwise. I want something—so much that I dare not ask for it. You know what it is—Frances!"

"You said once that I reminded you—of her: is that the reason you—Am I consoling you?"

"Good God! I don't want consolation! *That* thing never existed; but here is the reality; I cannot part with it. I wish you had as little as I have, outside of this room where we two stand together!"

"I don't know that I have anything," she said under her breath.

"Then," said he, taking her in his arms, "I don't see but that we are ready to enter the kingdom of heaven. It seems very near to me."

QUESTIONING ROLES

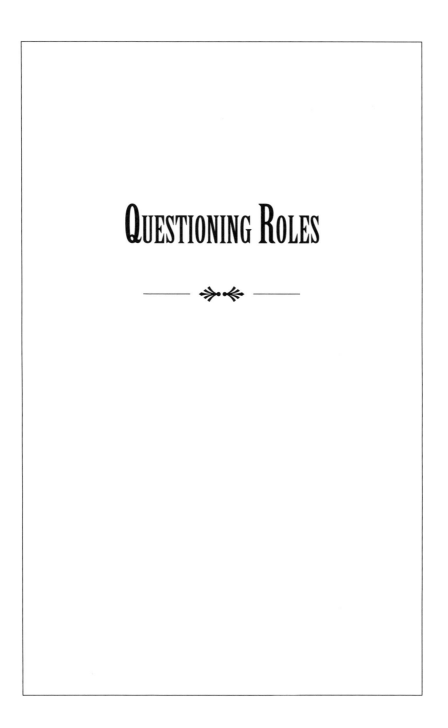

Charlotte L. Brown (1840?–?)

All but the most fundamental biographical information about Charlotte
L. Brown is lost in history, a fate all too typical of black women of the
time. Hers is a mysterious visage of courage and pride. Like Rosa Parks
nearly a century later, she suffered the humiliation of being removed
from a public conveyance, and similarly came to represent the hundreds
of thousands of black women who have endured abusive treatment at
the hands of a segregated society—and who have fought back. The
court decision of the 1860s which supported her right as a black woman
to use public transportation came 30 years before national legislation
upheld the segregation of public transport which lasted until Rosa Parks
and the 1960s. Charlotte's story is thus all the more remarkable.

Charlotte L. Brown was the daughter of James Brown and Charlotte
Brown of Baltimore, Maryland. The elder Charlotte Brown was a free
woman who worked as a seamstress and was able to buy the freedom
of her husband. Together they came to California, where James Brown
joined with four partners to establish the *Mirror of the Times,* a black
newspaper published in the Bay Area. It was he who persuaded his
daughter to file suit against the Omnibus Railroad Company for eject-
ing her from the streetcar; he paid the legal fees and saw to it that the
incident and the resulting legal decision in Charlotte's favor were
brought to the attention of the general public.

Today, Charlotte Brown's impressive oral testimony represents the
black community's demand for the rights implied when California
billed itself as a free state in its constitution. It took three years for the
court to rule in this suit—the case was initiated in 1863 and finally
settled in 1866. There was some negative press in San Francisco immediately after the decision in favor of Brown, including criticism of
Judge Pratt, who issued the landmark decision. Nonetheless, and even
though the award was only $500, a tenth of the $5,000 requested for
personal damages, it was a triumph for the California black community,
who used the suit to initiate legislation securing further legal rights for
the state's black citizenry.

Affidavit Of Oral Testimony

———— ❧•❧ ————

Istarted from home for the purpose of visiting my physician on Howard Street. On going down Filbert, one of the cars came along and the driver hailed me by giving me a signal of raising his hand. I returned the signal, the car stopped and I got in. It was seven or eight o'clock p.m. I entered from the rear platform. The car then started immediately. There were three passengers in the car at the time I entered, two gentlemen and one lady. I took my seat about midway and on the left hand side. I rode to the corner of Jackson and Stockton, between Union and Green. The conductor went around and collected tickets and when he came to me I handed him my ticket and he refused to take it. It was one of the Omnibus RailRoad tickets, one that I have purchased of them previous to that time. He replied that colored persons were not allowed to ride. I told him I had been in the habit of riding ever since the cars had been running. He answered, colored persons are not allowed to ride and I would have to get out. I answered that I had a great ways to go and I was later than I ought to be. At the same time he pulled the strap for me to get out, I said I would not get out. He then pulled the strap for the car to start on, telling me that I would have to get out further on. They next stopped to take on a lady passenger, and when she was being taken on board, the conductor told me again that I must get out. I then told him positively I would not get out. The car started again and went as far as Jackson and Stockton Streets, and between Pacific and Jackson

Streets, the conductor walked through to the driver. The conductor's name was Denison. After speaking to the driver he (the conductor) came to me and told me I must get out and took hold of me. The car had then stopped to take someone else in, at or near the corner, and I then asked him if he intended to put me out and he said yes, and at the same time let me out and I said I would seek redress, and he answered, "very good." I handed the ticket to the conductor, so that he must have seen it. I had purchased the ticket on the Sunday before that, while going to church, from one of the conductors of one of his company's cars.

I lived one block from where I took the car. When the conductor first came to me, and refused to take my ticket, I told him I thought I had a right to ride, it was a public conveyance; I told him I had a long distance to go, but didn't tell him that I had come a long ways. I told him I would not get out. He then said, "Madam, you will have to get out," and at the same time took hold of me, by the left arm, somewhere. He took hold of my arm. I made no resistance as he had taken me by the arm. I knew it was of no use to resist, and therefore I went out, and he kept hold of me until I was out of the car, holding on to me until I struck the walk. He didn't hurt me at all. I did not take the next car, but another one of the same company and went to the doctor's. I got into the second car afterward, and the conductor of that car did not object. I had a veil, but did not wear it down. I had it as I have it now. I never wore it down, at night, neither myself nor my family had ever been ejected from any car before that time.

Ella Sterling Cummins Mighels (1853–1934)

A woman of ambition and strong opinions, Ella Sterling Cummins Mighels wrote prolifically and also preserved much of the early literary history of California, fulfilling the goal she set for herself as a young woman: to be the "link between the Gold Rush days and the twentieth century's brave new world."

Born in 1853 near Sacramento in a gold rush mining camp named Mormon Island, Ella was rocked to sleep "in a goldrocker once used to wash the pay dust from the American River sands." Her mother was Rachel Hepburn Mitchell Clark, whose father was a wealthy Philadelphia businessman and county superintendent of schools. Ella's father, Sterling Benjamin Franklin Clark of Rutland, Vermont, came to California in 1849. He succeeded in unearthing enough gold to purchase property, and became a judge in the Sacramento district. Once he felt established in California, Clark returned east to marry Ella's mother. He brought his bride back to California, but just as they reached the golden state, he died. Seven months later, his daughter, Ella Sterling Clark, was born.

Ella's widowed mother opened the first school in the Sacramento area and in 1854 she married Dudley Haskell, a forty-niner who was a member of the first Nevada legislature. The Haskells moved around, from Nevada to California, and even for a time back to Pennsylvania, during which time young Ella developed a taste for writing. When she was ten, living in the Comstock mining town of Aurora, Nevada, she had a fairy tale published in the Aurora *Union,* and from then on she considered herself a writer. She especially enjoyed creating fairy tales and children's plays and stories—a pursuit she never abandoned.

In 1872 Ella Sterling Clark married Adley H. Cummins in Sacramento. Cummins was a philologist, researcher, author, lecturer and lawyer. Their daughter Genevieve (called Viva), Ella's only child, was born on October 17, 1875. The Cummins family traveled considerably from 1875 to 1889, while maintaining a home in San Francisco. It was in San Francisco that Ella's novel, *Little Mountain Princess,* was published, the first novel published by a native Californian. These were good years, but in 1889 Adley Cummins died of heart disease. With him Ella lost the love of her life. After the tragedy, she threw herself into a project

Ella Sterling Cummins Mighels (1853–1934), photograph circa 1870. Courtesy of the California Historical Society, San Francisco. FN-10754.

that took several years of research and resulted in her 1893 publication of *The Stories of the Files,* a literary and journalistic history of California. In the same year, she was named Lady Commissioner from San Francisco to the Columbian Exposition.

In 1896 Ella Sterling Cummins married Philip Verril Mighels, a lawyer, newspaper artist and writer. Together they moved to London, just after the marriage of Viva Cummins to Augustus Doan. Philip Mighels went on to become a noted novelist, playwright and newsman, but the first five years of the new century were painful for Ella. Her mother died in 1901, and then in 1905 both her daughter and her stepfather died. Adding to her misery, her marriage was deteriorating—the Mighels were divorced in 1910 and in the next year Philip died in a hunting accident.

Alone, Ella devoted the remaining years of her life to her writing and research, and to educating children in literature and ethics. She organized the California Literature Society that met at Ina Coolbrith's house for years, and also the Ark-adian Brothers and Sisters, "a program for the moral uplift of young people." Her program provided recommended books to young people, held "potlatches" (gift-giving parties), and also sponsored annual burnings of "bad" books.

Ella Mighels was opposed to women's suffrage, saying of women that "they have no caution, no principles, when it comes to voting." She was also opposed to birth control, stating that "parents who lend themselves to exercising 'birth control' are punished for interfering with Nature and they fall victim to epilepsy, nervous prostration, insanity or lingering death." During this period she wrote editorials and essays, many of which were published in San Francisco periodicals, on other subjects such as the "purity of the white race" and the "benign dominance of men."

After 1909, Ella produced five major works and a vast selection of short pieces. Her best-known fiction, *The Full Glory of Diantha,* came out in 1909, followed by the play *Society and Babe Robinson* in 1914, and *Literary California* in 1918. She had her father's travel diary, *How Many Miles from St. Jo?*, published in 1929. Her autobiography, *The Story of a Forty-Niner's Daughter,* appeared in 1934, under the pen name Aurora Esmeralda. The story that is published here, "Portrait of a California Girl," was taken from a collection called *Short Stories by California Authors,* published in 1885 by the *Golden Era.*

Raised amid the flurry of the Gold Rush, Ella Sterling Cummins Mighels observed and portrayed the pioneer West as an involved, life-long participant. Mighels' stories and novels portray California pioneers simply as they were—neither good nor bad, but rather human and hard-working. She reveled in the milieu of the West and did what she could as fiction writer and literary historian to preserve its original spirit. In 1919 the state legislature recognized her for these efforts, naming her "first historian of literary California."

PORTRAIT OF A
CALIFORNIA GIRL

———— ❧•❧ ————

A jagged horizon of frowning cliffs against the blue sky! Mountains to the east and west! Mountains to the north and south, a mammoth herd of mountains all crowned fantastically! Through the midst of this native wilderness ran a narrow cañon, the only outlet to the great world beyond, and here in this wild spot had been chosen a place for a habitation.

From the stage window, Judge Harville glanced out at the bevy of children that gathered round, and could not help but wonder at the refined mother of the group, and ask himself what fortuitous fortune had cast so beautiful and delicate a woman so far above the level of civilization. And then his eye had been caught by a strange young creature by his side, who resembled her as the fawn does the deer-mother. It looked like a child that was masquerading as a woman, dressed in matronly style, with trained skirts and ample crinoline, but showing in her childish face and undeveloped form the marks of extreme youth, and yet in the self-reliant pose of the head and utter unconsciousness of the gazing eyes bent upon her, was very different from the preconceived idea of the child who stands where brook and river meet.

She was dressed for traveling, and as she kissed them all farewell, her trunk was being strapped on behind the stage with tremendous energy.

"Is she coming in here?" asked one of the passengers with enthusiasm.

"No, she's booked outside with Dennis, the driver," was the reply. "She's one of the belles of Esmeralda. You wouldn't think it, would you. She's only fourteen, but she's had several proposals already. Women are mighty scarce in this part of the country, you know, and we don't let 'em waste much time."

"Good bye, Lorena, good bye!" cried the chorus of brothers and sisters as she mounted up the wheel and into the high seat by the driver, and they were off, the six horses prancing gaily down the cañon.

Judge Harville had listened amused to this little colloquy and at the Half-way House where they stopped for dinner he took a closer look at the girl.

She wore a string of pearl beads around her hair, a sailor collar turned down in the neck with a picturesque knot at the throat, very full gathered skirts over a large crinoline, and a saucy little brown felt hat like a boy's. Certainly she was all out in her clothes.

In the city, he knew the ladies affected very high chokers, and their skirts were rather slimpsey, crinoline having been dethroned for some time.

Still there was a certain sweetness and dignity in the fresh young face that was very attractive. He saw her eyes glisten as he took up his magnificent fur-lined coat, and knew she had never seen anything like it before.

He handed her into the coach, for it was now growing cold, and found her the easiest place, and watched her fall into a baby-like slumber. The night was bitter in its frostiness, and the shawl around her seemed scarcely heavy enough. Very lightly, he drew off his otter-lined garment, and put it around her, then wrapping himself in a blanket, he too had gone to sleep, maintaining meanwhile, however, a strong grip on the straps—those kindly-provided contrivances to keep passengers from mounting roofward at odd moments. In the grey light of the morning he saw her looking at him with an amused yet grateful pair of eyes, and patting the soft lining with evident enjoyment.

After breakfast they fell into a little chat, and he remarked the change in the landscape around them, for it was much more level and open on the road to Carson.

"It is very different," she replied; "yesterday it was like home all the way, nearly, for they were my own mountains, my very own, but I don't know my way here, at all. Which way are my mountains?" and her eyes betokened the liveliest interest.

They were pointed out in the dim distance directly upon one side, for they had come in a sort of semi-circle. Air, light and shade commingling to invest them with a royal magnificence of color from the delicate pearl tints to rose and purple, and behind them the clouds lay piled like another succession of heavenly peaks till the eye could scarcely tell where earth left off and the portals of the sky began.

"Are those my mountains?" she said in surprise. "Why, they are more beautifully purple than any of them and I have always been envying the far away mountains for being so lovely and hazy, and there all the time my own mountains were just as purple as any of them. Doesn't that seem funny?"

He was much amused by her naive remarks, for she was not afraid to talk upon any theme from politics to poetry, having an unusual fund of information upon these subjects, and showing that she had grown up among people much older than herself. And yet the childish idea would make its appearance every now and then, giving a most unique turn to the conversation.

The stage jolted violently over the rough road, and they fell into silence again. The rosy cheeks of the girl seemed to whiten out as a faintly perceptible odor began to steal on the air. It was an ill-defined suspicious odor, that seemed to creep upon the senses insidiously, and yet not give the slightest clue to its origin. Being a man, perhaps it made less impression upon Judge Harville, but he saw the girl evince signs of the greatest discomfort.

When they reached the place for changing horses, and the men got out and stretched their limbs, he saw the girl bend forward eagerly, and with her teeth, bite the string that fastened a great demijohn of whiskey to the side of the stage, put it under her shawl, and, at an unobserved moment, pitch it out the window.

He smiled to himself, at her resolution, and wondered how she would make it straight with the owner, getting back into the stage with renewed interest in the "child-woman," as he mentally dubbed her.

She sat smiling, wickedly happy now; the color had come back to her round cheek, and she had a sparkle in her eye that told of her triumph. Presently the owner of the odorous treasure began to look for his demijohn. In a few moments he had accused the man next to him, which was resented on the instant. Words followed and a row seemed imminent, when, all at once, the girl laughed. They looked at her with indignation.

"I took it," she said, a little shame-facedly.

"You?" said, the man, astonished, yet doubtful.

"Yes, the horrid thing was making me sick with its awful breath, and so *I pitched it out*"; her whole manner breathed of defiance. Then realizing faintly the difficulty she had gotten into, she said, apologetically, "Besides it was good of me to keep you from drinking it. 'Tisn't good for you, you know it isn't. Whisky makes people ugly, and if you hadn't been drinking it all the morning, you would laugh and call it a joke. Now, wouldn't he?" She appealed to the other passengers.

"Of course he would!" they laughed back.

"Better give in gracefully, old fel," said one, "you're beat this time."

"Got to stand the drinks next place," said another.

"Oh, bah!" said Lorena, her eyes flashing, "we don't want any more drinking. That's what I pitched that old thing out for. Can't you brighten up and be nice for the rest of the trip? Tell me, haven't you some nice little children?" she asked interestedly of the owner of the lost treasure.

"Yes," said the man, rather sullenly.

"How many?" her voice was eager.

"Three," was the reply, less sullen.

"Oh! have you? Boys or girls?"

"Two boys and a girl," replied the man, looking at her curiously. "We have three of each at our house, and I have just the sweetest baby sister in the world," said the girl, joyously.

Judge Harville looked upon her with a new interest; she was certainly an odd little child-woman, with so much maternal affection in her nature. In a few moments she had found out the names of all the children belonging to the fathers there, and made a remark on each; then turning to him, she asked, artlessly, "What are your children's names?"

Judge Harville was taken by surprise. He was not over thirty years of age, was brown haired and brown bearded, and felt himself a very young man for the honors he had received. That he should impress any one as the father of a family struck him incongruously.

"I'm almost afraid to tell you"—he hesitated, yet in spite of himself, he smiled.

"Why?" she asked, emphatically.

"Because I haven't any." Everybody laughed, even Lorena herself, and good nature was immediately restored.

The rest of the stage ride was pleasant enough, and Judge Harville found himself more than once on the point of asking the bright little Lorena where she was going to stop in San Francisco, which she had inadvertently referred to as her destination. But there was a certain dignity underneath all that childish presumption and chattiness that made him hesitate. And when they arrived at Carson, he arrayed himself in his luxurious coat, and gathered together all his belongings and bade her good-bye, saying simply, "Farewell, Miss Lorena. I hope we shall meet again."

And she looked him in the eyes like a child, and said, cheerfully, "I hope so, too."

"You won't forget me, will you?" said he with a little touch of vanity. She seemed too unimpressed by the notice he had taken of her.

"I'm sure I'll never forget your beautiful fur-lined coat," she said, mischievously, and he went off amid a shout of laughter from the other passengers.

Four weeks passed by. He had almost forgotten the little girl in the stage, when one day, near Christmas time, with the rain pouring in torrents, he suddenly met her face to face on Kearny street in San Francisco. He stopped and looked at her with a very pleased expression.

She was clad in city fashion, short trim skirts, ermine-bordered velvet jacket, and Tyrolean hat to match, with a scarlet wing setting it off jauntily, really a very charming picture of youth and freshness. He held out his hand. She hesitated.

"Why Miss Lorena, you haven't forgotten me surely?"

"No," she said, rather unwillingly, "but you see I've never been introduced to you."

"Well, I'll be blanked," he said to himself.

"Well? what difference does that make. We're acquainted all the same."

"I know," said the girl, "but at home—up in the mountains—we don't think it nice to continue an acquaintance without an introduction. If I'm worth being acquainted with, I'm worth being introduced to. Besides, I don't know who in the world you are, you know." And she laughed.

Finished man of the world as he was, Judge Harville was speechless. He looked down in wonder on this curious little woman with the artlessness of a child, this child with the wordly wisdom of a woman.

"With whom are you staying?" he asked in a low voice.

"With my uncle, W. B. Lawrence of the firm of Lawrence and Chester," she replied with dignity. "Good morning," and she was on her way.

The spirit displayed by this comical little mountain belle, aroused his deepest respect. "If she is worth being acquainted with, she is worth getting an introduction to," he repeated. "The little girl is right, and I'll take the trouble to get a first-class introduction that will be without a flaw."

And then he fell to laughing at the absurdity of the situation, he a man of high position and eagerly sought after by the finest circles to grace their receptions, going to the trouble of getting an introduction to a comical little girl from the mountains in order that he might set himself straight, and prove that he was not a gambler or other suspicious character. "I don't know who in the world you are, you know." It would make a funny story to tell some time, he thought.

Nevertheless his pique was aroused and he sought the house of a mutual friend, who during the call, casually mentioned that the Lawrence family were to dine with them on Christmas day. "But I suppose it is of no use to invite you, Judge Harville, you are always engaged months beforehand," said the lady with a sigh, thinking of her own marriageable daughter.

"Well," said he, stroking his handsome mustache, "I will tell you what I will do. I will come late."

He resolved to dumbfound the nonchalant little Lorena, and teach her a lesson. He would rather enjoy a harmless little revenge on such a spirited young creature. In spite of his pride and high position, underneath all there was to be found a petty vanity in the breast of the otherwise admirable Judge Harville.

The dinner was over, and the several little families were gathered in congenial little knots, some singing at the piano, some looking at the new gifts; but in the bay window, solitary and alone, sat little Lorena. She had discovered already, in her short experience of city life, that she was no longer a young lady, but only a little girl, and was trying to adapt herself to the new position of being seen but not heard.

The door suddenly opened and the hostess came in smiling, leading Judge Harville as if he were a prize ox that had received the first premium at a county fair. She introduced him to the few who did not already know him, personally, while Mr. and Mrs. Lawrence beamed upon him, renewing the slight acquaintance that already existed between them, and the others gathered around to show him deference and respect.

All listened to his words of bright address, and responded with animation—all but little Lorena, who shrank back behind the curtains and wondered at this remarkable coincidence.

Judge Harville saw her sitting there all solitary and alone, and after he thought he had punished her sufficiently, he said, "By the way, Lawrence, I believe I came down in the same stage with your niece—a very bright little girl—is she here? I should like to be introduced."

And Mr. Lawrence had gone to the window and had said, "Lorena, Judge Harville wishes to be introduced to you."

"Does he?" she said, quietly.

"Yes. It seems he came down in the same stage with you from the mountains," and he waited for her to come out from behind the curtains.

"Well, why doesn't he come and *be* introduced then?" and she turned to look out the window again.

Uncle Lawrence was somewhat startled, and then he smiled to himself, remembering the trains to her dresses only a few weeks before, which had to be cut off in order to make her presentable. "She wasn't so much of a child as they had imagined."

In a moment the curtain was separated more widely than usual, and Judge Harville stood there, with a quizzical smile in his handsome eyes, repeating gravely, "Miss Lawrence," after the ceremony of introduction.

But the little girl, in her pretty short suit, with, however, the pearl bead fillet still around her head, did not seem dumbfounded in the least. She inclined her head with dignity, and then there came a bright sparkle of merriment into her eyes.

"You are lately from the mountains, I believe, Miss Lawrence."

"Yes," returned she, "like yourself."

"Did you have a pleasant trip down?"

"Delightful," returned Lorena, "especially when I pitched out that old demijohn! Didn't you?"

"Are there any more formalities to be got through with?" he asked, "if so, please mention them, and I'll try to secure them all."

"I can't help it," said Lorena, answering implied sarcasm of his words. "I have been taught that it is the only proper way."

"Do you know who I am yet?" His eyes looked mischievous.

"No," said she frankly, "I do not."

"Yet you talk to me."

"Ah!" said the girl, "but my uncle has assumed the responsibility, and I trust *him.*"

Judge Harville stroked his moustache a moment reflectively. There wasn't much satisfaction for his vanity yet. "This is a great contrast to the country we left behind us four weeks ago, isn't it," pointing as he spoke, to the garden in front, which revealed great, white calla lilies, bright-red geraniums, and graceful, drooping fuchsia blossoms of purple and red. "I suppose you would be very willing to make the change."

"I?" said Lorena, with a flash of her eyes, "no, indeed! The city stifles me; I love my own wild mountains best."

He looked down at this small young person with a half smile on his face—"Ah, but if those brothers and sisters of yours lived here, it would be different, and you would soon forget all about the dreary desolation up there."

"No, I shouldn't," she persisted; "my dear old Mount Chalcedony is worth a dozen of these hills here. And besides, I have all the wild flowers to myself, and name them whatever I please. And then, too, we meet some of the most talented men in the country, up there. Why, I know Governor Nye, and J. Ross Browne, the traveler—when he was writing up Bodie and Mono Lake, for *Harper's* he visited our house—and there's Mr. Gough, the nephew of the celebrated lecturer, who is almost as eloquent as his uncle; and there's Mr. Clagget, and Mr. Kendall and several other Congressmen, and O, judges! why I know ever so many judges! There's Judge Boring, who often lectures for us; and Judge Sewell, who is considered really very fine; and Judge Chase—a real brilliant judge, who used to be a student of Longfellow's, himself, and I guess that's more than you can say, isn't it?"

Judge Harville's vanity was wounded in more ways than one. He had no desire to be considered in competition with "those old fogies," as he mentally dubbed them.

"You must think me a regular old grandfather," he said, passing over this extensive list of notables, his pride hurt more than he would have confessed at her childish refusal to consider him of any particular value, and also at the implied sarcasm which intimated that he evidently felt he was condescending to talk with her.

"Oh! It's nice to be old," said she, reassuringly, "that's what makes *you* so pleasant and agreeable," and then with a sigh of self-importance, "I don't like *young* men."

Judge Harville took a long breath. He had thought to subdue little Lorena, but, instead, he was himself subdued.

When he had recovered his breath, he looked at her curiously. "I'd like to come across you about five years from now. I'd like to see what sort of a woman you would make."

He was about to ask some questions about her mother, when voices from behind appealed to him to settle some vexed question of trivial importance, and he was drawn away, the little girl with her pearl bead fillet looking out upon them from behind the curtains with an ill-concealed smile of amusement at the way the young ladies hung upon his words, and looked up into his eyes. It made him feel ridiculous rather than triumphant, his vanity had received a blow.

The rain was falling in torrents when the gathering broke up, and he could only say a conventional good bye to the well-equipoised, little Lorena, who gave him a bright little nod in reply.

The next day he sent her an exquisite bouquet and a magnificent box of confectionery, mingling the gifts suitable to a child and a young lady, but when he called a week or so later, little Lorena had flown back to her beloved mountains, and so passed out of his life and thoughts, leaving only a dim little memory of a strange child who played at being a young lady.

A number of experiences fell to Judge Harville's share in the years which followed, but fortune and fame continued to smile upon him, and the young ladies and their mammas. Still his heart remained his own, that touch of vanity made him well satisfied to remain as he was—the honored and welcome guest of a large circle of refined acquaintances.

Eight years had passed. He was still handsome with only a few silver hairs clustering in his brown locks. An intricate question of law had taken him up through the wild Sonora route into Mono county.

On setting out in the morning, some one had said, "Jedge, I'm 'fraid there's goin' to be a snow storm. Ye'd better stay over till tomorrer."

He only laughed at the would-be weather-prophet, and thought no more about it, urging his horse along at a pleasant canter till he came into the rough mountain road, and gave himself up to the reflections that naturally come to a solitary horseman who knows he is likely to travel for twenty or thirty miles without meeting a human being.

The road wound around the hills, and then took a line through the only natural egress or ingress—a long, dark canyon, two gloomy walls of solid rock, that once fitted evenly together in a solid mass, but in some great convulsion of nature, had separated, leaving this narrow space between—barely room enough for two teams to pass with a little stream of water running alongside.

Stories of waterspouts, very frequent in this locality, came to his mind, and he wondered if one should strike this cañon, whether the unfortunate caught between these walls could possibly escape drowning.

After a while, the walls lowered gradually, and he saw a wild horizon of jagged fantastic angles encircling him round. On the instant a picture came back to his mind of a house situated in the foreground of a wild mountain, and a group of children, and then a succession of pictures with a bright little girl figuring arching in the center.

"It must be the peculiar horizon that brings back such a faint little memory as that of Lorena," said he, musingly. "It was no wonder she didn't grow up like other children, with such a horizon as that around her. What's that? Snowflakes falling? The old man was a prophet, after all. I wonder if I can't make the quartz mill before it gets too heavy." And spurring his horse, he hastened along. The weather had changed, the bracing air had given way to that strange, heavy atmosphere that precedes the snowstorm, so imperceptibly that he had not noticed it.

On leaving this uncanny place, the road verged about several small slopes, but the snow increased so suddenly and so violently, with a sudden gust of wind blowing down the canyon, that he became confused. Once he thought he had struck the trail because of the fresh horses' tracks before him in the snow, but he soon found that, in his confusion, he had been merely following in a circle upon his own trail.

To add to his distress, his horse stepped into a sudden gully and fell beneath him with a broken leg. Darkness now seemed to encompass the earth, and Judge Harville stood gazing into space utterly bewildered.

The violent efforts of his horse in attempting to rise called him back to himself, and after a moment's hesitancy, he drew out his revolver and put the beast out of his misery, performing this action of cruel kindness promptly and effectively.

He felt sure that the quartz-mill was not far away, and that he could make it within an hour. He lighted a match, and looked at his watch. It was six. He felt the need of food and shelter, and resolved to press forward.

The night was coming on fast, and it was bitter cold. He could not think of staying in this desolate spot when a place of refuge was so near.

But he soon found himself at the mercy of the pitiless elements. The snow still fell madly, the wind was beginning to throw up little drifts. Still he struggled on. Once he plunged into the creek through the shallow ice, and although wet through, and his clothes immediately stiffened, he exclaimed, "Thank God!" for it showed that the road was not far away. Bit by bit, step by step, he makes his way. In three hours he has made a mile directly forward, though five or six has been lost in retracement.

He is no longer the elegant and dignified Judge Harville. He is only a man fighting for life—a pitiable object of humanity. His clothes are torn by contact with the rocks, or stiffened with frozen water, his hands are bleeding, his feet badly frozen. Shall he give up and lie down to sweet, coaxing sleep—sleep that knows no waking, or shall he struggle on?

A sound breaking on the freezing air attracts his wandering senses.

"Help!" he cries.

The sound comes again, repeated thrice. If he was desperate before, now he was like one transfixed.

It was the bark of a coyote—a sharp, insolent bark. What an answer to a freezing man's call for help!

"What! lie down to die, and be devoured by those cowardly brutes?" And in answer he plunged along again with renewed efforts, nerved with strength born of desperation. The barks increased around him; there was a pair of them; he could see their dark shadows on the snow, waiting at a respectful distance. His hands were so cold and numb that he could not get his revolver out, and even then the water had frozen it stiff. "Great Heaven!" he cried, "was I born for this?"

His ears now told him the voices were three, he wasted no time looking for the shadowy forms on the snow. "I will keep them out of their feast as long as I can," he thought, his natural stubbornness coming to his aid. And he did, but his powers were nearly exhausted, his endurance overtried. Gradually the stiffness was creeping on him, he felt no more arms or legs, he was only a human clump struggling onward. Still the snow fell. "Heh! heh! heh!" barked the cowardly chorus. Each moment seemed a year as they gained upon him. One crept close to him; in an agony of despair he made one great effort and struck at it, the cowardly thing slunk back. It feared even the semblance of a man as long as there was a spark of life in it.

{ 275 }

Suddenly upon his ear almost dulled in its sense of hearing, came another sound, he roused himself to listen. Could he be losing his mind already, or was it a mocking human voice imitating the coyotes? "Heh, heh, heh!" called the chorus around him. "Heh, heh, heh," called out a clear mocking voice from a distance.

"God!" said the man, and with soul swelling within him, forgetting his poor cumbersome, solid body he strove once more, with hope inspiring him. That mocking human voice was the sweetest sound he had ever heard. But his feet failed him, they would no longer do their master's bidding. Accepting this new distress, he fell upon hands and knees and crept painfully along in the direction of the voice, which seemed to take delight in mocking the voices of the night. "If it should cease!" thought the man in despair.

One more little turn of a bend, and there he saw, very near, a light; with one loud cry born of agony and despair, he cried, "Help, help!" and at that moment felt the breath of the coyotes upon his cheek.

He struggled to show there was still life in him, and in the breathing spell thus obtained, the door flung wide open and the figure of a woman rushed out, a lamp in her hand.

"Where! where are you?" she cried. "Heh, heh," cried the chorus. "Here, here," cried the man with his last strength. "Merciful Heavens!" with this ejaculation, not pausing a moment she ran directly towards them, the coyotes shrinking back out of sight at the appearance of so much life and vitality. She found a clump of frozen humanity in the snow, speechless but with grateful eyes that looked up in her face and told of life.

Hurrying to the house, she brought out a flask of liquor, and by the light of her lamp made him drink. "There is no time to waste," she said in a quick way, "I shall have to depend on you to help me. My husband is at the mill, I can't wait to go for him." Putting a rope around his waist, she gave him instructions what to do. "Now when I pull, lift a little of your weight." Foot by foot they struggled along. The fire obtained from the whisky as well as the light so near him, and the encouraging voice, gave him new energy. Who can tell where the strength comes from that enables a woman to grapple with burdens beyond her powers? No one could ever tell how she got the helpless man into the cosy domicile where warmth and comfort awaited him. There was not much to remind one of the elegant scrupulously attired Judge Harville, in the poor piece of humanity before her eyes. Cold water was used to take the first agony out of the frozen limbs, and then warm drinks to comfort the inner man.

Then with a sigh of relief she said, "I guess you will do till morning, and then we'll have the doctor."

Judge Harville's eyes had been resting upon her questioningly through all this tedious process.

"It seems to me that I've seen you somewhere before;" he said slowly. "Very likely," was the response; "I've traveled all over California and Nevada since I was a child." "No, but it seems as if I had known you."

"If you will tell me your name," she said hesitatingly. A faint smile crept over his face with recognition. "You are the little Lorena who wouldn't speak to me without an introduction. Will the old one do, or must I get a new one?"

"Judge Harville!" she exclaimed, "can it be possible? I never expected to see you again, much less under these circumstances."

"How is it you are here, all alone?" he asked.

"Oh, my husband, Aleck Westbrook, is night engineer at the Silver King mill, a quarter of a mile away. I've lived here over a year. I never think of such a thing as being afraid.

"I often mock the coyotes just to amuse myself, they are a sort of company; but your cry, tonight, quite horrified me. They must have been starved to be as bold as they were tonight, but we won't talk of that anymore. You had better get some sleep before the doctor comes."

"What time is it?" "It is two o'clock, Aleck always gets a light lunch about twelve, and that accounts for my being up at such an hour and very fortunate it was." Judge Harville accepted all these statements as the most natural in the world, dining at twelve o'clock at night, and mocking coyotes to amuse one's self, why, of course, he wondered why he had never done these things himself, and in the sleep which crept drowsily on, dreamed he had turned into a coyote, and was tracking something to death.

Aleck Westbrook proved to be a tall, manly fellow, a little reserved, though cordial in congratulations to the stranger he found housed upon his return, and very prompt in bringing the doctor who pronounced the quick and efficient care the night before as likely to bring him through without an amputation, but his recovery from the shock and all would be slow.

Seeing that it was to be a long siege, Judge Harville sent for choice groceries to the city, as his contribution toward the household expenses, for provisions in the town where supplies were bought were incredibly high. He also sent for music and books.

Lorena Westbrook, as a woman, was the same arch, bright creature, with a strange dignity and fearlessness all her own, that Lorena Lawrence had been, and with the self-reliance that comes from frontier life.

Judge Harville from his place upon the bed-lounge watched her curiously in all her little duties, as she sewed, or tidied up the room, or in caring for the year-old child which clung to her skirts. He was lost in admiration of her. To his weary, sated eyes, in her freshness and vivacity—she was a revelation. Day after day crept by, and his admiration grew till it passed the limits of admiration. He allowed himself to break the tenth commandment. He coveted.

"Do you never wish that fate had placed you in a beautiful home in the midst of civilization?" he asked Lorena, one day.

"O, I don't know. I'm very happy here. I have my piano, and baby and husband. I don't know of anything else I want very much. I love this wild place better than the trammels of society."

"But you would find congenial society, and an opportunity for these accomplishments which make a woman so charming and delightful," said Judge Harville, insidiously. Lorena gave a little sigh. "It *is* nice to be accomplished," she said.

Many were the visitors that came in of an evening. Mrs. Westbrook's simple little parlor seemed an earthly paradise to those rough diamonds who had left civilization far behind them with all its comforts to battle with the wilderness. Some of them were fluent talkers, some were geniuses, some were bores, yet each was respectful and kind in his admiration of the engineer's wife. Occasionally a lady from the town, four miles distant, favored her with a call, or a family who lived a mile away, but these were exceptions, and men almost exclusively formed the society that gathered around her.

This curious state of affairs was not altogether new to Judge Harville, but it had never affected him as unpleasantly as now. "A bright, intelligent creature like Lorena to be wasted on the desert air," he though to himself, impatiently—and even a species of jealousy took possession of him, to see how freely and frankly she met them, and how sweetly she talked to them all.

"Say, Westbrook," said he, one day, after they had been discussing one of the habitual bores, "aren't you afraid you'll have to straighten out some of these fellows some day. First thing you know some of them will be in love with your wife."

"Oh, no," laughed back Westbrook, "Lorena straightens them out as she goes along. I'll never have any duels to fight for her."

The fierceness of the winter was over, and spring began to assert her sway, sending down great freshets ladened with boulders from the mountains, and touching into life the sparse vegetation. "Here is the harbinger of spring," said Lorena, one day, bringing in a branch of willow, which had commenced to sprout in tiny buds of wool. "And in California the roses are blooming, the lilies shining white, and the whole earth covered with green," said Harville.

She turned upon him fiercely, "Why are you always trying to fill me with discontent? I never thought of such a thing till you came."

Harville smiled to himself. "Because I cannot bear to see you satisfied with such a life." Lorena looked at him in bewilderment. But he said no more, and she had nothing to say, being puzzled to catch his meaning.

The roads were now in good condition, and Judge Harville's crutch almost unnecessary, everything pointed to there being no further excuse for his remaining in such a wild, desolate spot. But Aleck told him to be in no haste, he was glad to have such good company for his wife, and had enjoyed the time spent together. They did live delightfully in that strange place, with music (Harville was an accomplished musician), with reading (he was a fine reader), with communions with Nature and the charming little suppers at twelve every night, and sleeping in the morning, turning day into night, and night into day, with no bustle of the outside world, no weary seekings after pleasure, no mingling with great crowds of people, utterly indifferent to each other, but each new human being a study and a revelation.

One day, together, they went to the Indian Camp, quite near, and watched the dark-faced creatures prepare their meals, and try the steps of the Indian dance, preparatory to the grand pow-wow on Walker's river.

"I wish we both were savages like these," said Harville, in a low tone.

"Why?" she responded, "what idea have you in that?"

"So that we should not be bound by these laws civilization puts upon us."

"I am glad that your wish cannot come true, for I love law and order," she laughed back in reply. But something in his tone alarmed her.

The next day, with her baby, she went out seeking new flowers that she knew where to find, and stayed beyond her time. Meanwhile, Aleck, who had waked before his usual hour in the day, was out of temper for no particular cause, as a man can easily be sometimes, and stepping into the kitchen, saw the bread, forgotten in its capabilities for expansion, a great frothy roll over the sides of the pan, and even dripping on the floor.

At this moment Lorena and the baby came in the back door, both trimmed with wild flowers, a pretty bloom on their faces, and a smiling look in their eyes.

"You had a d—n sight better stay home and tend to this bread," said Aleck, crossly, yet touched by the pretty picture of his wife and child, and regretting his temper on the instant.

Without a word, but the bloom blanched in a moment, Lorena walked past him into her room.

Judge Harville observed this little scene and wondered what she would do, but in a moment she came out and got supper quietly, after Aleck's departure taking up her sewing.

Harville sat and watched her. Since he had allowed himself to covet that which was his neighbor's, he had, with many dallyings with conscience, proved to himself that his ultimate object was a good one, a real kindness, cruel perhaps—like the shooting of his horse to put him out of his misery—but a kindness, a good deed, after all; such tricks does pure, unadulterated reason, untouched with conscience, play with a man's judgment! He was no worse, no better, than many men we know and believe to be honorable.

He would not sully by a word Lorena's purity of soul; he loved her too deeply for that; he wanted her for his wife. He was a lawyer and a crafty one, and knew well the meshes of the law and how he could disentangle her from her present position and make her his own. And he had convinced himself that it would be a kindness to her in the end.

"To think of such a rare creature condemned to these dismal things of life, such a barren, miserable outlook! I'll place her in a sphere more fitted to her charms and graces, for where will not Judge Harville's wife be welcome?"

And so he sat there, thinking all these things, how lovely she would look in a beautiful home, and what a joy to free her from all this toil and hard work, this lovely creature who had saved his life—what would he not surround her with to soften life for her?

"Lorena," he said softly.

"Well," she responded, as if nothing strange were suggested by his familiar method of address.

"Do you ever think of this as a dreary life?"

She looked at him a second, as if measuring him. "Oh, no," she responded, carelessly.

"Lorena," he said again, and his voice was thrillingly low, "listen to me."

"I'm listening," she repeated, carelessly again.

"Lorena, don't you see the love shining out of my eyes? Don't you see that I adore you?"

"That's nothing new," she laughed back; "I've always been adored. I can't remember when I wasn't adored."

"But I want you for my own," he whispered, yet not coming any closer—he knew he dared not.

"That's nothing new, either," she laughed again, "there's always been somebody who wanted me for their own; in fact, if that's intended for a pleasant remark, I'm dreadfully tired of it."

"But seriously, Mrs. Westbrook," said he, in a different tone, "how can you be happy in such a place as this, and with a man who swears at you?"

The pretty chin quivered, still she kept up her play of speech, and said, most innocently, "One would suppose that you had never heard anybody swear before," and then, rising, "I must see to Aleck's supper; poor fellow, he'll be very hungry when he returns." And soon she was busied with the fire, and preparing an oyster stew for him.

His step was soon heard, and after a bright little talk around the table, he went back again to his work. Lorena, hurrying away the dishes, and clearing up, retired to her own room and locked the door.

Judge Harville soon sought his own couch, but not to sleep. He was restless, irritated, but more determined than ever.

In her room, Lorena acted very strangely; she seemed suffocating; she kissed the sleeping babe, then, drawing a shawl over her head, cautiously opened the window and crept out, and dropping to the ground noiselessly, she walked up the narrow road in the waning light of the old moon.

"Oh, I could kill him, I could kill him!" she cried to herself, passionately, "but I shall have to deny myself that pleasure." For an hour she walked up familiar pathways over the rocks, looking down upon rocky gorges and black, abysmal shadows between the mountains, and sat down to rest a moment.

She heard a faint rustle, a chasing movement, and in its terror, a white rabbit that had not yet changed its winter coat for grey, crouched close to her foot, and from behind the rock below came a shadow—a coyote. Quickly she threw a handful of stones, which made the ugly beast skulk away. Lorena stooped to stroke the trembling, terrified little creature at her feet, but in an instant it had leaped away and was gone.

"O God!" exclaimed the lonely little human creature on the rock, as a similar picture to the scene just enacted before her, came to her vision. "Can I come close to your foot for protection, as this rabbit has done to me? You are so far away, God! If you had left me mother she would have helped me. I am so lonely, and the Bad is so near."

This solitary, little human-being on the bleak and craggy Sierra, without knowing it, expressed, in her deep despair and anguish, the true Persian theory of belief—that Good and Evil (Ormuzd and Ahriman) are contending for the mastery, and the human being is free to choose one or the other; and no worshiper, at the old-time altar of incense, could have prayed more earnestly nor passionately to be delivered, than this untaught mountain child of the wilderness, trusting to her intuitions alone.

The wise and cynical may smile or sneer, but to the end of time, the despair of prophets and philosophers can never carry them beyond the Persian theory of belief, nor the despair of hunted souls find greater consolation than that strange instinct which bids them creep close to His foot.

Suddenly her tears ceased, she laughed hysterically, "If I haven't mother, I have my baby," and her tears flowed again, but they were sobs of joy. Those tears washed out all blur or spot that, like mould or rust, was beginning to faintly touch that pure, young soul.

She arose, and with impatient step made her way down from the frowning mountain, with its abysmal shadows and deep gorges, and running down the road to the little cabin home in the canyon, hastened in, and with the key which she had taken with her, unlocked the door and seized her treasure. Wrapping it warm in shawls with motherly instinct, she carried it out into the night, and kissed it again and again. What an experience for a babe! But it was used to its mother's eccentricities, and was always ready to accompany her to the deepest gorge, the highest peak. It was sent to be her comforter, and its trust in her was infinite. The darkest night it looked up in her face and smiled, not knowing whither it was going, and caring not whither so that it was with her.

Harville could not sleep, and the sound of her coming in and going out attracted his attention. Looking from the small-paned window, he saw her hurrying away. In an instant he had flung on his clothes and was following. What rash thing was she about to do—three o'clock in the morning straying through that bleak wilderness? He would follow and protect her from a distance.

What a picture of strangeness and unreality! The waning moon shone with a sickly glare, and looking down saw amid the rocks and fantastically-heaped mountains, a little open gulch, through which passed a small woman with a large baby in her arms, hurrying alone, small but brave, and at a distance a man following, anxious and full of dread. But the moon faintly smiled as she saw the red light beaming from the mill, and the mother and child seek entrance.

But the man frowned, and hastening, saw, unobserved, a picture of domestic bliss—Aleck with his arms enfolding the two, Lorena, whose head was pillowed on his shoulder, and the babe which crowed its joy in the strange accents of the baby language, that tongue which doubtless contains cognate sounds with the first and original language of the human race.

The protective feeling first aroused in his breast gave way to jealous hatred and ugliness of feeling, and he swore an oath to himself—an ugly oath—that he would destroy this happiness, or—"

Human nature is so strange! From love comes hate, from protection, destruction, in only a moment. From the kindly, loving friend of five minutes before, wishing to avert danger from Lorena's path, he became transformed into a subtle enemy determined to destroy her happiness. Love is an awful thing. It cooes like a dove, it coils like a serpent.

Not daring to trust himself at the window farther, he returned to the house, his iron will bent relentlessly on subjugation.

"Lorena," said Aleck, "you don't know how badly I felt today—and you took it so quietly, and did the work so cheerfully. You have a hard time, little woman," he said with feeling. "And I've been thinking it all over. I'm going to made a dead set to get out of this business, and let you see something of the world. And we'll go to San Francisco, and go to all the operas and concerts—how we'll enjoy the music—and baby there shall grow up a civilized child instead of a savage. How did you know I was wanting you so?"

"O, Aleck," cried Lorena, full of happiness, "I wanted you." What truer answer could be born of love?

They sat there in the flickering light of the lamps, the ponderous fly-wheel whirling around, the shining steel machinery sliding backward and forward with its subtle intricacies of mechanism, and pleasant noise, so strangely out of proportion with the clamp, clamp of the stamps and the hissing of the pans in the body of the mill. The engine-room was retirement in comparison.

Aleck made a little nest in the corner with his coat and a blanket, and the baby was allowed to finish its nap, going to sleep as obediently as it had wakened.

"I never realized until to-night, Lorena, how you would shine in society, you have such good taste and are so bright and clever. And I thought if I didn't tell you of it, somebody else might get in ahead of me, sometime. And the first thing I'd know, my little Lorena might be running away with some other fellow;" and Aleck laughed.

"Oh, Aleck," said Lorena, reproachfully.

"Well, we'll fix that all right, I'm going to run away with you myself; I'm going to be that other fellow."

Then they both laughed. Was it a childish happiness that made the rafters of that mill re-echo with merry laughter!

"Say, Aleck," said Lorena, "how much happier we are alone. I wish Judge Harville would go. If he speaks of it again, don't urge him to stay, will you?"

"Why, no!" said Aleck, looking surprised, "but I thought he made it pleasant for you. Why? has he commenced to talk silly? *If he has forgotten himself*"—what a threat of vengeance was conveyed in that tone!

"Oh, no," laughed Lorena, "only he bores me, a little of his style goes a great way, you know. It is six o'clock, isn't it? How fast the time flies in this dear old engine-room. Come, baby, it is time to go." And together the three wended their way home in the grey and chilly dawn. Certainly her husband's love was a charm that encompassed Lorena round, yet if he had not been so kindly, she would possibly have fought her good fight against Ahriman, though not so well armed for the fray. She had resolved to meet him in open fight, disarm and overcome him if she could. There must be no scene, no trouble, no scandal, it must be subtly, silently done.

Judge Harville was courtesy itself all day. Aleck almost forgot Lorena's instructions on the matter, and certainly his faintest suspicion.

But when evening came and Aleck was gone, he turned to her with supplication in his eyes that was almost irresistible. He commenced to tell the story of his life, garnished with brilliant bits of philosophy, it had even an element of pathos in it. Lorena's fancy was kindled unconsciously. Her work lay neglected in her lap, the baby, after sleeping all day, refused to sleep any more and amused itself tumbling blocks around upon the floor.

He went on, the deep love he felt for her coloring everything he touched upon, the impression she had made upon him as a little girl, till finally he reached the snow and her strange appearance with the light. "Oh, Lorena, Fate has ordained this from the beginning of the world, that we should meet and mingle our lives. You cannot escape from fate."

"Well," said she laughing, though it sounded strangely hollow, "I shall spoil fate for once—I'm just stubborn enough to defy it where my will is concerned."

"It seems wrong to you now," said the voice of the tempter, "but a year from now in a high and noble position, Mrs. Judge Harville shall find that she has escaped from a galling slavery and bondage. In her beautiful and lovely home with congenial friends and time for culture and improvement, she will wonder at the tame and profitless existence she led in the years forever past, and rejoice that she had had the ambition, the wisdom to grasp the opportunity which had lifted her from that condition which presented happiness as the happiness of a sheep, dull, quiet, aimless; enough to eat, but nothing else." Harville was nothing if not subtle.

"Is this what I saved you from the coyotes for?" asked Lorena quietly, yet a little dazzled by the picture he so brilliantly painted her.

"I know I stand in a bad light at present," he said rapidly, "but you are too lovely and dainty a blossom to blush unseen, and should see something of the world."

"That's what Aleck said, to-day," said she artlessly.

"I am the instrument of fate sent to interfere in your behalf, and in the years to come you will thank me for the interference. You have saved my life. It belongs to you rightfully; take it then and do what you will with it."

Lorena looked into his eyes hopelessly. Where were her subterfuges, her little arts to cover her feelings, where were the subtleties with which she was going to disarm him? All seemed in a daze around her.

"All conventionalities shall be observed. There shall be no scandal. I know enough of the technicalities of the law to set you free from this bondage without a mar to sully your fair name; and after that—for I shall be patient—the justice or the minister, which ever you like, shall give me the right to care for you." He spoke in a low, thrilling tone.

"Judge Harville, it has always been the great desire of my life to exert a good influence on those around me. Are you deliberately going to make me feel that I am responsible for all this terrible, terrible thing that you are talking about?" It was a direct appeal, and should have awakened his better self. But that vanity of his was underneath all, strong and exacting. He was irritated by her resistance, and threw off the mask which he had so carefully worn.

"I don't know anything about your good influence, I only know that you waken the very devil in me when you come near me. And I cannot endure to see you tied to a stupid dolt of a man who cares nothing for you. It simply maddens me." His voice was hoarse and his eyes were full of evil light.

Lorena's eyes were riveted on him, a strange little red flame seemed to burn in their depths. Was she going to succumb?

"If I should be in great distress," she said in slow, measured tones, her pupils dilated beyond their usual size, "if some one was hounding me, and driving me to death, could I claim your protection?"

"Claim my protection?" he repeated in surprise, and rising to his full height, he spoke, "Lorena, I'd protect you with more than my life if there were anything more to offer."

"Then, Judge Harville," said Lorena, slowly, rising also, *"I claim your protection"*—her voice faltered, her eyes fell, sobs choked her while her heart surged up in mighty throbs—*"I claim your protection from yourself."*

Turning to the table, she fell upon her chair, burying her face upon her arm, and cried like a broken-hearted child, the babe at her feet clinging to her dress, and sobbing in unison with its stricken mother.

Judge Harville drew a long breath. He walked up and down the room a moment. The evil light died out of his eyes. He felt himself a black-hearted fiend—a Mephistopheles—all the false reasoning in his premises stood out like lightning in the black night—his vision became clearer—his selfishness more apparent. He walked to her side, laid his hand gently upon her soft hair.

"Don't grieve," he said, *"you have my protection."*

And that was all.

Daily lives must go on, and daily tasks must be done, though the heavens fall, or earthquakes rend the world. Very quietly Judge Harville took his departure, but he never forgot for a moment, a certain purpose which took possession of him, and after much wire pulling and utilizing of secret influence, he had the pleasure of hearing that Aleck Westbrook had received an appointment from the Governor of the State, which placed him in a position of trust and well on the road to fortune.

Years have passed since that act of self-abnegation, and last winter Judge Harville was called to Washington to attend to an intricate matter of law.

At one of the receptions, where he went merely as a spectator, he stood gazing at the gay throng with weary, careless eyes, when suddenly a profile among the throng carried him back eight years in his life.

He saw the gloomy cañon covered with snow, a light shining from a window, he felt again the breath of the coyotes upon his cheek.

The face turned. It was indeed Lorena, bright, arch, as ever he pictured her, clad in a shimmering satin robe of white, leaning upon her husband's arm, and leading by the hand a beautiful little girl in daintiest lace, erratic a mother as ever, taking the child as naturally with her to a reception, as out into the blackness of the night in the wild Sierras.

A gladness came into Judge Harville's heart, and overflowed at his eyes. He felt a strange sensation of nearness to that beautiful, womanly figure. It was Lorena, and she was resting under his protection still.

*Adah Isaacs Menken (1835–1868). Courtesy of the San
Francisco Performing Arts Library and Museum.*

Adah Isaacs Menken (1835–1868)

Although she was in San Francisco for only a year, Adah Isaacs Menken created great excitement in San Francisco art circles as an actress and as a poet.

Joaquin Miller endorsed her as "the most soulful poetess" he had ever met. Described as dark-eyed with crisp black curls, plump curves and a pleasing voice, Menken had a flair for the dramatic in whatever she did, yet only tidbits are known about her life before San Francisco. She had three husbands and divorced two, one of whom was prize-fighter "Benicia Boy" Heenan. She spoke Hebrew and was probably Jewish; had danced with the New Orleans ballet in Havana; had taught school, perhaps German, Spanish and French; and had started a newspaper in Texas. She had also performed Shakespeare, done vaudeville and published poetry in New York's *Sunday Mercury*. It is easy to see why she was tagged a brilliant woman almost as soon as she arrived in the Bay Area.

She came to San Francisco in 1863 with her third husband, Robert Henry Newell, a well-known humorist who was invited to California to write the Orpheus C. Kerr column for the *Golden Era*. Adah was to write along with him, but she was soon writing poetry instead and becoming immersed in an acting career, creating a stir that San Francisco had not felt since the days of Lola Montez. Meanwhile, her husband was not as well received, being something of a disappointment as a journalist and also almost totally lacking in charm in the eyes of San Franciscans. One local resident commented that he had "little respect for a man who was less important than his wife, who was married to a woman who stripped her body and her soul . . . daily." This comment was in reference to one of the six plays Adah performed during the year she was in San Francisco: for authenticity and effect in *Mazeppa,* an adaptation of a Byron poem, Menken rode a galloping horse across the stage, clad only in a gossamer body stocking. She was not a conventionally beautiful woman, but she was definitely and overtly sensual, and with her cropped dark curls and arousing athletic body, her audiences loved her, going into a frenzy wherever she appeared. But this was not exactly what Adah sought. She did not want to be sensational, she said, but rather respected and admired for her strict insistence on authenticity and realism.

She held the same position on her poetry. She was among the first to recognize the importance of Walt Whitman, who was a controversial young poet at the time. Her own style was free verse, influenced by Whitman, compelling and frank in its call for meaningful, honest human interaction.

Although San Francisco literary audiences usually preferred metered verse, they gave Adah Menken the endorsement she deserved—far more than they gave her husband for his column in the *Era*. This imbalance may have helped drive the couple apart, for they were soon separated and Adah Menken was seen around town with another unmarried woman writer, Ada Clare. The two women socialized with Mark Twain and other well-known male literary figures of the time, and generated more than a little gossip.

But matters more significant than gossip drove the vivacious, sensitive, free spirit of Adah Menken. She obviously questioned her role as a woman, drinking sometimes with men in saloons, able to ride a horse as well as most men on the frontier, not shy of competing with her male literary counterparts. She was not afraid to broach taboo subjects such as sexuality, death and emotional pain in conversation or in her poetry. Like her sensational stage performances, her poetry was raucous, sensual, often shocking, always passionate. Her unhappiness in love was often the subject of her verse. She hyperbolized the highs and lows of human interaction and aloneness, and her lack of restraint was unique and appealing to nineteenth century readers caught in the era of Victorian morality. The reviews of her work were complimentary, praising her emphasis on emotion and her stark, symbolic natural voice. In 1863 a critic described her work as the "frantic soul cries of poetic aspiration, shrieked, as it were, out of the Darkness into the ear of Humanity and God."

Adah Menken found considerable artistic success in San Francisco, but not fulfillment, so she traveled alone to England and later to Paris, where she was entertained by Charles Dickens, George Sand, Alexandre Dumas and others. She was immortalized as "Dolores" by playwright Algernon Swinburne. She died in 1868, at thirty-three, and is buried in Paris under the inscription "Thou Knowest," from Swinburne's play.

Walt Whitman was probably right when he labeled her "another woman born too soon." Some of her poems were published in the *Overland Monthly* and the *Golden Era*. "Resurgam" and "Genius," included here, are taken from *Infelicia,* a posthumous collection dedicated to Charles Dickens and published in 1887.

Resurgam

— ✤ —

I.

Yes, yes, dear love! I am dead!
    Dead to you!
    Dead to the world!
    Dead for ever!
It was one young night in May.
The stars were strangled, and the moon was blind with the
    flying clouds of a black despair.
    Years and years the songless soul waited to drift on:
beyond the sea of pain where the shapeless life was
wrecked.
    The red mouth closed down the breath that was hard
and fierce.
    The mad pulse beat back the baffled life with a low
sob.
    And so the stark and naked soul unfolded its wings to
the dimness of Death!
    A lonely, unknown Death.
    A Death that left this dumb, living body as his endless
mark.
    And left these golden billows of hair to drown the
whiteness of my bosom.
    Left these crimson roses gleaming on my forehead to
hide the dust of the grave.

And Death left an old light in my eyes, and old music
for my tongue, to deceive the crawling worms that would
seek my warm flesh.

But the purple wine that I quaff sends no thrill of Love
and Song through my empty veins.

Yet my red lips are not pallid and horrified.

Thy kisses are doubtless sweet that throb out an eternal
passion for me!

But I feel neither pleasure, passion nor pain.

So I am certainly dead.

Dead in this beauty!

Dead in this velvet and lace!

Dead in these jewels of light!

Dead in the music!

Dead in the dance!

II.

Why did I die?

O love! I waited—I waited years and years ago.

Once the blaze of a far-off edge of living Love crept up
my horizon and promised a new moon of Poesy.

A soul's full life!

A soul's full love!

And promised that my voice should ring trancing
shivers of rapt melody down the grooves of this dumb
earth.

And promised that echoes should vibrate along the purple
spheres of unfathomable seas, to the soundless folds
of the clouds.

And promised that I should know the sweet sisterhood
of the stars.

Promised that I should live with the crooked moon in
her eternal beauty.

But a Midnight swooped down to bridegroom the Day.

The blazing Sphynx of that far off, echoless promise,
shrank into a drowsy shroud that mocked the crying stars
of my soul's unuttered song.

And so I died.

Died this uncoffined and unburied Death.

Died alone in the young May night.

Died with my fingers grasping the white throat of many
a prayer.

III.

Yes, dear love, I died!

You smile because you see no cold, damp cerements of
a lonely grave hiding the youth of my fair face.

No head-stone marks the gold of my poor unburied
head.

But the flaunting poppy covered her red heart in the
sand.

Who can hear the slow drip of blood from a dead soul?

No Christ of the Past writes on my laughing brow His
"Resurgam."

Resurgam.

What is that when I have been dead these long weary
years!

IV.

Silver walls of Sea!
Gold and spice laden barges!
　White-sailed ships from Indian seas, with costly pearls
and tropic wines go by unheeding!
　None pause to lay one token at my feet.
　No mariner lifts his silken banner for my answering hail.
　No messages from the living to the dead.
　Must all lips fall out of sound as the soul dies to be
heard?
　Shall Love send back no revelation through this
interminable distance of Death?
　Can He who promised the ripe Harvest forget the
weeping Sower?
　How can I stand here so calm?
　I hear the clods closing down my coffin, and yet shriek
not out like the pitiless wind, nor reach my wild arms after
my dead soul!
　Will no sun of fire again rise over the solemn East?
　I am tired of the foolish moon showing only her haggard
face above the rocks and chasms of my grave.
　O Rocks! O Chasms! sink back to your black cradles
in the West!
　　　Leave me dead in the depths!
　　　Leave me dead in the wine!
　　　Leave me dead in the dance!

V.

How did I die?
The man I loved—he—he—ah, well!
There is no voice from the grave.
The ship that went down at sea, with seven times a
thousand souls for Death, sent back no answer.
The breeze is voiceless that saw the sails shattered in
the mad tempest, and heard the cry for mercy as one frail
arm clung to the last spar of the sinking wreck.
Fainting souls rung out their unuttered messages to the
silent clouds.
Alas! I died not so!
I died not so!

VI.

How did I die?
No man has wrenched his shroud from his stiffened
corpse to say:
"*Ye murdered me!*"
No woman has died with enough of Christ in her soul
to tear the bandage from her glassy eyes and say:
"*Ye crucified me!*"
Resurgam! Resurgam!

GENIUS

—— ❧·❧ ——

"Where'er there's a life to be kindled by love,
   Wherever a soul to inspire,
Strike this key-note of God that trembles above
   Night's silver-tongued voices of fire."

Genius is power.

The power that grasps in the universe, that dives out beyond space, and grapples with the starry worlds of heaven.

If genius achieves nothing, shows us no results, it is so much the less genius.

The man who is constantly fearing a lion in his path is a coward.

The man or woman whom excessive caution holds back from striking the anvil with earnest endeavor, is poor and cowardly of purpose.

The required step must be taken to reach the goal, though a precipice be the result.

Work must be done, and the result left to God.

The soul that is in earnest, will not stop to count the cost.

Circumstances cannot control genius: it will nestle with them: its power will bend and break them to its path.

This very audacity is divine.

Jesus of Nazareth did not ask the consent of the high priests in the temple when he drove out the "money-changers;" but, impelled by inspiration, he knotted the cords and drove them hence.

Genius will find room for itself, or it is none.

Men and women, in all grades of life, do their utmost.
If they do little, it is because they have no capacity to do more.
I hear people speak of "unfortunate genius," of "poets who
never penned their inspirations;" that

> "Some mute inglorious Milton here may rest;"

of "unappreciated talent," and "malignant stars," and other
contradictory things.

It is all nonsense.

Where power exists, it cannot be suppressed any more than
the earthquake can be smothered.

As well attempt to seal up the crater of Vesuvius as to hide
God's given power of the soul.

> "You may as well forbid the mountain pines
> To wag their high tops, and to make no noise
> When they are fretten with the gusts of heaven,"

as to hush the voice of genius.

There is no such thing as unfortunate genius.

If a man or woman is fit for work, God appoints the field.

He does more; He points to the earth with her mountains,
oceans, and cataracts, and says to man, *"Be great!"*

He points to the eternal dome of heaven and its blazing worlds,
and says: "Bound out thy life with beauty."

He points to the myriads of down-trodden, suffering men and
women, and says: "Work with me for the redemption of these,
my children."

He lures, and incites, and thrusts greatness upon men, and
they will not take the gift.

Genius, on the contrary, loves toil, impediment, and poverty;
for from these it gains its strength, throws off the shadows, and
lifts its proud head to immortality.

Neglect is but the fiat to an undying future.

To be popular is to be endorsed in the To-day and forgotten in the To-morrow.

It is the mess of pottage that alienates the birth-right.

Genius that succumbs to misfortune, that allows itself to be blotted by the slime of slander—and other serpents that infest society—is so much the less genius.

The weak man or woman who stoops to whine over neglect, and poverty, and the snarls of the world, gives the sign of his or her own littleness.

Genius is power.

The eternal power that can silence worlds with its voice, and battle to the death ten thousand armed Hercules.

Then make way for this God-crowned Spirit of Night, that was born in that Continuing City, but lives in lowly and down-trodden souls!

Fling out the banner!

Its broad folds of sunshine will wave over turret and dome, and over the thunder of oceans on to eternity.

"Fling it out, fling it out o'er the din of the world!

    Make way for this banner of flame,

That streams from the mast-head of ages unfurled,

    And inscribed by the deathless in name.

And thus through the years of eternity's flight,

    This insignia of soul shall prevail,

The centre of glory, the focus of light;

    O Genius! proud Genius, all hail!"

Ada Clare (1836–1874)

Ada Clare came to San Francisco as the "Queen of Bohemia." She had already broken ground as a feminist in New York City, and to San Francisco she brought a burning desire to start a small, egalitarian conclave of academics and artists in the new frontier. But she was a hundred years too early. Had she come to San Francisco in the 1960s she might have realized her greatest dreams.

Born in the deep south as Jane McElheny, Ada Clare was in New York publishing lurid poems that shocked even cosmopolitan audiences when she was only nineteen. She gained some respect there, but dreamed of more, so at twenty-one she moved to Paris, to the Latin Quarter, where she sent provocative letters back to New York papers detailing her unorthodox life. When she returned to New York she brought with her an illegitimate son by musician-composer Louis Moreau Gottschalk. Uncompromising in her self-determined standards, she challenged and shocked the more staid members of society by announcing herself in print and in person as "Miss Ada Clare and Son."

Ada Clare intended to set up an American version of the Paris Latin Quarter in New York, but was unable to interest a large enough group of like-minded artists. Nonetheless, she was a main attraction at Pfaff's, a local artists' cafe, where she read her columns and poetry to large audiences. She attracted praise from many notables, including William Dean Howells and Walt Whitman.

In 1864, unable to fulfill her dream of a new Bohemia in New York, Ada Clare came to San Francisco, hoping her plans for a liberal community could be realized in the new west. She had an invitation from the *Golden Era* to write a weekly column. The *Era* editor had titillated his audience prior to her arrival, intimating that she would add an air of New York sophistication and European culture to San Francisco journalism. This build-up was hard to live up to, but within weeks she commanded a respectably large audience, and for some time she was noted as one of the three top columnists in the city.

In the end, though, Ada Clare and San Francisco readers were not a good match. Perhaps it was because, by the time she arrived, Californians desired a more conservative society than Clare proposed, wanting to get away from the rowdy reputation San Francisco had acquired. Or

Ada Clare (1836–1874). Courtesy of the Bancroft Library.

perhaps she represented the frank, liberal views that were becoming popular in New York and Europe, but which clashed with the rather stalwart, middle-class, sometimes romantic values which were prevalent on the west coast. Whatever the reason, the mismatch seems clear, and the breach was a mutual one. Ada Clare's opinion of Californians—a "people without any remembered past"—was not flattering.

Ada Clare and Adah Isaacs Menken became friends in San Francisco. Both were southern women, had survived New York City, and were frank in their approaches to sex, human need, and women's rights. On one occasion they hosted a party for Dan deQuille and Mark Twain, both reporters for the *Territorial Enterprise*. As later related by deQuille, the men fell under the spell of the two attractive women, whereupon Twain began to croon tunes from his home state, Missouri. All was festive until Twain, thinking to kick one of Menken's ten dogs under the table, accidentally inflicted a painful gash to Menken's leg instead.

Clare even followed Menken to the stage, performing *Camille* for San Francisco audiences, but without great success. The play closed after only a few weeks. At the same time, her disappointment was reflected in her column, which became increasingly ironic and critical. Discouraged by her perceived failures in San Francisco, and perhaps frustrated by life in general, Ada Clare left San Francisco for the Sandwich Islands with local poet Charles Warren Stoddard in the winter of 1864, just less than a year after she had arrived.

Her weekly columns for the *Golden Era* covered a variety of topics—fashion, theater, local color, tradition, food and humor. In them, she presents a candid, unique and refreshing point of view, and a master's command of style. Her works, besides uncollected poetry, include columns and reviews for the *Sunday Press* and the *Sunday Mercury* in New York City. The selections reprinted here were all published in the *Golden Era* in 1864 and 1865. Clare also completed an autobiographical novel, *Only a Woman's Heart*.

Perhaps Walt Whitman was right. Admiring her courage to be herself and her frank poetry, he labeled Ada Clare a "new woman born too soon." This may explain why those who read her today find in her ironic humor so much relevance to contemporary life.

THE PAST

— ❧❦ —

March 27, 1864

As I see more of your California I discover new traits of character and person to attract my study, or exercise my curiosity.

Wherever I observe these present holders and possessors of the Golden State, whether in the drawing room, at table, in the theatre or on the steamboat, I notice a something about them all that strikes me as very peculiar.

They seem to be people without any remembered Past, save as it may sometimes come to themselves and their neighbors in a confused sense of having been born in some other place at some vaguely remote period.

Though I cannot exactly specify why, there surely is a certain something in their general expression of countenance, tone of converse, movements and aims, which suggests to me, either the anomaly of matured human beings circumstantially created of the Present exclusively, or the novelty of sentient creatures whose entities are all in the present hour, and inseparable from the present place.

Perhaps I, too, shall become one of these iconoclastic Californians, by magnetic sympathy, if I stay here long enough; but just now there is too much of the old reflective style of humanity in my mental composition to make me feel entirely at home with the Pastless around me.

Scarcely an hour ago I forgot that I was in California.

The present lost its distinctness to confer it on the absent. And, led by the angel Memory, glided before me the shadows of the Past.

Old hopes whose eyes are now closed in death. Old griefs which have been transfigured into guardian spirits. Old disappointments which are subjects of thanksgiving.

Old thoughts and opinions that I now recognize to be illusions, and old sins that, like the elder gods of story, have been dethroned by their children.

Ancient resolves yet to be executed. Ancient faiths with dust upon their garments. Ancient happiness to console me for the future, and ancient misery to teach me how to endure it.

The friendships and enmities, the books and the battles of girlhood. The dreams and doubts, the thousand fancies and purposes of youth. And one sweet face that I loved without tumult, and kissed without passion, which I have now lost sight of forever.

Are these all? Ah, me!—I could fill pages with the records gathered from the red-leaved tablet in my bosom, but I mind me of the poet's words—

> "Not easily forgiven is he, who,
> Setting wide the bridal chambers of the heart,
> Lets in the day."

Few of us value our past sufficiently. Most people look upon it as a game that has been played, and ought to be forgotten.

In reckoning up their sum total of happiness, they add the present to their hopes in the future; but the past is spent money, and does not enter into the result.

They can hardly be said to live a life, or they live it only by fragments. Is not this a sort of daily death? It would be better to think of that past as a part of our present existence, as property still in our possession, which like the purse of Fortunatus, is full of exhaustless pleasures.

So we should be no longer cramped within a single pin-point of time, but enjoy the past, the present and the future together.

THE MAN'S SPHERE
AND INFLUENCE

— ❯·❰ —

April 3, 1864

I noticed one thing that grieved and annoyed me. That is, seeing so many gentlemen out without any body to take care of them, expressing their opinions without asking any body's leave, and enjoying the music without begging any lady's pardon. But is it strictly proper that a man should take care of himself, mind his own business and act like a rational, sincere and responsible human being. All this might do very well if it would end here; but alas! may it not lead the man into the rostrum, the pulpit, the auctioneer's desk and finally into the editor's sanctum.

I confess that though I often admire the writings of men, it always pains me to see a man exposing himself to public remark and to the gaze of women, by coming publicly forward in print. The sacred precinct of home is the real sphere of man. Modesty, obedience, sobriety are the true male virtues.

We love to see the sweet male violets hidden under domestic greens.

I don't mean to say that men have never succeeded in writing, but compare them with the great pen-women of the present, past and future, and where are they? Echo answers "gone out for an hour; in case of fire, keys may be found next door."

There is something effeminate in the literary or artist man, that our sex repudiates. We do not want man to be too highly educated; we want him sweet, gentle, and incontestibly stupid.

There are many things he can learn with impunity—the multiplication table for instance. He should learn to read, also; because the works of T. S. Arthur and the publications of the American Tract Socity should sometimes beguile his weary hours. But, above all things in his education, let not the sacred dumpling be neglected.

But why puzzle his brain, built for the cultivation of the moral sense and the adaptation of virtue, with such abstruse sciences as geography, history, grammar, spelling, guaging, etc.

It must not be supposed that we despise men; in their proper sphere we are willing to love, cherish and protect them. But we do not want them as rivals; we wish them low, in order that we may be able to come down from our dignity and stoop to them. Their strength must lie in their weakness. When we draw them under the wings of our protection, let them not take to crowing.

TAKING LEAVE

— ❧❧ —

April 24, 1864

I have discovered one curious thing about California, and that is the strange pleasure they have in getting rid of people.

For that reason, California is the best place I know of to die in. For in taking leave of them for the undiscovered country, from whose bourne no traveler returns, they are sure that no tide of fate or fortune will ever drift you back to them.

In this respect, it reminds me of a grand old Roman custom. A certain way, leading out from the city, was set apart for the statues of those men who, exiled or persecuted during life, were here deified after death.

For this reason, nothing excels the kindness, generosity, and gallantry of the Californians when you are parting with them.

In a short time from this, when I am going away, I expect they will find out, not, of course, that I write well, but that I know how to spell, and have a speaking acquaintance with Lindley Murray, which will be some praise, if not a very enthusiastic kind.

The Bureau of California and Nevada, unlike that of most young couples, has not a pin-cushion upon it, with "welcome little stranger" worked thereon.

The invocation here is "go, and God bless you," "and if you must call again, call when you can't stay quite so long."

Now I like this in California. Of all the traits in national character, I like this the best. It shows how much she is in advance of other new countries. In fact, I never saw so much wisdom, justice and forbearance in so short a time, as I have seen in the few weeks I have been here.

No wonder people are anxious to get away from California, for they feel that they cannot by any amount of mental tip-toeing rise up to her standard. They can never, unless they came here in the mining days, display that courage, intelligence and taste which so runs riot here. Modesty and a true appreciation of the surpassing merits of California, alone cause people to hanker after leaving the Golden Gate behind them.

California is pledged to prosperity, is bound over to keep success, and the more people that come here and go away, the more profitable will be the steam navigation of the Pacific, and navigation is the thief of time.

Moral: Rolling mosses gather no stones.

ABOUT THE FASHIONS

— ❧·❧ —

April 24, 1864

Fashion is by no means an absolute monarch in this country. In fact it is hard to tell what are the exact fashions here. Dresses are worn of every kind of stuff, (more especially of the costly ones,) and made in every conceivable way. They are made with short waists, with long waists, and with round ones. They are made with long, short, round, double or triple points. They are shut, open or double-breasted in front. And with complete basques, postillion basques, lappelle basques, and hip basques. All of these fashions have either lived their season, or are living them, in the great cities of the world. But here they are all worn simultaneously and with perfect originality. Everybody tries her own taste, and sails under her own independent colors.

You meet long talmas, jackets, sacques of a hundred different patterns, scarfs, shawls and mantillas floating down Montgomery street. Any one of them as much in favor as another, proudly and I think wisely unconscious that its prototype is not to be found on the Boulevards or Broadway.

For my part I like and esteem this characteristic. It gives such a chance to sensible people.

Now in New York the fashions spread like a wildfire or an epidemic. If it were for instance a tall bonnet, or a postillion basque, or a square sacque that came into fashion, it stood as it were on the street corners and took you by the throat. In a week it swept over Broadway in one smooth unbroken stream, and bore down all opposition like a flood tide.

The evil of that lay in this fact, that you must adopt a style although it obscured your good points and exaggerated your bad

{ 310 }

ones. For instance, if you had a long thin face you were forced to elongate it still further with a tall narrow bonnet that made your face look like one of those toy india rubber heads, that children stretch out until it is almost an illustration of a straight line, length without breadth. So if you happened to be short and pudgy, you must put on a postillion basque to diminish your length and increase your breadth, till you shaped yourself like a pumpkin with three frills around it.

That's the reason why I like the independent fashions here, for though it may cause women without good breeding and taste to make themselves still more ridiculous, yet it opens the way for common sense to assert itself, and gives a fair field that will always in the long run, win the day.

But I see here a disposition to discard hoop-skirts, as in most other large cities. I don't like it. I am as much opposed to the immense, swaggering hoops as anybody, but I think the small ones not only a blessing but a necessity in a lady's toilette, if the public insists that she shall wear a long dress.

As long as the public modesty is such that even the most indistinct symptom of limbs in a woman is considered a dangerous and demoralizing thing, the hoop-skirt will remain a beauty and a blessing. The attempt to disguise the shape of the woman by hanging innumerable heavy skirts about her hips has ever been disastrous to her health and spirits. A few years ago the weight which women were expected to carry suspended in that way, threatened to decimate the ranks of beauty.

Just as that barbarous weight was increased by the quilt, the rope-skirt, the corded skirt, the flounced skirt, and woman's burden had become greater than she could bear, an angel came lightly up to her and in expanding its wings, snatched from her the grievous burden and bade her go and suffer no more. This angel was in the shape of numerous rows of light and well covered steel, all linked together with narrow tape, and so nicely adjusted with bands, etc., that the waist, the hips and the shoulders were equally intrusted with carrying it—commonly called the hoop-skirt.

At this angelic approach, away fled the savage garments so long the torture of our sex, and the reign of the light weights began.

If ladies were allowed to wear short dresses, the hoop-skirt could be done away with, immediately, but with the present flowing robes—never.

But even with the blessing of the hoop-skirt, the woman's costume entirely indisposes her for out door exercise. For before she can go out into the street, she must go through with a series of manoeuvres as tedious as a military drill.

A man has nothing to do in going out, but to put his hat on and he is in full dress, but the number of things a woman has to put on and take off, involves such a sacrifice of time and patience as puts many premature wrinkles on her brow. The consequence is, regular exercise is very rare among women, and no wonder that men, their offspring, have such weak digestions and such selfish habits.

The new Dio Lewis system of gymnastics is calculated, I think, to teach women how to combine beauty, good taste and hygiene in dress. For to a well-informed mind, nothing can be beautiful that is injurious to health. It is only gross ignorance that could find any beauty in tight lacing and tight boots, and paper-soled shoes for winter. The adaptation of the costume to the unalterable laws of nature is the very marrow of good taste.

Some day when I am punctual, I am going to go round and visit the principal emporiums of fashion, and give some descriptions (for the benefit of the ladies, no gentlemen need apply,) of the new styles of importation.

I have no doubt that any man who reads this, will consider me a graduated and titled idiot. They always speak of woman's love for dress and all the departments of the toilette, as an evidence of the enormous inferiority of our sex as regards his.

A woman's love for dressing, decorating or ornamenting herself, is often the only way she has of developing her artistic tastes. In this way she exhibits her power of blending colors, of softening blemishes and throwing out beauties, of combining cause and effect. Often it is her blind groping out after the beautiful, an undefined longing after all that is harmonious and graceful.

Women do not all adorn themselves out of vanity by any means.

And then when men complain about our being wrapped up in trifles, I would like to know if cigars are not also trifles, if drinks are not trifles, if clubs are not trifles? That is, trifles as compared with the most serious questions of life, and with the momentous questions of the future.

The trifles of womanhood are at least innocent trifles, whereas the trifles of manhood are too often guilty trifles.

THE FATAL PIE

—— ❧·❧ ——

May 15, 1864

In these days when philanthropy is so followed, a new invention added to her stock in trade is a blessing.

Temperance, anti–lunatic asylumism, anti-slavery, anti–capital punishment, anti-greenbacks and anti–women's rights, are getting to be very tedious insects. I offer to any enterprising reformer, as a gift, my new branch of philanthropy—a crusade against the fatal pie.

I enroll myself as the first *anti pieatist.*

By the pie, I mean that dense leaden-hued or flakily unctuous (as the case may be) concavity of dough, within which certain substances are forcibly imprisoned, called generally after respectable fruits. This awful thing has found its way into most private dwellings and all public houses.

Its use in many places supersedes that of brandy, but the two horrible drugs are oftener consumed together.

The outer walls of the fatal pie are composed in many instances of musty and incapable flour united to the lard of hogs, grown too rabid even for the consumption of that animal. Into these domestic coffins are placed masses of superannuated preserves doctored with any or many of the acid family, and the whole hermetically sealed with a cover of the insidious dough. I have seen fathers of families preaching against the horrors of spirituous liquors, while they were building up dyspeptic mountains on the plates of their children, in the shape of the demoniac pie.

Once in New York I visited one of those pie-cellars, in which the clerks of the busy city come down to swallow a hasty lunch of the pie.

Innocent young men with blue eyes and corn-like hair, intrusted with banking business, with brokerage, with speculations in stocks, with commission business, with flour and grain, with book-publishing, all, all sucked into this whirlpool, all standing in their spotless innocence and ardent faith to feed on the accursed food.

One fair young man, with eyes as blue as a corn-blossom, demanded a pumpkin pie, a blear circular thing apparently moist from the breaking out of a horrid perspiration through its ghastly pores, and covered with a light yellow glue which looked as though it had been fabricated from the union of soft soap and sugar, through which ran intersecting streaks of dark orange, swelling out like angry veins. Into the innocent mouth this thing is thrust, crammed, nay jammed, and lo! in an instant it has joined the invisible! The glass of cheap brandy which followed the pie, seemed to me in comparison to it, a mild form of madness.

While traveling in England a fearful accident occured to me on the train for Oxford. Even now I tremble and turn pale in relating it.

It was near dusk; it was hailing slightly, it was raining a good deal and the wind moaned drearily through the screams of the engine.

In the midst of a very short nap, I was awakened by the wild cry "ten minutes for refreshments." In a few moments after stopping, one of the gentlemen who occupied the same rail-carriage with me, returned and begged me to eat a certain something it was too dark for me to see. Supposing it to be a respectable cake or roll, I bit into one side of it, and instantly felt as though my teeth were like those of Cadmus' Dragon, and were about to rise up and alay me through outraged personality.

Reader, I had tasted an *Eel Pie*.

Years may snow their whiteness upon this head; this hand may become palsied; this heart may lose the faculty of admiration—but never will I forget the emotions of that moment.

You have all of you—born to trouble as the sparks fly upward—tasted the eel, and you have doubtless remarked that alas! too many of them suggest the unmitigated whale-blubber. These are the ones usually devoted to the pie, after having been served as a fish, and refused by the indignant eater. They are then shut up in opaque and air-tight walls of dough, and left to intensify and aggravate their own implacable spermoiliness.

When these have remained on the counter three or four days, imagine the emotion of one who opens them.

That emotion was mine.

The feeling of the Arabian Night Fisherman, who opened the casket on the sea-shore and let out of it the tallest of the Genii, was mild in comparison.

I am going to close this article with the melancholy confessions of a wrecked and beaconless pie-eater.

It was in a private and select circle that he rose up suddenly and spoke: "Oh, my friends," he cried, "I have had youth and strength, and friends, and hopes like you; but where are they all?—buried under the fatal pie. Avoid the pie, for it leadeth to destruction; it seemeth brilliant, and fair, and fascinating, but it leadeth to ruin and shame.

"My father was a noble soap-boiler. Methinks I see him now, as he stood the proud lord of many tons of bones and soda. The lien of the lye vat evoking the yellow bars from the machinery as the furnaces of the Pacific burn off the bars of gold or silver whose presence causes the Californians to snub the green leaves of the goodly tree of national currency, which is getting greener and healthier every day.

"Of that tender soft soap-boiler's heart I was the hope and pride. One miserable day I met with evil companions, who persuaded me to eat oyster-pie,—a pie peopled with oysters in their dotage, delivered over in their second childhood to the tender mercies of dough.

"O, wretched pie! Thou wast the rock upon which the bark, aye and the bite, of my hopes struck and went down. From that moment I became a slave to pie. My wife entreated. My child held up its little hands. My friends reasoned. The pastor prayed for me. But the demon had entered my soul and would not be dispossessed.

"I went on eating and eating to my own ruin. Day after day, night after night, I haunted the pie-cellar, with staring eyes and disheveled hair, eating, eating, until the friendly policeman conveyed me to my abode.

"Ah, that abode! how had the loveliness of its walls fallen away! Pie was written on every fragment of my broken hearth-stone and fire-irons—pie on the haggard hysterical face of my wife—pie on the rickety raggedness of my children! I had now eated up all my substance; through the medium of pie I had masticated whole acres of landed estate and thirteen brick houses.

"Finally the last sad act of the drama remains to be told.

"One night I returned home in a state of madness, and unable to sleep, ordered one of my children forth to purchase more pie, in order to stifle with it the gnawings of conscience. Heedless of the child's entreaties, I forced her forth. She returned with pie in her trembling hands. While I devoured it, I heard the sound of sobs and cries proceeding from my family, who now slept on the floor, their bed having been pawned the preceding week. A fiendish thought suddenly swirled into my mind. Enraged by their grief, I determined to make them eat of the pie. I seized my wife by the hair, and dragged her to the middle of the room.

" 'Wretch,' I cried, 'eat, eat!'

"Vain were her tears, her entreaties, her anguish. By force she gobbled the pie; by force the children devoured it. Suddenly smitten by remorse and terror, I left them swooning on the floor, and fled forever the wretched hovel.

"I know not, I inquire not if death then claimed them for its own, but from that hour I was a changed man, and pie has not passed these lips.

"Oh my friends, my young friends, take solemn warning by me, and when you see the remorseless tin plate with the syren pies thereupon, singing in dulcet tones, 'I am thine if thou hast ten cents, a bit for a bit, chink down the dime and claim me with yonder carving knife,' then I say stay not upon the order of your going, but lift up your feet and go. Remember that the feet of the pie-eater are planted on dough, and waves of tartar emetic roll around him. On one side yawns the dyspeptic Charybdis, on the other towers up the erysipilistic Scylla!"

Here the voice stopped, and I was looking around for my reticule to find my handkerchief, to burst into tears, when some one cut off the flood gates of my emotions, saying, "Pay no attention to that stupid old dyspeptic. He gets the night-mare occasionally and talks in that way. To-night he has overeaten, nay, he has gorged himself with mince-pie, and this is the result."

This, indeed staggered me, for everybody knows that none of the reformed drunkards ever preach eloquent and tear-drawing temperance under the sunset glow which the human anatomy is said to receive from Jamaica rum.

Ah, no; never!

ROBINSON'S GYMNASIUM

— ❯·❮ —

June 19, 1864

The new system of gymnastics, originated by Dr. Dio Lewis, is one of the most marked movements of the age. As a blessing to women, there are no words to express its calibre. Useful as it may be to men, it is for women that it most legislates. For men have a thousand ways of feeding and building up their physical lives, which women never have. The great distinguishing feature of this new gymnastic movement is its establishing the fact, that women have a right to be healthy, and emancipating her from the dogma that it was feminine and womanly to be sickly.

Once upon a time it was considered almost immoral to be healthy. The worn woman, with feeble step, thick lips and wrinkled skin, with one or two organic diseases, was the ideal of feminine virtue and the woman after the moralist's own heart. For a married woman to be healthy, and what was worse, happy, was a dark sign indeed. Women had come to think ill-health their birth-right.

In this world where we must wander, tangled and tied up in the mazes of the tyranous long dress, nothing temporarily is of so much importance to us, as our health and general physical condition. Half of the cases that occur of ill-treated women, are cases in which the woman is in ill health, for the man above all things most dislikes the sick woman. In reading those horrible cases of male brutality, the women who are knocked down with flat-irons, whose heads are trodden upon with iron-heeled boots, whose countenances are perforated with three-pronged forks, and whose chests are flattened with heavy knees, are generally weak women with a half-dozen depressing diseases, with a swarm of scrofulous, neglected babies whom the poor mother is too ill to care for.

Much, nay, half of the ill-health of women, is the result of their own imprudence. There is a horribly pernicious sentiment prevailing among novel writers, which always represents the interesting heroine as being fragile, delicate and unhealthy. This sentiment has found its way into boarding-schools, so that the fat and healthy girls are regarded with an insulting pity, by their dyspeptic companions.

My own experience will serve as an instance of what is occurring every day and every minute. When about thirteen years of age, I was what was called in extreme scorn by the school misses, a hearty girl. A great deal of exercise in the open air, a devotion to running, swimming, climbing, wrestling, etc., rather than to sewing, reading and worsted work, had produced in me a physical development, a vigorous health, an exhuberant flow of spirits, which is, alas! too rarely found in girls. I ignored sentiment, nerves and sickness; and the time when most girls are just budding in coquetry, I spent in climbing fig-trees, turning somersaults in the grass, riding unsaddled horses, swimming in the open stream, paddling leaky little boats, and making myself the rough and tumble companion of boys.

But alas! I had female relatives, brought up in the old girl-slaughtering style. They remonstrated with me, threatened me, wept over me, warned me, prayed for me. I was told that it was a sin for a girl of my age, grown, as I was, to persist in being a hoyden, and was unceasingly entreated to become that devitalized and automatal thing, a perfect lady. I was told that it was my pious duty never to do anything for myself that I could tease a man into doing. I must become a serious annoyance and an unnecessary care to the male, before I could become a well-bred female.

Well, I tried my best to become "a lady;" I drank a glass of vinegar before breakfast to diminish my healthy appetite. I devoured sugar-plums with the ostensible object of acquiring a well-bred headache, and lemons in the hope of becoming thin. Everything injurious, in fact, that would be taken into the human stomach, I boldly consumed, with the hope of sickening myself, and I succeeded in losing my appetite, but health would not go.

Then I gave up feebleness in despair, and did my duty only in bidding good-by to climbing, wrestling and shinny sticks. But alas! how deeply I regret it now; I would I had played the hoyden to the very last moment that mental carelessness would allow. Animal spirits should be cultivated to the extreme, since the toils and pains of female existence so soon bring heaviness of spirits, and burden the nature with the weary carrying of useless but enfeebling weights.

Happily, for a few years, a great change has been going on in the public standard for women. Organic disease has ceased to be cherished by sentiment, the heroine of romance no more wears the hectic flush, and the perforated lung is no longer admired in the female bosom.

After all, I believe that when women become generally healthy, that brutal husbands will be much rarer than they are now; for what is more adapted to stimulate all the worst impulses of a bad man, than union to a miserable, pining, ill woman. None but the higher order of men can be intimately associated with a sick woman without despising her.

Encouraged by the wonderful success of his much admired sister, Mrs. Plumb, Mr. Robinson determined to establish a similar gymnasium here, and with what success may be seen by the number of scholars who have already flocked under his banners.

The exercises in some manner resemble those of a military drill, and are chosen with the view of bringing out those muscles that lie inert in the action of ordinary movements, raising them to the standard of those necessarily used in living, and thus establishing the balance and unison of the whole system. It is a simple and beautiful theory for developing elasticity, suppleness, accuracy, courage, dash, presence of mind and strength in so much as these qualities express it. To set every muscle and sinew free, as it were, and round the whole physical life off into perfect harmony, are its objects, not the mere ridiculous lifting of weights and performance of the ring-man's tricks.

Perhaps the greatest charm of the whole affair is the regulation of all these movements to music; music which is the very soul of order, which from confusion evolves harmony, and from discord unison. The very spheres must move to music; the planetary orbs, the central suns, the swift-whirling comets, each must march to the strains of divine melody, to the sublime choral sweeps of eternity, lest they clash in awful discord, and dash themselves dead down the fathomless steeps of space.

No sight could be prettier than a group of fifty or sixty ladies dressed in the jaunty and piquant bloomer dresses which the exercises demand, with the glow of health on their faces and the light of a healthful interest in their minds, and exhibiting in every movement a suppleness and a grace which only thorough liberation of the muscles could give.

Gentlemen are also admitted to Mr. Robinson's class, and some very fine specimens of the same I saw at his exhibition, handsome, manly and courteous. These exercises will be found peculiarly advantageous to lawyers and professional men of all ranks, who are continually using the brain without a corresponding use of the rest of the body, who are drawing steadily upon the reservoir of the nerve force, without feeding it from without. For such, this system is peculiarly calculated to restore the balance of power.

But bachelors who call themselves "not marrying men" had better take care of their hearts on such occasions. They may resist the ladies in the ball-room or the streets, but in this pretty, bewitching attire, and involved in the mazes of such graceful and natural movements, they will be almost irresistible. And you may travel a great many miles and not find as many pretty, sweet faces as that class of Mr. Robinson's will show.

THE TENDER PASSION

— ➤•◄ —

June 26, 1864

I have been accused of paying no attention to this very interesting subject. The fact is no body can write in the abstract about it, without appearing, if not being very foolish. What is true to one on the subject is ridiculously false to another.

A very dainty little rose-colored note, signed "Euphenia," has inquired of me this week whether I believed that people could love twice.

My answer is that it depends on the temperament. With some people, love is a sensation created in the mind, by the contemplation of an object, fitted to produce the mental state. This kind of love is not often found twice in the same career.

With others, love is the natural essence of the being, and these go about to shape an object to fit the already existing sensation. This kind of love can occur and re-occur, as long as the life of the being holds together.

Yet it must not be supposed that the removal of the affections from one object to another is attended with no disagreeable and inconvenient consequences. My grandmother used to say with regard to the wear and tear of one's furniture in moving from one house to another, that three moves were equal to a fire; so in affectional migrations three changes of the object of the tender passion is equal to a broken heart.

There would be none of these perplexities and removings of the affections if that old saying were true that "love begets love."

This ought to be true, and if the world were in a healthy state it would be, but the world has planetary indigestion and the dyspepsia of continents, therefore all the machinery of inner life is at sixes and sevens and seventy times sevens.

But if love alone begot love, it would be a delightful family indeed of pure blood and high texture. But, alas! 'tis not so. Love very seldom begets love. Pride, vanity, egotism, interest, pique, oppositions and even hate quite as often give rise to it.

If to love were to be loved, what would become of broken hearts, general tragedy, woman's tears, seducers' hellish designs, and all that family of agitations that make the fortune of the dramatist and romance writer?

There is still another infamous old saw that declares that "women and spaniels love you better the more you ill-treat them."

That is about equal to saying, that the greater the weight you suspend upon a rope, the stronger it is. The rope, on the contrary, is not strong because of the weight, but in spite of it.

Of spaniels I will not aspire to speak, but for women the only grain of truth in the remark is this,—that their love is such a tough, obstinate, and strangely endurable thing that it will bear up very heavy weights. But that weight is not the less a drag upon it, and when it gets a little too heavy, happily the cord must snap and precipitate both love and burden into the abyss where they belong.

THE "BLUE STOCKING"

— ❧·❦ —

July 3, 1864

Once upon a time, I'm told the Blue Stocking was a living fact; now she exists only in the minds of the fogy-men old enough to remember her. Some of these curious old fossil-fellows are still extant, and through means of these eye-witnesses and the copious analyses of various male writers, I am thus taught to conceive of her exact picture. For both the minds and works of such male beings kindly retain an unfailing fund of the noxious scales from this fish, in order that we may know how the horrid creature sported herself in the slimy waters of her existence.

Thus to my eye she is painted. The Blue Stocking is an intellectual woman. She is a female who possesseth mental gifts. These mental gifts, of whatever nature they be, she weareth in the manner the porcupine doth his quills and with the same intention. She hath wrenched the curves from her form and her body is thus bounded with square lines, with the occasional diversity of a wildly acute angle. Her hair calleth the brush and comb its direct foe. A threatening pen gapes at each ear. Her claw-like hands are long, scraggy and immortally ink-spotted. Her feet are clothed in maimed stockings, and forlorn slippers flap their wings about her heels as she walketh. Such is the seediness of her attire, that the scavenger claimeth her for his own, the sympathetic ash-barrel singeth to her "come rest in this bosom," and the scare-crow waggeth at her the corn-stalk of scorn as she passeth.

Doubly an Amazon, she hath seared her two breasts, in order to plant upon them the iron muskets of literature; yea, and lest the blueness of their veins should draw to her the softening influence of the blue-eyed angel of love.

She hath been known to bear children, but there is no record that she hath known the maternal sentiment. She cannot rank so high as the weazel in the treatment of her offspring. She feedeth them on sour meal and musty bread, for the pen has dried up the sources of milk in her breast, ere they were seared.

She delivereth them over to the devouring elements. Naked are they thrust forth to the cruel winds. Hungry dogs attack them before her eyes, and she waiteth to close her sentence, ere she reacheth them from the canine clutches. She seeth them creep into the fire and crisp themselves into carbon before her eyes, but her only emotion venteth itself in a "hum," and a nib of the impatient pen.

She feedeth on strange flesh and mysterious bread. Her food cannot attract caloric; it is cold and clammy even during the process of cooking. A needle causeth her to foam at the mouth. All that is hard and harsh, and graceless in nature clustereth around her. Even the blue-bottle-fly she calleth a coquette and crusheth with ireful heel. Her eyes are optical Gorgons whose glance turneth the heart into stone.

But with the male sex lies the chief terror of her coming. When she beholdeth the male, she mocketh at him in her wrath. Her mane is erect, her eyes vomit flames, her feet are pawing the ground, and her mouth snorting tempest-making words. Tall, thundreth and terrible, she driveth the male shrieking before her.

Now, alas! how painful the contrast. The male sex has ceased to fear her entirely, not a sign of a retreat at her coming, and nothing like swooning if she speaks to him. Nay, there is a fact still more astonishing, they are beginning to accuse the literary woman of over susceptibility, and of vanity, of a love of finery and luxury.

How painful indeed is the contrast between these literary women as we now see them, and the glorious picture of the blue-stocking of the past as the male has portrayed her.

As far as genius is concerned it is so much above and beyond us that we cannot legislate for it. What it will do we know not, any more than we can predicate what riot an earthquake or a whirlwind may run, but as far as *talent* is concerned, if a literary woman does not show a little more common-sense, forbearance, patience and dexterity in life than the majority of her sex not literary, then really she is not fit for her profession. For the habit of thinking and of going through the mechanical effort of arranging such thoughts into writing, should discipline the whole mental force of the woman, and in fact should teach her to make the best use of all materials whether mental or physical.

Now-a-days the woman of brains is generally the woman of specially acute emotional nature. Thus have the mighty fallen, and the literary woman is no longer to be distinguished from the rest of her sex.

Alas, me! how degenerate hath the age become, for in these modern days, the truly great woman hath her heart so fused into her head, that all the fires of hate, and envy, and calumny, and persecution, cannot unlock that God-sealed embrace.

VERDINA

— ❦ —

January 8, 1865

"Then, as a hunted deer, that could not flee,
I turned upon my thoughts, and stood at bay."

How long had I known that he loved her?
I cannot tell. I was voluntarily blind for so long. I knew I
was walking directly toward an abyss, but it seemed better to be
plunged into it blindfold than to wear the living death of consciousness as I was driven to its dreadful verge.

But a moment of revelation came, which shook all my senses
from their willful torpor to the extremity of sensation and pain;
a moment in which my life seemed to have sprung a leak, and to
be fast filling up and going down.

Why, why did Fate torture *me?* Was it any triumph for it, so
strong, and I so bound and low, to crush me? It was not worth
the trial.

There are so many noble, wide natures to be exalted and purified
by suffering. Mine is not a high nature; pain degrades it; it cannot
rise with suffering. I did not even soar with my love. I could only
sensate, desire and adore.

It seemed that I hated something, I knew not what, with a
savage and greedy hate.

Yet is was not she. I could not hate her for having a white face,
and yellow hair, and sky-blue eyes. I could almost love her for
being so fair, though her whiteness was the shroud of my hopes.

I did not hate him, ah me! not those wildering eyes, that most
pathetic face.

I believe I hated love. I hated it as the power that had wrought out in me a thousand eager, hungry nerves, only to feed them all with pain.

Yet I did not murmur. I walked calm and silent over the sharp rocks. I did not even weep. Mine was a dry sorrow that slowly parched and withered up my life.

They were so wrapped up in reading each other's faces, and listening to each other's voices, that they did not even notice those long, long hours, in which I wandered out alone.

Then I would crawl among the trees, and prostrating myself, lips downward, would mutter meaningless words to the sullen, reeking ground.

Oh! how I cursed that equatorial sun that called me, a dark weed, up from its luxurious soil. If my face had been white, he might not have loved her's. But mine was dark; my eyes were purple black, and my face dark and sad as only dark things can be.

Dark, dark! a lightless dark. Every terror, every woe, every crime, is pictured as dark. The darkness of the tempest is its most appalling horror. Darkness is the symbol of despair, and so my face is justly dark.

I brooded over myself with a pity too hopeless for tears. Pity and nothing more. But to look only with deep, speechless pity, with no further faith, no further hope in myself, was to turn with cruel Fate and hunt myself—where, alas where! For it seemed to me that I hung suspended between life and death, but it was no longer possible for me either to live or die.

Then, in a very spirit of envy and emulation, I longed to die. I cried to myself continually, "When I am dead, when the purple blood ceases to labor through my veins, and lies still on my worn heart, if they will shroud me in black for the sombre contrast, I think that so bloodless and black-swathed, I shall seem white. Let him come and look upon me then. Let him know that my spirit, whiter than ever her cold cheek was, bends triumphant over him."

But that triumph would not have given me his love. Without him, even though I were fair, where should I go, what should I do?

I dreamed sometimes of a sullen vengeance, of tearing her from him, because I had what is called a right to him, but what gain would that have been? I might have had a look of scorn and contempt from his most dear eyes, and that was the only drop from the cup of gall that had been spared me.

No, I could do nothing but stand dumb and marble-eyed, and see the blood of my spirit ooze slowly and ceaselessly through the vital wound.

To me he was always kind and gentle, his voice never hardened, his eyes never grew cold. If I could have known that he had not forgotten me; that he pitied and grieved for me; for who could know so well as he, how much I had lost when he took his love from me! I could have accepted his pity. It had been a cup of pure water held to the parched lips of the dying.

One moonlight night, as I wandered in the garden among the flowers, I met him suddenly, face to face. I tried to pass him, but he held me fast, held me with strong nervous hands, and looked down upon my face with that strange, thrilling, luminous smile. I would have struggled with him, but some subtle, languid perfume from his person, rushed across my senses, and smote them with a thrill of ecstatic pain.

I felt myself melting away into his bosom.

He drew my face up to the moonlight, holding it with both hands and saying:

"What is it troubles you, my own, poor little girl?"

My only answer was a burst of tumultuous, passionate tears.

Ah! that night! snatched from the gulf of hell, and borne up, up—what place is high enough to stand for it?—it yet burns like a great flaming jewel on the night of my despair.

Day after day, night upon night, that sullen cloud hung over my heart's sky. I do not know whether 'twas my manner or my face that most changed. But one of them gave a history of inward tempest that drew curious eyes upon me. I even heard it whispered that I grew stranger as the moon waxed to its full.

No wonder; when the moon was at its full they came out to gather roses in the garden and smiles from each other's eyes.

{ 330 }

If I had been a little less self-conscious or a little more self satisfied, I might have been saved. But I was too much and too little. The very strength of my passions put the rest of me to shame. To be nothing but a weak, confused, morbid and trembling child, in the presence of him I loved with such savage energy, caused me to look down upon myself with surprise and scorn.

He never knew with what ferocity I loved him; how could he know that the little, restless, timid, easy-blushing creature at his side, had her veins filled with melted lead instead of pure and quiet blood?

I was the fawn and the panther in one. Sometimes when the cruel hurt in my breast made me angry for very anguish, I felt my mouth turning to the hue of ashes and my eyes expanding and growing tawny, like a panther's, with a blind and impotent rate. But at the least consciousness of his presence, I was the fawn again, with the deadly gun-wound in its breast, hiding mute among the trees, till I should drop without a moan and dumbly die.

Ah, me! how the melancholy Autumn chilled me, the purple flower of the tropics, as it crept on towards ghastly Winter. All my habits, all my pleasures, all my instincts were torrid, and this was the first time I had been blasted with that terrible curse of nature—cold. It was almost with a superstitious terror, that I saw the flowers begin to wither, and the leaves turn yellow and sickly.

On one of those Fall evenings, I went out into the garden and glided listlessly down its paths. A low wind stirred the trees, and shook their dying leaves upon me. And with these fading leaves a thousand soft and sorrowful memories fluttered down upon my fond, agonizing soul. I was again in the clime of immortal Summer. I—he and I—were under the orange trees. He was speaking words of love to me, and my head was lying on his knees, and my life hung rapt and panting on his words; and the orange flowers fluttering thickly down, were crushed upon my breath and mouth; and his face was breaking my heart with its beauty, and—they were out—it leaped suddenly into my eyes—walking close together, sauntering to the rock on the bank of the river, where the moonlight rolled languid down its tide.

The torture in my soul seemed to take the form of a ring, to whirl outward with regular and ever increasing thrills, till it burst in one intolerable spasm.

I was upon them in a second; I swooped upon them like a hawk. I had thought to thrust one or both of them into the deep, rapid stream—they were so exactly on the verge of the rock, not dreaming of danger or of me. But in the very act, his eye caught up mine, and held it, not sternly, but with a sweet confiding surprise.

At one glance, my heart flung down its arms, and crouching in the dust, surrendered itself to him forever.

"Live, live!" I cried; "live and love—the ugly river is only fit for me—it will hug me close in its arms, till it run to hide my dark face in the sullen bosom of the sea." Then flinging my arms aloft, I leaped up and out.

An awful moment, and the waters foam over me.

Another moment, and I am snatched up by two strong arms. We rise to the surface, and half strangled, struggling to be free and dreading like a branded wild beast an angry look from his eye, I turn upon him a glance of pitiful supplication. By the melancholy light of the moon, drowning his face in its softness, I could see no anger, no reproach there, only a look of passionate pity and unutterable tenderness. Lost to all other sensation, I only feel how sweet it is to die in his arms, and my heart staggers, pauses, and goes to sleep in my breast.

How many hours or days I remained sundered from Life I never knew. It seemed to me that I lay in a dreamy delirium for months, and only she, the grand, fair beauty, did I ever recognize beside me. It seems to me, too, that I longed for her always; that I was never easy for a moment when she was out of my sight. Sometimes I took her for an angel, sometimes for a marble monument, but I always clung to her, and moaned for her.

One day I heard her saying, as if to herself, "Verdina, Verdina!" and I opened my eyes and looked feebly into her face. She started away from me, when she first saw I was conscious, and then, coming near to me again, told me I had been very ill, and must lie quiet and ask no questions and not excite myself.

What question, indeed, had I to ask of Fate, and what agitation had she reserved for me? I was as quiet as the smallest pebble that the unconscious foot trod into the garden walks; she had no need to be afraid of me.

All that day I lay half-conscious, half-dreaming, looking up at the dead white ceiling, which seemed to have as much blood in it as her white face.

I think she was kind to me; I know I exaggerated her beauty and her attractions, with a feverish generosity. I thought she was an angel, a chill and spotless angel; but when she pressed her large, cool hand on my fire-bound brows, it felt to me like a circlet of stone.

I did not ask for him. I had read a leaf in the red-leaved tablet in his bosom that would never be opened to her. It satisfied me; I could wait.

The next day I found myself alone for a moment. I was tired of lying inactive. I arose from the bed and tottered to a chair. It seemed to me at first that I was about to faint from the exertion, but I had not sat there long before I felt a new strength creeping over me. I rose out of the chair, and this time walked, feebly enough, but without fear of falling. I was so weary of the room in which I had been ill, that I thought I would go into the next one. I opened the door and walked in. I had scarcely advanced six steps, when my eyes fell upon a heavy, oblong table. A bronze sarcophagus was upon it.

I knew—I knew what was lying in it.

I walked slowly and composedly toward it, and looked quietly upon what was sleeping cold and silent there.

I noted that the undertone of melancholy that lay dormant in his face in life, had now swayed up upon the surface; that the heavy hair had been blown slightly over his forehead; that the long eyelashes trailed over his cheek with a languishing effect, and that a look of deep disquiet had got sealed into the mouth.

I took up the small, strong hand, wherein were united so strangely strength and delicacy—in the short, firmly-knitted fingers, in the fine bluish-white skin with its film of black hair, and in the iron-textured wrist its graceful tracery of purple veins. How was it that in that soft, caressing hand lay the strength of a giant? This was the temper of the man's soul: in it were the two poles, and between them lay all the world's possibilities.

I laid the hand back upon his breast, and crawled up upon the table, beside that piece of iron that held him.

I remembered nothing but my cold, cold feet, and the sharp burning torture in my head.

I crouched up beside him, wrapping my shivering feet in my garment, and laying my fiery brow against his cold cheek.

At once it began to draw the fire out of my head, and finally seemed to drink it all out of my whole body.

Thus relieved from pain, my eyelids gradually drooped beside his, and so I fell asleep.

Conscious and unconscious, passive and struggling, agonized and senseless, dead and alive, for a day, for weeks, this was my awakening. Sometimes it seemed that I hung in an awful night-void of space, conscious only that I was the focal point where pain concentrated itself to spread its rays out through the world.

Then would come hours of helpless, mute consciousness, in which I could hear all that was said about me. Then I heard them talking of him, speaking of a long-existing malady of the heart, of a hurt received on the sharp rocks in reaching me, of great agitation about my fate, and my eyes closed and I was the revolving centre for pain again.

Then I would swim back into weary consciousness. Once I heard them talking of me—wondering why he had married me—saying that I was so small and dark, and childish, and silent, and had nothing but my lustrous eyes to recommend me. Then they whispered that I was not in my right mind, and they had noticed long since the morbid tendencies of my nature, running directly into madness. And they wondered whether it had been home-sickness, or sullenness, or general insanity, that had made me keep alone for several weeks. Not one of them ever suspected, except herself, that I might have been jealous.

I never lost sight of her; when she was not beside me, I still saw her. Sometimes when I lay there, all dumb and broken, the yellow sunlight would steal in upon my bed, creeping up warily like a great tawny serpent, and when, in the act of springing upon and strangling me, it would change into coils of her yellow hair, and I would shudder at them, more than at the serpent's spring.

I know that I was mad all those days, but I cannot believe that I was the wild beast they said I was. I cannot believe that I plucked my own hair out by the bleeding roots, that I tore at my own breast with savage cruelty, that I lacerated with sharp teeth and nails every hand that approached me.

I cannot believe it, for who was ever so gentle, so patient as I, who so grateful for a tender word or smile? See how patient I was beside him in that horrible suit of death-mail, that had locked him in its arms. What complaint did I make? Did I ask anything more of Fate than to put out the ravening fires that burned in my brain? Is it likely that I should have grown suddenly so fierce? I do not believe it.

One night I heard them say I was dangerous—ought not to be allowed to go at large, and should be removed to an asylum as soon as I was well enough. I heard and understood them well; all my senses were sharpened with fright, for it was the night of the first snow; I saw it beating whitely against the windows, and everything white had come to strike me with a chill and sickening terror.

Hearing this, I feigned a deep and tranquil sleep, hoping I might be left alone for a time.

I was not disappointed; after a while, I found myself alone.

I got out of my bed, and laughed at them. Lock me up! I that could climb like a cat, swim like a fish, run like a hare, hide like a fox! I laughed at them.

I opened the window; the snow beat harshly against my face, and for a moment took away my breath; but there was a net-work of liquid fire under my skin, that soon melted it away.

The window was not very far from the ground, and a tree grew close up to it. I could easily descend by that.

I looked around for something to wrap myself up in, but could find nothing but a crimson silk shawl. I gathered that about me, and grappling with the tree, soon found myself in the garden.

Naturally fleet of foot, and with a terrible fear to urge me on, I sped before the wind. I ran at random, not knowing, not caring whither I went. I passed out of the garden, through a little piece of forest, across a field, through a brook, then across a wide and desert piece of land, till I came to a low hedge. Fancying that people were pursuing me, I crept under the hedge and lay still.

I am so small; so small and dark, that they cannot find me here; I can hide like a bird among the leaves.

After a while I tried to rise, but my knees refused to bear me up, and I sank down again.

There were thorns in the hedge, and one of them wounded my cheek. I smiled at its little malice, as if it could hurt me! I let my head sink in among many more of them, only to taunt them with their impotence to hurt me, and I forget whether they ceased to tear me, for the wind rushes up now, blowing fierce cold against me. The snow strikes sharp upon me, and then whirls whitely away.

Ah me! how cold I am; even the fire in my head is blown out, and its ashes lay stifling my brain.

Ah me! how cold my feet are; they are so little—such a poor little morsel for the great hungry wind—why should it gnaw them so?

My own, own torrid land, would you but take me back into your warm bosom, beneath your burning stars, your sleepy palms! I am your true child, the exhalation of your fiery breath, the fruit of your luxurious soil—take me back to you, take me back!

Something presses upon my eyelids—can it be sleep? I think

that the wind is dying away; it no longer gnaws these little feet, and there is no more white snow.

What is this that lifts my head from among the thorns, and drowns it in sweetest flowers? The cruel wind melts into soft airs. The black skies break up, and a whole flood of lustrous stars rush into them. A vertical moon, encircled with a violet rainbow, hangs in torrid splendor, in the very heart of the heavens. These are sleepy palms, that sigh over me, these are voluptuous orange flowers that ravish the winds with their breath.

And now the air breaks up in melody, resonant melody that runs up in long shivering chords through the sighing of the palms, through the breathings of the orange flowers, and mingles itself with the stars.

There are arms that hold me close; this is a most dear breast that my head sinks upon.

I am drawn down a tide; I float away, away—and—.

Bibliographic Sources

Introduction:

Bean, Walton, and James J. Rawles. *California History.* New York: McGraw Hill Book Co., 1983.

Boynton, Searles R. *The Painter Lady—Grace Carpenter Hudson.* Eureka: Interface California Corp., 1978.

Brown, Charlotte L. *Manuscript #228A.* Unpublished manuscript of trial testimony, California Historical Library, San Francisco.

California Historical Society. *Ella Sterling Mighels,* biography, Manuscript #1470. California Historical Society Library, San Francisco.

California Historical Society. *Hipolita Orendain de Medina,* biography, Manuscript #1441. California Historical Society Library, San Francisco.

Carpenter, Helen McCowen. *Helen Carpenter Diary.* Unpublished diary. Held Poage Research Library, Ukiah.

Carpenter, Helen McCowen. "The Mitchells," in *Overland Monthly.* San Francisco, September 1895.

Clapp, Louise Amelia Knapp Smith (Dame Shirley). *The Shirley Letters.* Salt Lake City: Peregrine Smith Books, 1983.

Clare, Ada. *Ada Clare,* column, *The Golden Era,* San Francisco, 1864.

Clifford, Josephine Wompner. *Overland Tales.* San Francisco: Bancroft Library, 1877.

Coolbrith, Ina. *Songs from the Golden Gate.* New York: Houghton Mifflin Co., 1895.

Cummins, Ella Sterling (Mighels). *The Story of the Files.* San Francisco: World's Fair Commission of California, Colombian Exposition, 1893.

Cummins, Ella Sterling (Mighels). "Portrait of a California Girl," in *Short Stories by California Authors.* San Francisco: Golden Era, 1885.

Bibliography

Esmeralda, Aurora (Ella Sterling Cummins Mighels). *The Story of a Forty-Niner's Daughter*. San Francisco: Harr Wagner Publishing, 1934.

Etulian, Richard. "Mary Hallock Foote, 1847–1938," *American Literary Realism*, 5 (Spring 1972), 145–150.

Farnham, Eliza W. *California In-Doors and Out*. New York: Dix, Edwards & Co., 1856.

Ferlinghetti, Lawrence, and Nancy J. Peters. *Literary San Francisco*. San Francisco: City Lights Books and Harper and Row, 1980.

Foote, Mary Hallock. *The Last Assembly Ball and The Fate of a Voice*. Boston: Houghton Mifflin, 1889.

Frémont, Jessie Benton. *Mother Lode Narratives*. Shirley Sargent, ed. Ashland: Lewis Osborne, 1970.

Gabriel, Ralph Henry. "*Concerning the Manuscript of Sarah Royce.*" In *A Frontier Lady*, by Sarah Royce. Lincoln: University of Nebraska Press, 1977.

Hamann, Skee. "Edith Murphey: Pioneer Botanist in Mendocino County." *Fremontia*, California Native Plant Society, July 1984.

Harte, Bret, ed. *Outcroppings—Being Selections of California Verse*. San Francisco: A. Roman and Co., 1866.

Held Poage Research Library. *Helen Carpenter*, biography. Ukiah: Held Poage Research Library.

Herr, Pamela. *Jessie Benton Frémont*. Norman and London: University of Oklahoma Press, 1988.

Jensen, Joan M., and Gloria Ricci Lothrop. *California Women: A History*. San Francisco: Boyd & Fraser Publishing Co., 1987.

Kennedy, Susan. *If All We Did Was to Weep at Home*. London: Indiana University Press, 1977.

Kirby, Georgiana. "A Tale of the Redwoods," in *Overland Monthly*. San Francisco, March 1874.

Kirby, Georgiana. *Journal of Georgiana Kirby*. Unpublished personal journal. California Historical Society Library, San Francisco.

Kirby, Georgiana. *Years of Experience; An Autobiographical Narrative*. New York: Lippencott, 1887.

Levy, Jo Ann. *They Saw the Elephant—Women in the California Gold Rush*. Hamden, Connecticut: Archon Books, 1990.

{ 339 }

Loosley, Allyn C. *Foreign Born Population of California,* Master's thesis. University of California, 1927.

Maguire, James. *Mary Hallock Foote.* Boise State College Western Writers Series, 1972.

McCrackin, Josephine Wompner Clifford. *Overland Tales.* San Francisco: Bancroft, 1877.

Medina, Hipolita Orendain de. *Manuscript #1441.* San Francisco: California Historical Society Library.

Menken, Adah Isaacs. *Infelicia.* New York: Lippencott, 1881.

Mighels, Ella Sterling Cummins, ed. *Literary California.* San Francisco: Harr Wagner Publishing Co., 1918.

Newman, May Wentworth, ed. *Poetry of the Pacific.* Hartford: Case, Lockwood and Co., 1866.

O'Brien, Robert. "Riptides," *San Francisco Chronicle,* December 18, 1946.

Oglesby, Richard E. "Introduction" in *The Shirley Letters* by Dame Shirley. Salt Lake City: Peregrine Smith Books, 1983.

Oliver, Catherine. Manuscript #1596. California Historical Society Library, San Francisco.

Paul, Rodman. "In Search of Dame Shirley" in *Pacific Historical Review.* No. 2, May 1964.

Rhodenhamel, Josephine DeWitt, and Raymund Francis Wood. *Ina Coolbrith—Librarian and Laureate of California.* Provo: Brigham Young University Press, 1973.

Royce, Sarah. *A Frontier Lady.* New Haven: Yale University Press, 1977.

Sargent, Shirley, ed. *Mother Lode Narratives,* by Jessie Benton Frémont. Ashland: Lewis Osborne, 1970.

Smith, Eric. "Lucy Young or T'tcetsa—Indian/White Relations in Northwest California, 1846–1944." Master's thesis. University of California, Santa Cruz, 1990.

Smith, Henry Nash. *Virgin Land—The American West as Symbol and Myth.* Cambridge: Harvard University Press, 1978.

Templeton, John. *Our Roots Run Deep—The Black Experience in California, 1500–1900,* Vol. 1. San Jose: Aspire Books, 1991.

Victor, Frances Fuller. *The New Penelope and Other Stories and Poems.* San Francisco: A. L. Bancroft & Co., 1877.

Walker, Franklin. *San Francisco's Literary Frontier.* Seattle: University of Washington Press, 1939.

Young, Lucy. "Out of the Past: Lucy's Story." California Historical Society Quarterly, October 1978.

Sarah Royce:

Gabriel, Ralph Henry. "Concerning the Manuscript of Sarah Royce." In *A Frontier Lady,* by Sarah Royce. Lincoln: University of Nebraska Press, 1977.

Royce, Sarah. *A Frontier Lady.* Lincoln: University of Nebraska Press, 1977.

Lucy Young:

Hamann, Skee. "Edith Murphey: Pioneer Botanist in Mendocino County." *Fremontia,* California Native Plant Society, July 1984.

Smith, Eric. "Lucy Young or T'tcetsa—Indian/White Relations in Northwest California, 1846–1944." Master's thesis, University of California, Santa Cruz, 1990.

Young, Lucy. "Out of the Past: Lucy's Story." *California Historical Society Quarterly,* October 1978.

Dame Shirley:

Clapp, Louise Amelia Knapp Smith (Dame Shirley). *The Shirley Letters.* Salt Lake City: Peregrine Smith Books, 1983.

Oglesby, Richard E. "Introduction" in *The Shirley Letters* by Dame Shirley. Salt Lake City: Peregrine Smith Books, 1983.

Paul, Rodman. "In Search of Dame Shirley." *Pacific Historical Review,* 2, May 1964.

Helen Carpenter:

Boynton, Searles R. *The Painter Lady—Grace Carpenter Hudson.* Eureka: Interface California Corp., 1978.

Carpenter, Helen McCowen. Unpublished diary. Held Poage Research Library, Ukiah, California.

Held Poage Research Library. *Helen Carpenter,* biography. Ukiah: Held Poage Research Library.

Frances Fuller Victor:

Cummins, Ella Sterling (Mighels). *The Story of the Files.* San Francisco: Co-Operative Printing, Co., 1893.

Ferlinghetti, Lawrence, and Nancy J. Peters. *Literary San Francisco.* San Francisco: City Lights Books and Harper and Row, 1980.

Walker, Franklin. *San Francisco's Literary Frontier.* Seattle: University of Washington Press, 1939.

Josephine Clifford McCrackin:

Cummins, Ella Sterling (Mighels). *The Story of the Files.* San Francisco: Co-Operative Printing Co., 1893.

McCrackin, Josephine Wompner Clifford. *Overland Tales.* San Francisco: Bancroft, 1877.

Rhodenhamel, Josephine DeWitt and Raymund Francis Wood. *Ina Coolbrith—Librarian and Laureate of California.* Provo: Brigham Young University Press, 1973.

Jessie Benton Frémont:

Herr, Pamela. *Jessie Benton Frémont.* Norman and London: University of Oklahoma Press, 1988.

Sargent, Shirley, ed. *Mother Lode Narratives,* by Jessie Benton Frémont. Ashland: Lewis Osborne, 1970.

Hipolita Orendain de Medina:

California Historical Society. *Hipolita Orendain de Medina,* biography, Manuscript #1441. California Historical Society Library, San Francisco.

Medina, Hipolita Orendain de. *Manuscript #1441.* California Historical Society Library, San Francisco.

Georgiana Kirby:

Cummins, Ella Sterling (Mighels). *The Story of the Files.* San Francisco: Co-Operative Printing Co., 1893.

Farnham, Eliza W. *California In-Doors and Out.* New York: Dix, Edwards and Co., 1856.

Kirby, Georgiana. *Journal of Georgiana Kirby.* Unpublished personal journal. California Historical Society Library, San Francisco.

Bibliography

Kirby, Georgiana. *Years of Experience: An Autobiographical Narrative.* New York: Lippencott, 1887.

Ina Coolbrith:

Ferlinghetti, Lawrence, and Nancy J. Peters. *Literary San Francisco.* San Francisco: City Lights Books and Harper and Row, 1980.

Rhodenhamel, Josephine DeWitt, and Raymund Francis Wood. *Ina Coolbrith—Librarian and Laureate of California.* Provo: Brigham Young University Press, 1973.

Walker, Franklin. *San Francisco's Literary Frontier.* Seattle: University of Washington Press, 1939.

Mary Hallock Foote:

Etulian, Richard. "Mary Hallock Foote, 1847–1938," *American Literary Realism,* 5 (Spring 1972), 145–150.

Foote, Mary Hallock. *The Last Assembly Ball and The Fate of a Voice.* Boston: Houghton Mifflin, 1889.

Maguire, James. *Mary Hallock Foote.* Boise State College Western Writers Series, 1972.

Charlotte L. Brown:

Brown, Charlotte L. *Manuscript #228 A.* Unpublished manuscript of trial testimony. California Historical Society Library, San Francisco.

Templeton, John. *Our Roots Run Deep—The Black Experience in California, 1500–1900,* Vol. 1. San Jose: Aspire Books, 1991.

Ella Sterling Cummins Mighels:

California Historical Society. *Ella Sterling Mighels,* biography, Manuscript #1470. San Francisco: California Historical Society Library.

Cummins, Ella Sterling (Mighels). *The Story of the Files.* World's Fair Commission of California, Columbian Exposition, 1893.

Esmeralda, Aurora (Ella Sterling Cummins Mighels). *The Story of a Forty-Niner's Daughter.* San Francisco: Harr Wagner Publishing, 1934.

O'Brien, Robert. "Riptides," *San Francisco Chronicle,* December 18, 1946.

No Rooms of Their Own

Adah Menken:

Ferlinghetti, Lawrence, and Nancy J. Peters. *Literary San Francisco*. San Francisco: City Lights Books and Harper and Row, 1980.

Menken, Adah Isaacs. *Infelicia*. New York: Putnam's Sons, 1887.

Walker, Franklin. *San Francisco's Literary Frontier*. Seattle: University of Washington Press, 1939.

Ada Clare:

Clare, Ada. "The Past," *Ada Clare,* column, *The Golden Era,* San Francisco, 1864.

Ferlinghetti, Lawrence, and Nancy J. Peters. *Literary San Francisco*. San Francisco: City Lights Books and Harper and Row, 1980.

Walker, Franklin. *San Francisco's Literary Frontier*. Seattle: University of Washington Press, 1939.

Photograph by Susan Forrest.

ABOUT THE EDITOR

A Californian whose roots go back to pioneer Santa Cruz, Ida Rae Egli was raised in Potter Valley in Mendocino County, and has been enjoying stories and tales about California since she was a child. An English instructor at Santa Rosa Junior College in Santa Rosa, she graduated from Sonoma State University before earning a Master's degree in American literature from San Francisco State University. The mother of a daughter and a son, she lives with her husband, an instructor of political science, in Santa Rosa.